THE HISTORY OF EVENTS

RESULTING IN

INDIAN CONSOLIDATION

WEST OF THE MISSISSIPPI

ANNIE HELOISE ABEL

AMS PRESS
NEW YORK

THE HISTORY OF EVENTS RESULTING IN INDIAN CONSOLIDATION WEST OF THE MISSISSIPPI.

By ANNIE HELOISE ABEL, Ph. D.

(TO THIS ESSAY WAS AWARDED THE JUSTIN WINSOR PRIZE OF THE AMERICAN HISTORICAL ASSOCIATION IN 1906.)

Library of Congress Cataloging in Publication Data

Abel, Annie Heloise, 1873-
    The history of events resulting in Indian con-
solidation west of the Mississippi.

    Reprint of the 1908 ed., which was issued as v. 1,
ch. 13 of the 1906 Annual report of the American
Historical Association.
    Bibliography: p.
    1. Indians of North America--Government relations
--1789-1869. 2. Indians of North America--Indian
Territory. I. Title. II. Series: American
Historical Association. Annual report, 1906, v. 1.
E93.A26 1972   970.5   76-158219
ISBN 0-404-07116-3

Reprinted from the edition of 1908, Washington, D. C.
First AMS edition published in 1972
Manufactured in the United States of America

International Standard Book Number: 0-404-07116-3

AMS PRESS INC.
NEW YORK, N. Y.   10003

THE HISTORY OF EVENTS RESULTING IN INDIAN CONSOLIDATION WEST OF THE MISSISSIPPI RIVER.

By Annie Heloise Abel, Ph. D.

Sometime Bulkley Fellow in History at Yale University, later Associate Professor in History at Wells College, and now Instructor in History at The Woman's College of Baltimore.

PREFACE.

The germ of this thesis was a task, apparently an insignificant one, assigned to me in the college class room, several years ago, by Prof. Frank Heywood Hodder—a task that eventually developed, under influences the most favorable, into an earnest and prolonged study of Indian political relations with the United States. Later on, the special subject of Indian removal was offered and accepted in candidacy for the degree of doctor of philosophy at Yale University. The present paper is that dissertation thoroughly revised, rearranged, and enlarged, so much so, indeed, that the fifth chapter is wholly new and some of the other chapters are scarcely to be recognized.

In pursuit of detailed information regarding Indian migrations to the westward of the Mississippi, I have consulted books, periodicals, and newspapers of all sorts, not only in the university libraries of Columbia, Cornell, and Yale, but also in the Lenox Library of New York City and the Congressional Library of Washington, D. C.; yet, in the final result, I have used the information thus obtained only to secure general impressions of the period, the setting, or historical perspective, so to speak, and have recorded very few facts that have not been found in primary sources.

These primary sources have been enumerated and commented upon in the bibliographical guide, but there remains this to be said, that, in the body of the work, reference to them has followed one unvarying principle. For instance, where, on any subject, there are parallel authorities, such as the Clark Papers, the Jackson Papers, and the Indian Office Records, the last named has been made, for the sake of simplicity, the court of last resort and, usually, the only one appealed to. Then again, Indian Office manuscript records have been preferred to copies of or extracts from them found in the "American State Papers." Sometimes, however, these same "American State Papers" constitute the original source. Documents are found therein of which there is no longer any trace in the official files at Washington, D. C., yet there seems no reason to question the authenticity of the documents since it is only too evident that none too much care has been taken to preserve the Indian Office files and the original manuscript may easily have been destroyed, while, most fortunately, the printed copy of it remains intact.

In connection with the third chapter, attention should be called to the recent monumental works of Captain Mahan. Long before those works appeared and quite independently of them, from a careful perusal of Yonge's "Life of Liverpool," the Castlereagh Correspondence, and Wellington's Supplementary Despatches, I had reached, with respect to the Indian buffer State, a decision considerably at variance with the published opinions of the best secondary authorities. Captain Mahan has most gratifyingly dwelt upon and sanctioned that decision, at least, in part; but he had access to an additional great authority, the unpublished memoirs of Castlereagh.

Sometime since, Mr. Ulrich Bonnell Phillips, of Wisconsin University, published a monograph on "Georgia and State Rights," to which I am immeasurably indebted; inasmuch as it contains an exhaustive treatment of the "Creek Controversy" and of the "Cherokee Expulsion." It is true, I had already arrived at the same facts and conclusions by personal investigation, but I had not yet brought them together in a finished product. My studies had, however, rendered me competent to judge of Mr. Phillips's work, and I at once recognized its very great merit. Naturally enough, I felt some hesitancy about introducing similar chapters into my own thesis, but continuity of thought demanded that I should. The Creek and Cherokee troubles have a place in the history both of State rights and of Indian removal, and can not logically be omitted from either. Besides, I have gone further into the primary sources than did Mr. Phillips; for he does not seem to have used J. Q. Adams's Diary, the Jackson Papers, the Curry-Schermerhorn Papers, the "Missionary Herald," the Indian Office files and letter-books, nor even the manuscript reports of Andrews, of Crowell, and of Gaines. None the less, he had a slight advantage over me in personal access to the Crawford, Draper, Hawkins, and Wilson Lumpkin Papers, although they were not especially productive. At all events, Mr. Phillips offers no data as coming from them that I have not found more adequately elsewhere. Nevertheless, I have noted their titles in the bibliography; because no account of sources for the period could be considered complete without them.

It is sincerely to be regretted that various travel narratives, particularly some of those recently issued under the editorship of R. G. Thwaites, did not appear in time for their exceeding interest to be reflected, and, perchance, an occasional incident from them to be embodied in the present paper. Indian removals were to so great an extent brought about by the pressure of western settlement that even the faintest of lights thrown upon the conditions of that settlement may be, in reality, a guiding star to further research. Hopes are entertained that at no distant day I may be able to continue the present work along the line of the effect of the actual removals and then an opportunity will be given for a more extensive inclusion of descriptive material.

Both in the course of the long years of investigation and in the months of final revision, I have met with courtesies great and small from librarians, clergymen, government officials, and colleagues, to all of whom I take this opportunity of expressing my most sincere thanks, such thanks, indeed, as are especially due for generous cooperation in the reading and copying of the manuscript to my sister, Lucy E. Abel; and, for helpful suggestions to E. B. Henderson, of the Indian Office, to Charles H. Hull, of Cornell University, and to A. C. McLaughlin, of Chicago University.

In a more particular way I wish to acknowledge my indebtedness to the Rev. Joseph Hooper, of Durham, Conn., who has furnished me gratuitously with carefully made copies of all such Hobart Papers as bear upon the movements of the Oneida Indians; to my father and mother, whose sympathy in the undertaking has made its completion possible; and also, to my instructors, Professors Edward Gaylord Bourne, George Burton Adams, and Frank Heywood Hodder, who by precept and example have been a constant inspiration to steadiness of purpose, thoroughgoing work, and sound scholarship.

TABLE OF CONTENTS.

CHAPTER I.

THE ORIGIN OF THE IDEA OF REMOVAL.

The Louisiana purchase is justly regarded as one of the most important events in American history. Studied as it has been from every conceivable point of view—economic, political, constitutional—it is remarkable that no one has as yet determined its true relation to the development of the United States Indian policy. This can be accounted for only on the supposition that the native tribes have played but a sorry part in national affairs. Their history, except at rare intervals, has excited little comment; and in a very few instances only has it aroused enough interest to make it the subject of special study. Such study has recently shown that the purchase of foreign territory in 1803 brought out the first explicit statement of the removal idea. The importance of this can not be overestimated; for removal is the significant thing in later Indian history. The term itself implies the interference of the Government in Indian migrations, and is the expression of a distinct policy that sooner or later modified the whole character of official relations with the tribes.

Whatever may have been Jefferson's private views on the legality of expansion, it is certain that he did his best to validate the purchase of Louisiana. In fact, he took it upon himself in July of 1803 to draw up a rough draft [a] of a constitutional amendment which should cover that questionable exercise of the treaty-making power. The proposed amendment is cumbersome, heavy with details, and has little historical value beyond the light which it throws upon Jefferson's personal opinions. It failed to become a part of the supreme law of the land and would be unnoticed here were it not for the fact that it contains the first direct and, at the same time, an official advocacy of Indian removal. Indeed, it has Indian removal for its central idea, and therefore deserves, in spite of its awkward style to be quoted in full:

The province of Louisiana is incorporated with the U. S. and made part thereof. The right of occupancy in the soil, and of self-government, are confirmed to the Indian inhabitants, as they now exist. Pre-emption only of the portions rightfully occupied by them, & a succession to the occupancy of such as they may abandon, with the full rights of possession as well as of property & sovereignty in whatever is not or shall cease to be so rightfully occupied by them shall belong to the U. S.

The legislature of the Union shall have authority to exchange the right of occupancy in portions where the U. S. have full rights for lands possessed by

---

[a] Ford's "Jefferson," Vol. VIII: pp. 241–249.

Indians within the U. S. on the East side of the Missisippi: to exchange lands on the East side of the river for those of the white inhabitants on the West side thereof and above the latitude of 31 degrees: to maintain in any part of the province such military posts as may be requisite for peace or safety: to exercise police over all persons therein, not being Indian inhabitants: to work salt springs, or mines of coal, metals and other minerals within the possession of the U. S. or in any others with the consent of the possessors; to regulate trade & intercourse between the Indian inhabitants and all other persons; to explore and ascertain the geography of the province, its productions and other interesting circumstances; to open roads and navigation therein where necessary for beneficial communication; & to establish agencies and factories therein for the cultivation of commerce, peace, & good understanding with the Indians residing there.

The legislature shall have no authority to dispose of the lands of the province otherwise than as hereinbefore permitted, until a new Amendment of the constitution shall give that authority. Except as to that portion thereof which lies South of the latitude of 31 degrees; which whenever they deem expedient, they may erect into a territorial Government, either separate or as making part with one on the eastern side of the river, vesting the inhabitants thereof with all the rights possessed by other territorial citizens of the U. S.

An analysis of the proposed amendment will reveal some interesting particulars. It is a fair illustration of what the American Constitution might have been had it been framed exclusively by the party that believed in the doctrine of express powers. Such things as are discussed at all are discussed in detail. Topics of slight and transient importance receive as much attention as those that are fundamental in their nature. With respect to the subject-matter, it may be said that the greater part is devoted to the Indians. The purchase of Louisiana is not mentioned and, except in the first, or incorporating, clause, there is no indication that any change whatever had taken place in the ownership of the province. This seems strange; because, apparently, the chief object of the amendment was to validate the recent acquisition of foreign territory.[a] The real difficulties that confronted the strict constructionists seem to have been dodged. Only one constitutional impediment is referred to, and that is the question touching naturalization. Such an amendment, had it ever been accepted, would scarcely be considered as conferring a grant of power to acquire any other territory. It might even be seriously questioned whether it legalized the one under discussion. From one point of view it complicated matters. As events have turned out, precedent has been the authority for later acquisitions. Had there been a special amendment to validate the purchase of Louisiana, similar special amendments would have been necessary for the subsequent incorporation of Florida, Texas, the western country, Alaska, Hawaii, Porto Rico, and the Philippines.

In at least one respect Jefferson was, contrary to his custom, consistent with himself. He prepared a document that would permit of literal interpretation only. This makes the new amendment, when compared with the Constitution proper, seem to contain a good deal of irrelevant matter. Why, for example, should Jefferson have taken advantage of the occasion to exploit his favorite scheme of traversing the western country and of establishing trade relations with the Indians of the plains? Surely it was not necessary to burden a fundamental law with the details of an exploration. The truth is that Jefferson was, for some reason, intent upon giving what must have seemed undue attention to the Indian side of the Louisiana purchase. He also looked forward to the future condition of the lower part of the province; that is, to its territorial organization and eventual admission to statehood.

As has been already intimated, the greater part of the proposed amendment was taken up with a provision for the Indians and the substance of that provision was the removal of the eastern tribes to upper Louisiana. That meant the planting of Indian colonies north of the thirty-first parallel. The idea marks an epoch in Indian history. It seems to have been spontaneous with Jefferson; [a] for, in all preceding communications,[b] official or otherwise, he appears to have regarded absorption, or perhaps, amalgamation, as the only possible solution of the Indian problem. Even as late as February of 1803 [c] he advocated this most strongly in a letter to Benjamin Hawkins. In the following April he wrote [d] to John Bacon, with whom he was conferring on Indian affairs. The cession of Louisiana had then become an assured thing; but still there was no mention of Indian removal. It is true there is in the letter to Bacon an ambiguous statement to the effect that settlements, strong enough to ward off

[a] As far back as 1800 (Ford's "Jefferson," VII: 457), he had discussed with James Monroe, governor of Virginia, the advisability of transporting fugitive and insurgent negroes. A year later (ibid., VIII: 103–106, 152–154; 161–164) he went the length of proposing to colonize them on land purchased in the northwest, in Canada, or in the West Indies; but, before the issue of the constitutional supplement in the summer of 1803, there is positively no trace of a plan for doing the same thing with the Indians.

[b] Some writers, notably Charles C. Royce (Annual Report of the Bureau of Ethnology, 1883–84, p. 202), attribute the origin of the removal idea to the confidential message which Jefferson sent to Congress January 18, 1803 (Richardson, I: 352–354); but there is really nothing in the document to support the claim. Mr. Royce seems to have mistaken the desire to establish trading posts on the Mississippi and its branches as a desire to plant colonies. It must be admitted, however, that Jefferson's phraseology in this particular instance is a trifle misleading. Were the evidence not so strong in favor of the assertion that the Lewis and Clark expedition was an early dream of Jefferson's, we might be led to believe, as Mr. Royce was, that when he spoke " of planting on the Mississippi itself the means of its own safety," he was referring to the planting of Indian colonies and not to the establishing of trading posts. There is nothing else in the message that could be construed as relating in any way whatsoever to removal. Jefferson's correspondence does not serve to deepen, in the slightest particular, the impression that the idea of removal had been conceived in the beginning of the year. In January the Administration had not been approached on the subject of buying the whole of Louisiana. The eastern bank of the Mississippi was the only one in the possession of the United States, and it is not to be supposed for a moment that the western people would have consented to let the Indians control it. The confidential message of January 18, 1803, has about it an air of secrecy. Jefferson was plotting to secure the monopoly of the valuable fur trade of the far west and northwest. His language was circumspect, and it had need to be.

[c] Ford's "Jefferson," VIII: 213–215.

[d] Ibid., VIII: 228–229.

intruders, ought to be planted on the Mississippi; but the context shows that the writer had reference to white settlements only.

Removal, as the term is technically used in American history, was apparently not only spontaneous, but absolutely original with Jefferson.[a] The inception of it has been credited to General Knox,[b] but his correspondence, voluminous as it is, is silent on the subject. It would seem more natural to think of his successor in Washington's Cabinet, Timothy Pickering, as the originator; for he was known to be greatly interested in the Indians and to hold very advanced ideas with respect to their civilization.[c] The fact is, prior to 1803, the carrying out of any such project would not have been practicable. Even with Jefferson the idea was probably not the result of long study but was called forth by the conditions of the Louisiana purchase. There are a few colonial precedents for Indian removal on a small scale.[d] With these Jefferson may have been familiar, yet he could well have been independent of their influence; because his scheme was so entirely different from anything that had thus far been undertaken. Jefferson contemplated the organization of what would have become an Indian Territory, perhaps an Indian State, to which all the tribes might be removed, while the colonies simply provided reservations, more or less distant, for fragmentary bands. All such schemes may, however, have had their rise in the familiar nomadic tendencies of the aborigines. The Indian, it was thought, could be easily uprooted and transplanted; for was he not a wanderer by nature, a voluntary exile?

Various theories may be advanced to explain Jefferson's interest in the Indians at this particular time. It is quite likely that he was seeking a legitimate use for what the Federalists chose to call a *wilderness*.[e] This may account for the subordination and even for the omission of constitutional matter in the proposed amendment. The constitutional objections to the purchase of foreign territory would naturally come from his own party. He was sure of its support, therefore he turned to meet, as best he could, the objections of his enemies. The objections were, to say the least, absurd. They covered exaggerated accounts of the magnitude of the price, of the uselessness of the land, and of the disadvantages, yea, disasters, that might come from too great an enlargement of the Union and disintegration of its people.[f] Jefferson's own reflections show that he wished at the same time to remove the immediate cause of Indian wars. He had always held that they were an unnecessary drain

---

[a] The honor of suggesting it to Jefferson was claimed for the Tennessee legislature. ("Nashville Republican and State Gazette," December 18, 1830.)
[b] Otis, p. 92.
[c] Upham's "Pickering," III: 156.
[d] Osgood, I: 536–540; Annual Report of the Bureau of Ethnology, 1896–97, pp. 573, 590.
[e] McMaster, II: 630–632.
[f] Ford's "Jefferson," VIII: 243, note.

upon the public treasury, and, in introducing his system of public economy, he aimed at diminishing the number of Indian expeditions. In a sense, removal was the logical outcome of such a policy. Could the Indians be moved westward, Indian wars would cease; because encroachment upon Indian land would cease. In this way the cost of Louisiana would soon be offset.

Furthermore, Jefferson must have had a clear impression of the obligation that had been put upon him and upon the nation by the Georgia compact of 1802.[a] He was a strict constructionist. He believed in State rights. To him the compact with a sovereign State could not have been a dead letter—a mere ruse to enable the Federal Government to get possession of the western lands. It must be admitted, however, that there is not the slightest allusion to the Georgia compact in his correspondence of this period, yet it is fair to suppose that he could not have forgotten a circumstance so recent. The disputes with Georgia, involving the title to the present States of Alabama and Mississippi, together with the resulting covenant and all that it entailed, were still a subject for discussion. Consequently Jefferson must have remembered only too well that the Federal Government, for a material consideration, had solemnly promised to extinguish, at its own expense, the Indian title within the reserved limits of Georgia as soon as it could be done " peaceably and on reasonable terms." The purchase of Louisiana paved the way for the immediate fulfillment of the promise. That this plan of keeping faith did commend itself to the statesmen of the time is shown by subsequent Congressional debates. There is an occasional reference, for instance, to the removal of the Creeks, who were almost exclusively Georgia Indians.

A further examination of the proposed amendment shows that Jefferson had other reasons for wishing to bring the Indians together west of the Mississippi. Pioneers, daring adventurers, had been wont to settle in isolated spots, far removed from each other. The detached homes proved an easy mark for Indian attacks. This was the condition of affairs on both sides of the river. Therefore, to avoid unpleasant complications and doubtless to guard against expense, Jefferson thought it would be advisable to consolidate the white men and forbid settlement except in compact form. He proposed that the white settlers west of the river should be induced to trade land with eastern Indians. This would leave the field open for the planting of Indian colonies in upper Louisiana. At the same time, another object, equally important, would be attained. The settlers, living on the frontier, had much to dread from the jealousy of Canadian trappers and from the rapacity of Mexican freebooters; but, if an Indian Territory were to be established west

---

[a] American State Papers, " Public Lands " I : 125–126.

of the Mississippi, the red men would shield the white.   No suspicion seems to have been raised in Jefferson's mind that the Indian and the Mexican had much in common and that they were likely to become allies, thus increasing instead of diminishing the danger.

It should be remarked that Jefferson, in providing for the disposal of upper Louisiana, was neither blind nor wholly indifferent to Indian interests.   The amendment secured possession to the Indian emigrant under constitutional guaranty.   The occupancy title could in no wise pass away by simple legislative act.   A new amendment to the Constitution would be necessary to effect a legal transfer to white people.   Yet everything goes to show that he regarded the Indian claim as provisional only.   The occupancy would be but temporary, which was wholly inconsistent with Jefferson's known views on Indian sovereignty.   As a State rights man, he should have been unalterably opposed to the recognition of Indian claims in perpetuity, yet we find him, as a Cabinet officer under Washington, pursuing an opposite course.   On one occasion, when in conference with General Knox, he actually argued that the Federal Government had no more right to grant land to the Indians than to cede it to a European power; inasmuch as the land so conveyed was just as likely to continue in the permanent possession of the one as of the other. His views had assuredly undergone a change before July of 1803. From what he wrote then it can be inferred that the Indian might be dispossessed at pleasure.   He might hold the land, but only until the white man had need of it.

A question may be raised as to why the southern line of Indian colonization was drawn along the thirty-first parallel.   European settlers had ventured still farther north, therefore their presence could not have determined the limit.   Had it been intended to place the Indians south instead of north of the line we might have been led to suppose that the thirty-first parallel was henceforth to mark the southern boundary of what was purely United States territory; or, in other words, that the line, running through the Louisiana purchase and separating the red men from the white, was to be a western extension of the old United States line.   Even then a difficulty would arise; for Jefferson had a notion that Louisiana included the whole of West Florida.   If the theory of arbitrary choice be rejected, one must seek an explanation in a detailed study of the geography of Louisiana, although it is quite possible that the line of thirty-one degrees was selected solely because the people of the United States had more reason to be familiar with that parallel than with any other, it having been the scene of contention in connection with the northern limit of the Floridas.

Jefferson submitted the proposed amendment for critical perusal to Robert Smith, Secretary of the Navy.   As it turned so largely on Indian affairs it would have seemed more natural to refer it to the

Secretary of War. Robert Smith had no official dealings with the Indians, and does not appear to have been particularly intimate with Jefferson. However, he criticised the draft at considerable length. Some of his remarks were exceedingly well made. He pointed out that, if the amendment were adopted as proposed, the Constitution would be burdened with unnecessary details. He objected to the preponderance of Indian matter on the ground that, if the Indians received a constitutional guaranty of possession in the western land, their occupancy might, at some future time, seriously embarrass settlement, and, perhaps, prove a source of endless trouble on the southern frontier. He therefore suggested such changes as would accomplish the object most to be desired—that is, gradual and compact settlement, and yet not insure to the Indians anything more than a temporary asylum. He omitted the specific mention of removal and ran the demarcation line one degree farther north. The change in the location of the line may have been unintentional; but it is more probable that Smith took careful note of the settlements north of the thirty-first parallel and purposely abandoned all thought of making an exchange with the eastern Indians.

JULY 9, '03.

SIR.—I am greatly pleased with the ideas suggested in the proposed amendment of the Constitution and I sincerely hope that they will be adopted by the Legislature of the Union. But I am rather inclined to think that they ought not all to be ingrafted upon the Constitution. Your great object is to prevent emigrations excepting to a certain portion of the ceded territory. This could be effectually accomplished by a Constitutional prohibition that Congress should not erect or establish in that portion of the ceded territory situated North of Lat. 32 degrees any new State or territorial government and that they should not grant to any people excepting Indians any right or title relative to any part of the said portion of the said territory. All other powers of making exchanges, working mines etc. would then remain in Congress to be exercised at discretion; and in the exercise of this discretion, subject as it would be to the three aforementioned restrictions I do not perceive that any thing could be done which would counteract your present intentions.

The rights of occupancy in the soil ought to be secured to the Indians and Government ought, in my opinion, to endeavour to obtain for them the exclusive occupation of the Northern portion of Louisiana excepting such posts as may be necessary to our trade and intercourse with them. But ought not this to be a subject of legislative provision? If the Indian rights of occupancy be a part of the Constitution might not the Government be hereafter thereby much entangled? Under such a Constitutional guarantee the Indians might harass our military posts or our settlements in the Southern portion or elsewhere in the most wanton manner and we could not disturb their rights of occupancy without a formal alteration of the Constitution.

Under the idea that so many & such undefinéd restrictions as you have proposed to be engrafted upon the Constitution might in process of time embarress the government and might not be acceptable to Congress, I have respectfully submitted to your consideration the enclosed sketch.

"Amendment proposed to the Constitution to be added to S. 3, Art. 4.

"Louisiana being in virtue of the Treaty etc. incorporated with the United States and being thereby a part of the Territory thereof Congress shall have power to dispose of and make all needful rules and regulations respecting the same as fully and effectually as if the same had been at the time of the establishment of the Constitution a part of the Territory of the U. States: provided nevertheless that Congress shall not have power to erect or establish in that portion of Louisiana which is situated North of the Latitude of /32/ degrees any new State or territorial government nor to grant to any citizen or citizens or other individual or individuals excepting Indians any right or title whatever to any part of the said portion of Louisiana until a new Amendment of the Constitution shall give that authority." [a]

Jefferson did not restrict the expression of his views to constitutional amendments; but, in correspondence with his friends, enthusiastically explained the removal project. On the 11th of July [b] he wrote to Horatio Gates enlarging upon the wisdom of inducing the migration of eastern tribes. A few days later he sent to Clark,[c] of New Orleans, and to William Dunbar certain queries bearing upon Louisiana, the Indians, and their land titles which indicate that the subject was engrossing his attention. His very enthusiasm seems proof positive that the idea of removal was a new one to him. It was an idea suggested by the acquisition of unoccupied land. Jefferson's opinions were still unchanged when he wrote to John Dickinson [d] and to John Breckinridge,[e] respectively, the 9th and 12th of August. He urged the attendance of Western members [f] at the coming session of Congress, in order that the matter might be brought to a successful issue. Within a week thereafter circumstances had changed the whole aspect of affairs.[g] News had come from Livingston that Napoleon was somewhat disturbed by French discontent, possibly also by Spanish protests. The terms of the secret treaty of San Ildefonso had not been complied with, and Spain, supported by Great Britain, was threatening to contest the title to Louisiana. Plainly the thing to do was to close the negotiations as soon as possible,[h] hasten ratification in the Senate, and trust to the future for a settlement of all disputes. Jefferson hastily prepared another constitutional draft [i] and sent it to Madison, to Levi Lincoln,

---

[a] Ford's " Jefferson," VIII : 241–242, note.
[b] Ford's " Jefferson," VIII : 249–251.
[c] Ibid., pp. 253–255, and notes.
[d] Ibid., pp. 261–263.
[e] Ibid., pp. 242–244, note.
[f] Ibid., p. 244, note.
[g] Ibid., pp. 244–245, note.
[h] Ibid., pp. 246–248, notes.
[i] Louisiana, as ceded by France to the U. S. is made a part of the U. S. Its white inhabitants shall be citizens, and stand, as to their rights & obligations, on the same footing with other citizens of the U. S. in analogous situations. Save only that as to the portion thereof lying North of an East & West line drawn through the mouth of Arkansa river, no new State shall be established, nor any grants of land made, other than to Indians in exchange for equivalent portions of land occupied by them, until authorised by further subsequent amendment to the Constitution shall be made for these purposes.

" Florida also, whenever it may be rightfully obtained, shall become a part of the U. S., its white inhabitants shall thereupon be Citizens & shall stand, as to their rights & obligations, on the same footing with other citizens of the U. S. in analogous situations."— Ford's " Jefferson," VIII : 241–245.

and to Gallatin. The excitement of the moment had not destroyed his interest in removal; but to some extent he heeded the advice of Robert Smith. The second draft aimed to be a grant of general powers; but it simply validated the purchase of Louisiana and provided for Indian occupation north of a line drawn east and west from the mouth of the Arkansas River. This ended the matter for the time being. Subsequent events prevented Congressional action and the Constitution was never amended along the lines laid down by Jefferson.

Whether or not Jefferson immediately abandoned his scheme for the colonization of upper Louisiana is impossible to determine. Neither his message to Congress, October 17, 1803,[a] nor his letters to confidential friends contain any reference to the subject that had so deeply interested him in the early summer, yet the Annals of Congress bear witness that his ideas had extended beyond the Cabinet circle. Both in the Senate debates [b] and in the House debates [c] on questions growing out of the cession, an occasional argument was given for or against Indian occupancy. The records are, of course, meager and much may have been said though little was reported. To all appearances, if removal was ever more than incidentally mentioned in the Eighth Congress, it was discussed as a secondary matter only and never once upon its own merits. Probably the statesmen of the day thought there were other things of far more importance. Nevertheless, the ideas of Jefferson must have carried some weight with them; for, when the Louisiana territorial act of 1804 [d] was finally passed, it contained a clause [e] which empowered the President to effect Indian emigration. The act likewise divided the province of Louisiana into two districts, separated from each other by the thirty-third parallel. Presumably the understanding was that the Indian colonies should be planted in the northern; but the people of Louisiana protested vigorously and their remonstrances may have been a determining reason why Jefferson's scheme had practically to be abandoned for more than twenty years. Its abandonment may, however, have contributed to produce such peaceful conditions in Louisiana that the so-called Aaron Burr conspiracy was, as McCaleb has so ably argued, an utter impossibility.

---

[a] Richardson, I : 357–362.

[b] Annals of the Eighth Congress, pp. 33–34, pp. 40–41.

[c] Ibid., p. 440.

[d] 2 United States Statutes at Large, pp. 283–289.

[e] Section 15. "The President of the United States is hereby authorized to stipulate with any Indian tribes owning land on the east side of the Mississippi, and residing thereon, for an exchange of lands, the property of the United States, on the west side of the Mississippi, in case the said tribes shall remove and settle thereon ; but in such stipulation, the said tribes shall acknowledge themselves to be under the protection of the United States, and shall agree that they will not hold any treaty with any foreign power, individual State, or with the individuals of any State or power ; and that they will not sell or dispose of said lands, or any part thereof, to any sovereign power, except the United States, nor to the subjects or citizens of any other sovereign power, nor to the citizens of the United States. * * *"

Chapter II.

UNSUCCESSFUL ATTEMPTS TO EFFECT REMOVAL DURING PRESIDENT JEFFERSON'S ADMINISTRATIONS.

Although the real history of Indian removal dates from 1803 it was a long time after that before the Federal Government saw fit to adopt systematic migrations as a part of its regular policy. The intervening years were years of development. Changes took place, not so much in the idea itself as in the conditions that gave rise to it. For a period immediately succeeding the purchase of Louisiana the United States was distracted by a divided interest in France and Great Britain. The very independence of the young western nation seemed to be involved in the disturbances of Europe. Sentimental regard for France, indignation against the United Kingdom on account of real or fancied wrongs, and the arbitrary sacrifice of New England commerce, divided the sections and threatened the integrity of the Union. It is not to be wondered at, therefore, that the idea of Indian removal failed, at the time of its origin, to appeal to the mass of the American people. Its development toward a national policy was exceedingly slow and practically covered a period that extended to 1817.

During a part of that time Jefferson himself was absorbed in other things. He had apparently forgotten his former advocacy of Indian colonization. Perhaps he had come to doubt its efficacy. Otherwise, why, in his inaugural speech of 1805,[a] did he so earnestly advise the old plan of amalgamation to the evident exclusion of any other? Contemporaries a little later sought to find in the march of emigration westward an explanation for the decline in his enthusiasm. They claimed that upper Louisiana[b] was not organized as an Indian Territory in 1803; because the white people anticipated matters by rushing across the Mississippi and establishing a prior claim to the land. This can hardly be accepted as sufficient excuse for the delay, inasmuch as the same obstacle must then also have existed, and in a greatly exaggerated form, twenty years later. Besides, the land was not needed for the white people in 1803. Emigration from Europe, except by army and navy deserters, was not particularly strong during the stormy period preceding the war of 1812, and the pressure of

---

[a] Richardson, I: 378.
[b] Gales and Seaton's Register, VI: 1064.

population was certainly not yet felt in the Eastern States. Moreover, had the Government been fully resolved to colonize the Indians, it would have been a comparatively easy matter to have dislodged the trespassers.

A much more satisfactory and, in a sense, confirmatory explanation of Jefferson's apparent indifference may be surmised from a letter of instructions which the Department of War addressed to William Henry Harrison[a] June 21, 1804. " On the subject of an Exchange of lands with the Delewares & other Indians, It is conceived it would be improper for the Government untill [b] it shall have obtained more particular information relative to the existing claims to the lands in Louisiana to enter into any stipulations with any of the Indian Nations on the subject of an exchange of the lands they respectively possess for lands in Louisiana and they ought not to be allowed to make any settlements on the Western side of the Missisippi without special permission from the Government of the United States. In the meantime it may be proper to inform such of the Nations as shall discover a wish to remove into Louisiana, that as soon as they shall have settled the limits of their present possessions with their Neighbors, so as to prevent any dispute hereafter in case of an exchange, and the Government of the United States shall have ascertained the just claims of the several Indian Nations, and others to lands in Louisiana, there will be no objection on the part of the U. S. to exchanging such lands with said Indians, West of the Missisippi for lands east of that river as shall be mutually agreed on; but it should be understood that they cannot receive lands immediately on the Missisippi unless they go some distance above the mouth of the Missouri. It is probable however the U. S. will be able to accomodate them with lands on some of the large branches of the Missouri or on the western Branches of the Missisippi, not verry far above the mouth of the Missouri * * *." c

Those who believe that from first to last Indian colonization was primarily a movement in the interests of the slaveholding power may find a deeper meaning in this letter than on the surface appears. It was not addressed in duplicate to any of the southern agents. Are we then to suppose that its discouraging tone was intended for the northwest tribes only? The impression conveyed by its contents is that the Indians to whom it referred were not only willing but really anxious to remove. Why then were they dissuaded? They were causing considerable trouble on the Canadian border, and unquestionably their

---

[a] William Henry Harrison was, at the time, governor of Indiana Territory and, like all other Territorial governors, was ex-officio superintendent of Indian Affairs. (" Indian Office Letter Books ; " Series I, A, p. 166.)

[b] It must be noted that whenever a letter or extract of a letter from the Indian Office Letter Books has been taken the spelling of the original Indian Office copyist has been followed.

[c] Indian Office Letter Books," Series I, B, p. 6.

departure from the British sphere of influence would have much allayed local apprehension. The question naturally arises, Did Jefferson postpone their emigration for the reason assigned? Later events would indicate that he did not, but judgment in the matter might well be suspended until later applications of his policy have been discussed.

On at least three different occasions previous to the war of 1812 an apparently honest effort was made to put the removal idea into practice, and the personal influence of Jefferson was strongly felt in each instance. The proposition in all seriousness was first submitted to a Chickasaw [a] delegation from Mississippi Territory that came to Washington, D. C., early in 1805. Jefferson seized the opportunity to enlarge upon the benefits to be derived from agricultural pursuits, and then delicately hinted at removal, saying in the most unconcerned way, without any unnecessary regard for the truth, "We have lately obtained from the French and Spaniards all the country beyond the Mississippi called Louisiana, in which there is a great deal of land unoccupied by any red men. But it is very far off, and we would prefer giving you lands there, or money and goods, as you like best, for such parts of your land on this side the Mississippi as you are disposed to part with. Should you have anything to say on this subject now or at any future time, we shall be always ready to listen to you." [b] There is no record of what impression this invitation to emigrate made upon the delegation or upon their constituents. Perhaps, they were as ill-prepared to comprehend its import as would have been Rabbit and his fellows who found their way to Washington in the fall of 1802, their only credential a captain's commission from General Washington and their only interpreter a little boy who understood neither the English nor the Chickasaw language.[c]

The Choctaws, whose headquarters were likewise in Mississippi Territory were the next to be experimented upon.[d] The actual " talks " may not have come down to us; but there are references enough in contemporary documents to show that, sometime in 1808, these Indians evinced a disposition to withdraw themselves from the encircling white settlements, and that the Government tried to take

---

[a] General James Robertson and Silas Dinsmore were commissioned in 1805 to treat for a cession with the Chickasaws. Their journal of proceedings, still extant among the Indian Office Manuscript Records, contains a reference to the Louisiana purchase, but none to removal.

[b] Jefferson's Works, Library edition, XVI: 412.

[c] " Indian Office Letter Books," Series I, A, pp. 293, 295.

[d] It is possible that the Choctaws were approached on the subject of removal even earlier than were their neighbors, the Chickasaws; for, in an address of December 17, 1803 (Jefferson's Works, Library edition, XVI, pp. 400–405), Jefferson alluded to a probable examination of a new home: " I am glad, brothers, you are willing to go and visit some other parts of our country." The context, however, does not indicate an exchange of lands or a permanent change of residence.

advantage of the situation. Secretary Dearborn [a] had prophesied that the Louisiana cession, particularly if it were held to include West Florida as he believed it would be, would place the United States " on strong ground with the Choctaws." Such, indeed had proved to be the case, and now, in view of approaching troubles with Europe, it was deemed advisable to consolidate the military strength of the United States on its southern frontier and to erect a barrier between the Indians and their Spanish neighbors.[b] Migration across the Mississippi was not a new experience with the Choctaws. They had become accustomed long since to make frequent hunting and predatory excursions into the valley of the Arkansas River.[c] Nevertheless, in 1808, they held out against a permanent removal. The Government was not yet ready to resort to force, and persuasion availed nothing. The tribe as a whole refused to emigrate. A few individuals went West on their own responsibility; the rest stayed in Mississippi.

The third instance of attempted removal is found in connection with the Cherokees, who constituted the most numerous, the most powerful, and the most highly civilized of the southern tribes. At one time their hunting grounds " were conceded to extend from the eastern slopes of the Blue Ridge to the neighborhood of the Mississippi River, and from the Ohio River almost as far south as central Georgia. * * * The settlement of the country by the whites and the acquisition of the Indian territory by them was naturally along the lines of least resistance. That is to say, the Cherokees first ceded away their remote hunting grounds and held most tenaciously " to eastern Tennessee and northern Georgia, " the section in which their towns were situated." [d] They had early divided themselves as a people into two classes, the Lower and the Upper Cherokees. The former lived in Georgia, the latter in Tennessee. It was more or less of an accident that the Lower Cherokees happened to be the less civilized of the two groups. One would naturally have expected the reverse to be the case. As it was, the Cherokees of Georgia still earned a precarious living by hunting and fishing, desired no innovations, and strenuously resisted every invasion of their territory by would-be settlers. They quarreled incessantly with the inhabitants of the upper towns, who appealed, in the spring of 1808, to the United States for an adjustment of their differences, particularly for a more equitable distribution of the annuities.

Antecedent and preparatory to this move the Cherokee agent, Col. Return Jonathan Meigs, had received some pretty definite instruc-

[a] Dearborn to Silas Dinsmore, September 7, 1803. " Indian Office Letter Books," Series I, A, p. 374.

[b] Message to Senate, January 15, 1808. Richardson I: 435; Message to Senate and House of Representatives, January 30, 1808, ibid. I: 438.

[c] Annals of Congress, XIV, Appendix, p. 1510 et seq.; McKenney and Hall, I: 31.

[d] Phillips, p. 66. See also Royce, " Cherokee Nation of Indians," p. 141

tions. " If you think it practicable," [a] wrote Secretary Dearborn, the 25th of March, " to induce the Cherokees, as a nation generally to consent to an exchange of their present Country for a suitable tract of Country on the other side of the Mississippi, you will please to embrace every favorable occasion for sounding the chiefs on the subject; and let the subject be generally talked about the nation until you shall be satisfied of the prevailing opinion."

Just to what extent the efforts of Meigs were successful we have no means of knowing; but in the beginning of May a delegation from the Upper Cherokees visited Washington and asked, among other things, that a permanent line of division might be drawn between their settlements and those of their less civilized brethren, to the end that such as wished might become husbandmen while the others remained hunters. The Upper Cherokees also expressed a desire to become citizens of the United States and subject, in all respects, to the laws of the white men. Jefferson personally interviewed the delegates and addressed to them the customary " talk " [b] taking care to introduce the alternative of removal. In the light of later events it is interesting to note that he admitted that citizenship could not be conferred upon the Indians without Congressional action. He further said that, prior to any territorial division of the tribe, the sense of the whole must be taken. " Should the principal part of your people," said he, " determine to adopt this alteration, and a smaller part still choose to continue the hunter's life, it may facilitate the settlement among yourselves to be told that we will give to those leave to go, if they choose it, and settle on our lands beyond the Mississippi, where some Cherokees are already settled, and where game is plenty * * *."

The delegates went home and again the furtherance of the removal project was intrusted to Colonel Meigs, with the advice that " the act of removal should be the result of their own inclinations without being urged to the measure." [c] Almost a year later Cherokee delegates again appeared at Washington, some to represent the upper towns and some the lower. Each party presented its case to Jefferson. To the Tennessee Cherokees he talked, January 9, in much the same spirit as the year before. [d] They were still desirous of citizenship and on that point Jefferson's remarks were anything but hopeful. To the Cherokees from Georgia he presented arguments for removal which were well taken. [e] Indeed, Colonel Meigs must have done some

[a] " Indian Office Letter Books," Series I, B, p. 364.

[b] " Indian Office Letter Books," Series I, B, pp. 374–375 ; Jefferson's Works, Library edition, XVI : 432–435.

[c] Dearborn to Meigs, May 5, 1808, " Indian Office Letter Books," Series I, B, pp. 376–377.

[d] " Indian Office Letter Books," Series I, B, p. 414 ; Jefferson's Works, Library edition, XVI : 455–458.

[e] Jefferson's Works, Library edition, XVI : 458–460.

good work since the preceding May in convincing the more nomadic that their only hope of earthly salvation lay in emigration beyond the Mississippi. The delegates had therefore come to Washington prepared to arrange the terms upon which the Lower Cherokees were to remove.

The plan was a very simple one but fraught with untold evil for the future, inasmuch as it served as a model for the treaty of 1817.[a] It was based upon an exchange, acre for acre, of the tribal land to which the individual Indian was proportionately entitled. Now it is very evident that there was no way of determining that proportionate amount of land except by allotment in severalty. The thing to do was to take a census of the Indians and at the same time determine the exact amount of land held by the tribe in common. As it happened, nothing of the kind was done. Interest [b] in Cherokee emigration lapsed with the incoming of President Madison.[c] The Federal

---

[a] 7 United States Statutes at Large, p. 156.

[b] It did not immediately die out but steadily declined. In the spring of 1811 about 2,000 Cherokee showed themselves desirous of emigrating west and Colonel Meigs wrote to Washington for instructions. In reply he was told "that a more gradual migration was preferred by the government. Time and circumstances (having their effect on this policy) render it expedient to ascertain whether such an exchange to any considerable extent, continues to be practicable * * * ." (Letter from War Department to Col. R. J. Meigs, March 27, 1811. Indian Office Letter Books, Series I, C, pp. 69–70.) A slight explanation for this change of policy appears in a letter to Silas Dinsmore and M. T. Wash, under date of April 20, 1811 : "The removal of the Cherokees and Choctaws to the Western Side of the Mississippi, as contemplated by Mr. Jefferson, has been considered by the present President. A gradual migration until some general arrangement could be made, has been prefered. Col. Meigs is about consulting the Cherokees on the Subject ; but it has occurred to me, from the circumstance of the murder of three Cherokees by a party of Choctaws, during the last year near Arkansas, that Similar Scenes might be repeated in case both Tribes Should migrate in considerable bodies. attention to this * * * ." ("Indian Office Letter Books," Series I, C, p. 78.)

[c] Although ordinarily somewhat indifferent toward the Indians, Madison seems, when especially appealed to, to have taken a fairly liberal view of their position. In 1816 he instructed John Rhea, United States Commissioner to the Choctaws, that the policy of the Government was a gradual acquirement of territory upon the basis of generosity and humanity. ("Writings," III : 6–7.) In 1817 he intimated to Monroe that the United States might push its claims of preemption a little too far and exaggerate the claims of civilized over uncivilized men to its own ruin. (Ibid., p. 54.) He fully indorsed Morse's scheme for benefiting the Indians (letter to Rev. J. Morse, February 16, 1822, and letter to Jefferson, March 5, 1822 ; ibid., pp. 259–261), and McKenney's also, though in more moderate terms : "The article in the North American Review concerning the Indians is evidently from one who, with opportunities the most favorable for his purpose, has made the best use of them * * * . I wish, as doubtless he does, that your comments on his distrust of the means adopted for new modeling the Indian character may be sanctioned by their success. If I am less sanguine of such a result than you are, I do not despair, and join in applauding the philanthropy and zeal that labor and hope for it. Next to the case of the black race within our bosom, that of the red on our borders is the problem most baffling to the policy of our country." (Ibid., p. 515.) In commenting upon Monroe's message of April 13, 1824, Madison showed clearly where he stood on the subject of compulsory removal and, in a dignified manner, blamed the Georgians severely for what he called their "egregious miscalculation" of the compact of 1802. (Ibid., p. 434.) His first direct opinion upon the subject of general removal was given to William Wirt in connection with the Cherokee case : "The most difficult problem is that of reconciling their interests with their rights. It is so evident that they can never be tranquil or happy within the bounds of a State, either in a separate or subject character, that a removal to another home, if a good one can be

Government was not prepared to advance funds as it had promised; so, left to their own resources, the Indians went or stayed as they pleased. Such of them as did emigrate came from the upper towns mostly and not from the lower, as had been anticipated,[a] and they journeyed, not as a compact body, but as individual families.[b] Neither the United States Government nor their own tribe had anything to do with their removal.[c] No definite tract of territory was assigned them west of the Mississippi. They wandered about or settled down whenever and wherever they could find room. The gap their several departures made in the tribe, probably never appreciable, because so gradual, was soon closed over. As far as the Cherokee Nation was concerned the absentees were as though they had never been.

Jefferson's real plans, respecting which a decision was heretofore held in abeyance, may now be arrived at with a measurable degree of certainty. In the beginning of 1805 we have seen him urging the Chickasaws, in seeming good faith, to move westward and assuring them of an unobstructed progress. How can this be reconciled with Secretary Dearborn's letter to Harrison in the June preceding? The Chickasaws were southern Indians, so were the Choctaws and Cherokees in whose favor the idea of removal was reasserted during the closing years of Jefferson's second term. The President personally interested himself in their migration; but he seems never to have similarly solicited the removal of the Northwestern tribes, although he readily fell [d] in with Harrison's plans for a rapid extinguishment of their title, which shows that the presence or absence of an economic need for territory had nothing whatever to do with his varying attitude toward removal. (As a matter of fact, Jefferson pursued a policy in the Northwest that tended in one way to obstruct and in another to disparage Indian colonization. Besides ignoring a Shawnee [e] dispo-

found, may well be the wish of their best friends. But the removal ought to be made voluntary by adequate inducements, present and prospective ; and no means ought to be grudged which such a measure may require." (Ibid., IV : 113–114.)

[a] Phillips, p. 68.

[b] Department of War to Col. R. J. Meigs, November 1, 1809. " Indian Office Letter Books," Series I, C, p. 6.

[c] At least we infer as much since the tribe as a whole had not sanctioned the movement in the first instance. Talk of Cherokee Council, July 2, 1817, American State Papers, " Indian Affairs," II : 142.

[d] Department of War to William H. Harrison, June 27, 1804. " Indian Office Letter Books," Series I, B, p. 7.

[e] About 1803, and again in 1807, the Shawnees begged for a grant of land where their entire tribe might congregate. (Miscellaneous Files, Indian Office.) At the later period they were even anxious for a union at one place with the Wyandots, Delawares, and Miamies. Prior to the purchase of Louisiana small parties of Shawnees emigrated to the vicinity of St. Louis, and when the United States took possession of the country Governor Wilkinson promised them a permanent home. (Address of James Rogers, chief of a band of Shawnees—Miscellaneous Files, Indian Office.) In 1811 Governor Clark interested himself in their cause and wrote personally to Madison, " I have been frequently solicited by small parties of Shawnees residing within this Territory on the subject of the governments assigning to them a permanent tract of country to live on, where the white people might not encroach on them. Those people wish to be situated so as to prevent disputes

sition to emigrate, he resorted to removal only as a threat [a] against insubordination.

It might very properly be contended that the purpose here was not removal in the ordinary meaning of the term. Had the threat been carried out the Indians would either have been exterminated or have been driven beyond the confines of the United States. The scheme of colonizing would have had no part in the concern at all. No similar threats seem to have been used against the more formidable southern tribes.

At first glance, considering how differently Jefferson, the originator of the removal project, dealt with the southern and northern Indians, respectively, and how prominently the Gulf States were destined to figure in the history of removal, we are fain to conclude with Henry Wilson that the whole course of the United States Indian policy was so shaped as to prove national subserviency to the slave power. Interesting as this would be, care must be taken not to place too much stress upon it, or even to give it entire credence, for it does not altogether accord with the historical facts. It is incorrect, in the first place, to think of the Southern States, in the days of Jefferson, as a " slave power," or to imagine that their interests as such were ever consciously considered by him. Removal had become an accomplished fact, in so far as the ultimate policy of the Government was concerned, long before slavery had been recognized as a serious issue in national politics. It is only when we take later and isolated instances of removal and study them apart from all their historical connections that the argument of the abolitionists can have any weight. Such a course would be manifestly illogical and unfair.

We can not even say that Jefferson's indifference or objection to the removal of the northwestern tribes was the result of partiality to his own section. His interest in the Indians turned on the Georgia compact of 1802, which was the key to the whole situation. Unless

---

which frequently take place between them and their nearest neighbours; and where the white people will not be permitted to sell them spirituous liquors. * * * A part of the Shawnee and Delaware nations have a claim under permission from the Spanish Govern[t] of a large tract of land situated immediately on the Mississippi about half way between this place and the mouth of Ohio, on which land a part of those Nations reside in Towns.—Several white families have settled promiscuously on those lands, as the unappropriated property of the United States which creates some discontent amongst the Indians of that quarter; who are anxious (as I am told by some of their chiefs) that the Government would confirm them in the possession of that Land or assign them another place outside the settlements. * * * " (Clark to Madison, St. Louis, April 10, 1811, Miscellaneous Files, Indian Office.)

[a] There are many instances of this. Jefferson's talk to the Ottawas, Chippewas, Pottawatomies, Wyandots, and Senecas of Sandusky, April 22, 1808, is, perhaps, one of the best. " * * * if there be among you any nation whom no benefits can attach, * * * that nation must abandon forever the land of their fathers, no nation rejecting our friendship and commencing wanton and unprovoked (war) against us, shall ever after remain within our reach, it shall never be in their power to strike us a second time * * * ." (" Indian Office Letter Books," Series I, B, pp. 372–373.)

16827—08——17

the design of that could be carried out by removal, he was under no
obligations to force a change in the Indian policy at a moment when
the national resources had need to be expended in other directions.
It required all the foresight of which he was capable to steer clear of
foreign complications. It was not a time to venture upon new and
untried methods in the settlement of domestic affairs unless, indeed,
a great purpose, like the keeping of national faith pledged to a sovereign State, could be subserved. Failing that, it was best to let matters take their own course.

There were other reasons and serious ones too why the impetus to
Indian removal, if it came at all, was bound to come from the neighborhood of the four great tribes. The Choctaws, Chickasaws, Creeks,
and Cherokees were no inconsiderable part of the southern population. They constituted a power that, if allowed to increase unchecked,
might be truly formidable. As it was, they blocked any widespread
and consolidated settlement south of the Mason and Dixon line.
Combination and effective resistance to encroachment were more likely
to come from them with their superior intelligence and superior political organization than from the scattered and scattering bands
dwelling north of the Ohio River. This was as true in 1805 as in 1830.

Moreover, until after the acquisition of East Florida, foreign interference, much as it was to be dreaded on the Canadian border, was
an ever-present and ever-increasing menace in the Southeast. The
political influence at Washington as exerted by States was, of course,
much more strongly felt than was that exerted by Territories. If
we leave New York out of consideration, as having interests distinct
from all the others, we may well suppose that the influence of Georgia
and the Carolinas combined, to say nothing of Tennessee and Kentucky, would greatly outweigh that of Ohio. Finally, if at the opening of the nineteenth century there was a land pressure any where, it
was rather in the South than in the North. Under the vigorous administration of such men as William Henry Harrison, the old Northwest was being cleared of its Indian encumbrance much faster even
than the economic needs demanded. The tribes there were numerous,
but individually too small to offer effective opposition. Their very
number was a source of weakness, as their frequent quarrels enabled
the white men to play off one faction against another, and in the long
run to reap the whole advantage for themselves.

In one important particular the removal idea as revived for the
Chickasaws presents a striking contrast to the idea as it was first pro-
mulgated by Jefferson in 1803. In 1805 it was separated and considered as something distinct from Indian colonization. It contemplated
the migration of individual tribes, or, to state it more nearly in accordance with what actually occurred, that of detached bands. Here again
we must seek an explanation in local and temporary conditions. At

the time of the Louisiana purchase, Jefferson probably did not dare to venture to hold out relief to the South only, not even though the national faith was pledged to Georgia. He therefore suggested removing the whole body of Indians westward. In 1805 and later, he was able to proceed upon narrower issues; and, by shifting the responsibility upon the Indians and making it appear as though they had taken the initiative, to depart from the broad lines laid down in the constitutional draft of 1803. It is well to remember this, because the two ideas of removal and colonization were very rarely brought together again; and, when they are associated in after years, they serve to distinguish the real philanthropists, like Isaac McCoy and, perhaps, Thomas McKenney, from the self-seeking and aggressive politicians who cared not what became of the aborigines so long as their presence was not allowed to obstruct the onward path of the white men.

CHAPTER III.

THE WAR OF 1812 AND INDIAN REMOVAL.

The outlook for an early accomplishment of a general Indian removal along lines of cheerful acquiescence is thus seen to have been, at the close of Jefferson's term of office, not very promising, and assuredly nothing else was possible; for the southern tribes were far too strong for anything that bordered upon expulsion to be successful and, if we are to judge from what was soon to occur under Tecumseh's influence, the same might be asserted of those of the Northwest. At all events the inauguration of James Madison brought a decided lull in the prosecution of the colonizing project. As has been already remarked, the new President, although inclined on occasion to be just to the aborigines, was not much interested in their affairs, and, therefore, had the conditions been ever so favorable, it is doubtful whether he would have given removal his cordial support. As it was, he had other and wider subjects to engage his attention, so that the idea might have been completely forgotten had not speculators chosen to remember it for their own aggrandizement and, in addition, had not various events conspired to intensify the hatred already existing between the two races.

Chief and foremost among these events was the reputed Indian alliance with the British who, both before and after the surrender of the western posts, controlled the fur trade around the Great Lakes. Their influence for good or ill extended westward beyond the Rockies and southward even to the Red River. Consequently they came in contact with the most warlike tribes dwelling wholly or partly within United States territory, and were suspected of inciting raids upon the defenseless American settlements. The charge in its extreme form as reflecting upon the policy of the British Government can be easily and satisfactorily disproved by research into the Canadian archives.[a] Even at the time of its greatest circulation the majority of thinking people must have doubted its accuracy. It was officially

[a] " Moreover, it has been constantly charged by our writers that England, from the vantage ground of these western posts, instigated in a secret, dastardly manner the Indians of the region to wage their horrible, barbarous warfare upon our frontier settlements. There has been little disagreement on this point among our own writers. The prima facie evidence is so strong that presumptions of insidious instigation from England are easily and naturally made. The revelations of the Canadian archives allow us to go further than presumption and to settle the question with some definiteness. * * * The results of such do not enable me to agree either with the American historians who lay this charge at the door of Great Britain or with the more recent writers of Canada

denied by the ministry,[a] discredited by the Department of War at Washington,[b] scouted by the Federalists [c] and war opponents generally both in and out of Congress,[d] and maintained on a large scale only among the anti-British westerners as a sort of justification for the renewal of hostilities with the mother country.

The more prominent Canadian officials can be equally exonerated; but, in deciding upon their guilt or innocence, it is necessary to draw a sharp distinction between inciting the Indians to warfare and taking pains to preserve their attachment to themselves. The latter was an element in sound policy, especially as, during the period of the later Napoleonic wars, Canada had good reason to look askance at the movements of both France and the United States. Her domestic difficulties coupled with a fear of invasion were a matter of no small

---

who endeavor to clear the skirts of the home Government and the province of all unworthy motive or infamous action * * * " (pp. 413–414). ("Annual Report of the American Historical Association," 1894.)

Prof. A. C. McLaughlin, the writer of the above, further remarks that it is unfair to charge the conduct of vagabond, irresponsible half-breeds and rovers to the British Government or to the Canadian authorities. (Ibid., p. 429.) Great Britain was indignant that the Americans should settle in territory organized as Indian and, as she hoped to use the savages in case of possible war, she constantly assured them that she would be their friend and that they were not to yield too easily to the allurements of the other party. (Ibid., p. 434.) In conclusion, he says : " I am glad to be able to state, after an examination of the Canadian archives, for the purpose, that England and her ministers can be absolutely acquitted of the charge that they desired to foment war in the West. I do not mean to assert that they were entirely without responsibility for a condition of affairs and for a state of mind on the part of the savages which made hostilities a certainty. * * * " (Ibid., p. 435.)

[a] British Declaration, January 9, 1813, " British and Foreign State Papers," Vol. I, part 2, p. 1519.

[b] William Eustis to W. H. Harrison, September 8, 1811, " Indian Office Letter Books," Series I, C, p. 113.

[c] Governor Strong, of Massachusetts, said : "A suspicion has been intimated that the hostility of the Indian tribes was excited by British influence ; as no proof has been offered to us on the subject, it might be sufficient to say, that a regard to vague and uncertain suppositions exposes a nation to become an unjust aggressor. But has not our conduct toward those tribes been often oppressive and unjust ; and have we not indulged an eager desire to obtain possession of their lands, when we had already millions of acres which we could neither cultivate nor dispose of? * * * " (Message, May 28, 1813, Niles's Register IV : 233–236.)

[d] Benton, in his "Abridgement of Debates," Vol. IV : 436–442, gives the substance of a speech by John Randolph, of Virginia, on this matter : "An insinuation had fallen from the gentleman from Tennessee, [Mr. Grundy,] that the late massacre of our brethren on the Wabash had been instigated by the British Government. Has the President given any such information? has the gentleman received any such, even informally, from any officer of this Government? Is it so believed by the Administration? He had cause to think the contrary to be the fact ; that such was not their opinion. This insinuation was of the grossest kind—a presumption the most rash, the most unjustifiable. Show but good ground for it, he would give up the question at the threshold—he was ready to march to Canada. It was indeed well calculated to excite the feelings of the Western people particularly, who were not quite so tenderly attached to our red brethren as some modern philosophers ; but it was destitute of any foundation, beyond mere surmise and suspicion. What would be thought if, without any proof whatsoever, a member should rise in his place and tell us, that the massacre in Savannah, a massacre perpetrated by civilized savages, with French commissions in their pockets, was excited by the French Government? There was an easy and natural solution of the late transactions on the Wabash, in the well-known character of the aboriginal savage of North America without resorting to any such mere conjectural estimate. He was sorry to say, that for this signal calamity and disgrace the House was, in part, at least, answerable. Session after session their table had been piled up with Indian treaties, for which the appropriations had been voted as a matter of course, without examination. Advantage had been taken

concern.[a] The loyalty of the French inhabitants[b] was a very uncertain quantity as was also that of recent immigrants from the States.[c] Early in the summer of 1808 there were rumors that Bonaparte contemplated an expedition to America, in which, were British dominions the objective point, he might or might not secure the cooperation of the United States since there had been some rather boastful talk about joining forces with the French and conquering Canada.[d] It was deemed important, therefore, for the British to strengthen all their defenses, and the good will of the Indians was certainly not the least of these, inasmuch as they were bound to fight on one side or the other, and if not with the British, then against them.[e]

The chances were that the Indians would much prefer fighting on the British side. Year by year they had become more and more enraged against the spread of western settlement and, as the Americans took no pains to propitiate them, they continued to plot revenge.[f] The Canadian authorities knew of this—knew also how likely, under the circumstances, blame was to fall upon them should any savage outbreak occur. They therefore resolved to act discreetly[g] so as not

---

of the spirit of the Indians, broken by the war which ended in the Treaty of Greenville. Under the ascendancy then acquired over them, they had been pent up by subsequent treaties into nooks, straitened in their quarters by a blind cupidity, seeking to extinguish their title to immense wildernesses, for which (possessing, as we do already, more land than we can sell or use) we shall not have occasion, for half a century to come. It was of our own thirst for territory, our own want of moderation, that had driven these sons of nature to desperation, of which we felt the effects."

[a] Craig to Erskine, May 13, 1808. " Report on Canadian Archives," 1893, p. 10. Craig to Edward Cooke, July 15, 1808, ibid., p. 13.

[b] Craig to Castlereagh, August 4, 1808, ibid., p. 14 ; Craig to Castlereagh, August 5, 1808, ibid., p. 14.

[c] Gore to Craig, January 5, 1808. Ibid., p. 3.

[d] John Henry to Ryland, March 6, 1808. Ibid., p. 6.

[e] Craig to Gore, December 6, 1807, ibid, p. 1 : " If the Indians are not employed with us, they will certainly be employed against us. Caution necessary in dealing with them ; the loss of the valuable Indian trade if they are not kept on our side. * * * " Gore to Craig, January 5, 1808, ibid., p. 3 : "Considers that could we destroy the American posts of Detroit and Michillimackinac many Indians would declare for us. Agrees that if not for us they will be against us." Craig to Gore, December 28, 1808 : " Repeats that they must be either for us or against us," ibid., p. 16. Letter from Downing street to Craig, April 8, 1809 : " Entirely concurs that in present relations with the United States, the Indians must be conciliated on the principle that if not for us they will be against us," ibid., p. 28. Letter from George Heriot to Judge Edward Winslow, Quebec, July 3, 1811. Raymond's " Winslow Papers," p. 671.

[f] Harrison wrote, in 1801, showing that the Indians needed little encouragement to war against the United States. They were incensed at the violation of treaties and at Indian wrongs unavenged, and were ready to unite with any power at war with the United States in whom they could trust. (Henry Adams, VI :73.) This state of feeling continued and measurably increased after it became apparent that the Treaty of Greenville was not to be respected.

[g] Craig to Gore, February 10, 1808. (" State Papers of Lower Canada " in " Report on Canadian Archives," 1893, p. 5.) "Advices abstaining as far as possible from irritating the public mind in the United States, though preserving the attachment of the Indians."

Craig to Erskine, May 13, 1808, ibid, p. 10 : " Will use every endeavour to avoid irritating our neighbours. * * * With the view of binding the Indians more closely, he has given directions that the officers of the Department be particularly attentive in all points and has also recommended that intercourse be opened with the most distant nations, with whom little communication has lately been had. * * * The instructions given particularly point out his desire that all means pursued should be such

to irritate the Americans. Their plan was to secure the friendship of the Indians, yet offer no encouragement should they, in their fiendish hunger for retaliation, wage war upon their own responsibility. Presents were distributed in greater quantities than usual, but the deputy superintendents were cautioned against letting the recipients know of the near prospect of strife between the English-speaking countries. As time went on and the Indians persisted in their intention of warring against the United States, thus resisting even the blandishments of Red Jacket who made a special endeavor to wean them from the British cause,[a] Sir James Craig went one step further and tried to conciliate them in the interests of the United States,[b] for he rightly surmised that a war provoked by savages upon the frontier would be very inconvenient in every way for the British.

Canada was not alone in the seeking after an Indian alliance. At the beginning of 1808 [c] the Americans were reported as sparing nothing to assure themselves of support, but the case was hopeless.[d] When once convinced of this, they pleaded for Indian neutrality but not because they were conscientiously opposed to the employment of savages. Indeed, the people of the two nations stand on much the same level with respect to Indian transactions generally. The differences in their conduct have been mainly differences of degree and not of kind. Whatever may be said to the contrary, neither had any very delicate scruples when it came to an actual test about allying themselves with red men.[e] The party that failed in a particular instance

as are of general conciliation and attachment, without allusion to possible hostilities. Is well aware that suspicion will be awakened, but adopts these measures to prevent the Indians from reporting that he was trying to instigate them against the States. Complaints on this head probable. * * * ”

Matthew Elliott to William Claus, Deputy Superintendent of Indian Affairs, October 16, 1810 : “ Believes that the Indians are more ripe than ever for war. Dreads they may of themselves commence hostilities and our Government be blamed for encouraging them. * * * ” (“ State Papers of Upper Canada ” in “ Report on Canadian Archives,” 1893, p. 26.)

Gore to Claus, February 26, 1811 : “ He is to instruct Elliott to be more than usually circumspect in his communications with the Indians so as to give no suspicion of favoring their hostile designs against the United States. * * * ” Ibid., p. 27. (Same in “ State Papers of Lower Canada,” p. 46.)

[a] Elliott to Claus, October 16, 1810. “ State Papers of Lower Canada,” p. 45.

[b] Craig to Gore, February 2, 1811 : “ Thinks upon consideration that our policy is to prevent a rupture between the Indians and the United States. A war so near our frontiers would* be very inconvenient in every way, and would expose us to suspicion on the part of the Americans, which would sooner or later involve ourselves. The bad effects inevitably attending such a war. The Indians must be advised that to avoid hostility is for their own good. They must be carefully managed * * * .” “ State Papers of Lower Canada,” p. 45.

Gore to Claus, February 26, 1811, ibid., p. 46.

Gore to Craig, March 2, 1811, ibid., p. 46.

Craig to Liverpool, March 29, 1811, ibid., p. 46.

[c] McKee to Prideau Shelby, January 8, 1808. “ State Papers of Lower Canada,” p. 3.

[d] Craig wrote to Lieutenant-Governor Gore on the 11th of May, 1808, that it would not be an easy thing to persuade the Indians to take part against the British, so incensed were they against the Americans. (“ State Papers of Lower Canada,” p. 9.)

[e] A very cursory review of the Revolutionary war proves that the Americans were no more adverse to the employment of savages than were the British. Matthew Griswold, of

to secure Indian aid liked to prate a good deal about the inhumanity of the practice and at the same time to redouble its own efforts for future success.

The strongest evidence implicating the Canadian authorities of incendiarism and the evidence most commonly cited is that contained in the " talks " addressed to the disaffected Indians by lesser officials. Such evidence is presumptive of very culpable conduct on the part of Indian agents,[a] army officers, and the like. Of itself, however, it is not sufficient to incriminate the Government. Indian " talks " by white men were seldom given in good faith, and their extravagant statements must not be taken too literally. No one, except the deluded Indians in the days of their first innocence, and white men who wanted something to support their own claims or charges, ever affected to believe that what they contained was true. Their object was to make a favorable impression for the time being upon the poetical sensibilities of the hearer—hence the rhetorical flourishes

Connecticut, advised encouraging their enlistment for defense. (American Archives, Fourth Series, II : 1588.) Ethan Allen earnestly invited them to fight with his Green Mountain boys (ibid., p. 714), and even John Adams thought that since they were not likely to remain neutral they ought to be induced to engage in the colonial cause. (Ibid., V : 1091.) Lord North claimed, indeed, that the British had had no intention or desire to use either negroes or Indians until the Americans started the practice (ibid., VI : 187), and that practice was the excuse for the issuance of the royal order of August 2, 1775 (ibid., III : 6). The British had a similar justification, if we may call it such, in the second period of strife (" Niles'· Register," XXVIII : 175–176). Men in authority on the frontiers, and more especially Lewis Cass (American State Papers, Indian Affairs, II : 13, 14), were provided with the means of distributing presents among such Indians as would take an active part in the war against Great Britain. Toward the close of that war and when the British threatened an invasion of Louisiana, Monroe wrote to Jackson : " You will not fail to secure the friendship and cooperation of the Creeks and Choctaws and other Tribes in our favour, should the menaced invasion take effect. To enable you to do this, blankets, &c. will be forwarded without delay to our Agents with those tribes *   *   * ." (Monroe Papers, V.) Jackson's whole military career was colored by the participation of savages so-called in warfare. In the Creek uprising he employed the friendly party against the hostile and in the Seminole war his main reliance was upon savages. His use of them on that occasion was ground for severe criticism and his line of defense has an interesting bearing upon the subject we are discussing. In his autograph memorial to the Senate, 1819, he says : " The Committee has been prodigal of its labour and research in order to prove the illegality of employing the friendly Creeks during the last campaign, it declares that no Legal authority for calling the friendly Indians into the field has existed since 3[d] of March, 1795. Whether this measure be sanctioned by Law, required by policy, or justified by necessity, I presume I need not say to an enlightened public that it has been the common practice of our Country during every Indian war in which we have been engaged since the first organization of our Government and there is not a friendly Chief of distinction on our extensive frontier who does not wear a meddle, or a sword, presented by our Government as a reward for his valour and fidelity in those conflicts, during the late war with Great Britain, the employ—of the friendly Indians was not only authorized at every point on our frontier, but I was directed to compel (by coercive measures if it became necessary) all the warriors of the fóur Southern Tribes to enroll themselves in our defence *   *   * ." (Jackson Papers, November, 1819.)

[a] Two of the most notorious of these agents, McKee and Elliott, were not in good standing even with the Canadian government. The former was addicted to intemperance (Gore to Craig, January 8, 1808 ; State Papers of Lower Canada, p. 3) and tne latter had some time before been discharged from the service for misconduct. Francis Gore, lieutenant-governor of Upper Canada, and Sir John Johnson, superintendent of Indian Affairs, both recommended his restoration because of his very great influence over the Indians. Governor Craig hesitated, but was finally obliged, apparently against his better judgment, to yield to the situation.

and the high-sounding, meaningless phrases about the "Great Father" and his "tender care for his beloved red children," which were their most marked characteristics.

The actions of the British traders[a] among whom the French element, with all that it promised for mutual good will, predominated, have also been exposed to censure; but, whether justly or not, is quite another thing. There is no question that everything possible was done by these traders to win the friendship of the Indians, but upon their own responsibility, quite independent of national politics. Like the Indian agents, they distributed gifts freely, supplied arms and "fire water," and made a fair return for peltries. Their real object can not be determined exactly. It may have been perfectly legitimate; nothing more, in fact, than the commercial advantage which all competitors take if they get a chance. Jealousy was rife between them and the American backwoodsmen; but, as peace was conducive to profitable trade, it is hardly likely that they would have been so blind to their own interest as to provoke an Indian war.[b] One thing is well worth noticing, and that is, their economic footing in the West. Their relations to the Indians was decidedly different from that of their rivals. Their purpose was the acquisition of wealth by trapping and trading, implying no real occupation of the land but merely a free transit through it. The purpose of the Americans was settlement, permanent occupation, and the dispossession of the natives. Is it any wonder, then, that the tribes saw in the one party a friend, in the other an enemy, and acted accordingly?

Supposing from what has been said that the conduct of the British at its very worst amounted to nothing more than commercial selfishness and a semi-official sympathy too freely expressed, it remains to explain how and why the charge of incendiarism ever originated. Is it too much to say that it had its beginnings in a desire to blind the eyes of the world to the real cause of Indian hostility toward the United States, and that it was started by the speculators and politicians of the Northwest for the double purpose of warding off suspicion and criticism from themselves and of increasing the popular prejudice against both the Indians and the British? Admittedly the evidence against these men is purely circumstantial. No definite statement is forthcoming showing what their real designs were. All we can do is to study the history of the years immediately preceding and draw our own conclusions.

---

[a] Professor McLaughlin, in his study of the subject, says that "The legitimate traders, the men, it is to be presumed, who had influence with the [British] Government, did not desire war between the Americans and the Indians * * * actual war was injurious to their business interests." ("Annual Report of the American Historical Association," 1894, p. 429.)

[b] The Department of War seems to have thought that the non-importation act had much to do with the attitude of the British traders. (Letter to Gen. John Mason, April 15, 1811, "Indian Office Letter Books," Series I, C, p. 74.)

In discussing two of the most prominent events occurring in the early history of the old Northwest, viz, the incorporation of land companies and the disastrous expedition of General St. Clair, writers almost invariably fail to give due weight to the intimate relation which they bore to each other. It was remotely that of cause and effect. Take, for example, the case of the Scioto Land Company [a] which, in 1787, received from the Confederate Congress an immense tract of land on the Indian side of the Ohio River. The Indian owners were not consulted in the transaction. Their rights were totally ignored. Not a cent were they ever offered in compensation.[b] They watched with indignation the steady progress of the pioneers. Finally, they entered upon a series of depredations which increased in frequency and seriousness as the white settlements advanced. They were accused of wantonly harassing the frontier. No one seems to have thought that they were at all justified in what they were doing. Alas for the inconsistency of human nature! When white men fight for home and country they are lauded as the noblest of patriots. Indians, doing the same thing, are stigmatized as savages. What a fortunate and convenient excuse the doctrine of manifest destiny has proved!

Matters in the Ohio region reached a climax during Washington's Administration; but it is unnecessary to enter here into details respecting the successive defeats of Harmar and St. Clair. The story has been too often told and told well. Let us rather pass on to a consideration of the Greenville treaty of 1795,[c] which the victorious Anthony Wayne forced from the Indians after the battle of Fallen Timbers. It has usually been regarded as one of the greatest of Indian treaties. It is certainly one of the best known, mainly because the dividing line which it established became a sort of basis for later territorial changes. In so far as it looked toward an amicable adjustment of Indian difficulties, it was very deceptive. Indeed, it was so framed as to be productive of the very evils it sought to avoid. Within the country conceded as of right to belong to the Indians, it provided for a number of reservations to which the native occupancy title was declared extinguished and to which citizens of the United States were to have an unobstructed right of way.[d] This arrangement could hardly fail to bring about collisions.

As a matter of fact, the treaty of Greenville proved to the Indians a delusion and a snare. White men invaded their country more un-

---

[a] E. C. Dawes, "The Scioto Purchase in 1787," in "Magazine of American History," Vol. XXII: 470–482.

[b] C. G. Herbermann, "A French Émigré Colony in the United States, 1789–1793," in "Historical Records and Studies of the United States Catholic Historical Society," I, part 1 pp. 77–96.

[c] 7 United States Statutes at Large, 49–54.

[d] Article III.

restrainedly, if that were possible, than before. In 1800 Indiana Territory was organized west of a line drawn from the mouth of the Kentucky River, through Fort Recovery, to the Canadian border,[a] and the Indians at once exhibited a restlessness that augured ill for the future. Certain methods of dealing with them, persisted in by Governor Harrison, simply fanned the flame. His civil administration provoked much opposition from the people of Indiana,[b] and, in order to win popularity,[c] he began to negotiate a series of Indian cessions. He made no pretense of extinguishing the title of all the claimants, but held treaties with factions, with isolated bands; in short, with any Indians over whom he could exert a temporary influence, quite in defiance of Indian usage, which required the consent of a general council. The second treaty of Fort Wayne, 1809,[d] the last and, in some respects, the most unjust of the series, is a fair illustration of the Harrisonian tactics. Its chief provision was the cession, conditional upon Kickapoo consent,[e] of a large tract of land on the Wabash, to which the Shawnees of all the Northwest tribes had probably the best title, yet not a single Shawnee signed it or was present at its negotiation.[f] The conduct of Governor Hull, of Michigan Territory, was scarcely less reprehensible than that of Harrison. To all intents and purposes, both men had a standing commission to extinguish Indian titles, and no evidence of dissatisfaction could dampen their ardor.

Jefferson strongly disapproved of such high-handed proceedings. Since 1805[g] there had been vague but constant rumors of an Indian conspiracy and, in May of that year, Harrison was ordered to make explanations to dissenting chiefs and to counteract the effect of his own questionable methods.[h] As time went on the condition of affairs along the Canadian line became less and less reassuring. Knowing this, and wishing the natives to be spared additional provocations, Jefferson cautioned restraint on the part of Governor Harrison. In 1809 the Department of War ordered that a certain treaty should be made, provided the " chiefs of all the Nations who have or pretend a right to these lands should be present." [i] Two years later Harrison received another rebuff and was told that it was not expedient to negotiate any new cession until " the discontents occasioned by the one lately concluded " had been quieted.[j] Jefferson must have real-

---

[a] 2 United States Statutes at Large, 58–59.

[b] McMaster, III : 137 ; " Letters of Decius."

[c] McMaster, III : 528, 529.

[d] 7 United States Statutes at Large, 113–115.

[e] Ibid., 117.

[f] Manypenny, p. 87.

[g] " Indian Office Letter Books," Series I, B, pp. 86–87.

[h] Ibid., pp. 78–79.

[i] Letter to W. H. Harrison, July 15, 1809, " Indian Office Letter Books," Series I, C, p. 2.

[j] Letter to W. H. Harrison, March 17, 1811, ibid., p. 66.

ized that the almost wholesale dispossession was altogether unnecessary. It simply encouraged detached settlements and was certainly not the way to effect the pacification which would count for so much should war break out with Great Britain. Besides, he felt that eventually, without any application of force, the land would be cleared of the Indian encumbrance; for, as the products of the chase diminished, the natives would be compelled, as a matter of course, to do one of two things—"incorporate themselves with us as citizens of the United States or remove beyond the Mississippi." The caution came too late. Events had already gone too far.

The Indians, aware of the strained relations existing between the United States and Great Britain, doubtless conjectured that the time was propitious for them to avenge their own wrongs. They might even hope for cooperation. The earlier failure of Thayendanegea could not discourage such a man as Tecumseh. As early as 1807 the Americans at Detroit had anticipated as much and had "issued a proclamation[a] threatening retaliation on the wives and children of those joining the British standard." As has been seen, the advantages to be derived from such an alliance appealed likewise to Governor Craig. For a time he wavered, scarcely knowing what course to pursue. The loss of the valuable fur trade was, moreover, a contingency that had to be considered. To expect that the Indians would yield to Governor Hull's persuasions and remain neutral was absurd.

It was at this juncture, when war with Great Britain seemed daily imminent, that Jefferson wrote to Henry Dearborn, asking that the Territorial governors of the Northwest be instructed to hold interviews with the refractory tribes and threaten removal as a punishment for any attempted alliance with the enemy.[b] In April of 1808 he had himself addressed a similar talk to the Ottawas and their friends near Sandusky,[c] telling them that "if they help the enemies of the United States" they "must forever abandon the land of their fathers." In January of 1809 he threatened "to extirpate" the same tribes "from the Earth or drive to such a distance as that they shall never again be able to strike us."[d] It would seem that some of the Sacs and Foxes, confederated from time immemorial, had misgivings as to their ability to refrain from hostilities. "At their own request therefore they were removed from Illinois to the interior of Missouri." This resort to removal as a precaution against treachery is interesting as a forecast of future developments. The time was to come under Andrew Jackson when the Indians were to be left no

[a] Gore to Craig, December 1, 1807, "State Papers of Lower Canada," p. 1.
[b] Ford's "Jefferson," IX : 132–133.
[c] "Indian Office Letter Books," Series I, B, pp. 369–373.
[d] Ibid., p. 412.

choice in the matter; but never before had Jefferson presumed to hint at anything beyond a strictly voluntary migration.

The uprising of 1811–12 possessed one feature that was almost, if not quite, unique in Indian history. Pontiac and Thayendanegea had each in his turn dreamed of a concerted action among the tribes that should result in the expulsion of the whites and the reestablishment of native power; but it was left for Tecumseh to advance the theory that no individual tribe possessed the power of alienation. His argument was, that originally the continent belonged to the red race as a whole and that therefore no part of it could be sold without the consent of all. The doctrine was radical but by no means inconsistent with the fact that, until the advent of the white man, the Indian had had no conception of an individual personal interest in realty. Each tribe, it is true, had had its own indefinitely defined hunting grounds; but a map outlining them " that would be correct for a given date would probably be sadly misleading in the study of events that took place a few years earlier or later. "[a]   With specific reference to recent occurrences, Tecumseh held that all the treaties made subsequent to 1795 that involved the transfer of land northwest of the Ohio were absolutely invalid unless it could be shown that each and every tribe interested in the treaty of Greenville had subscribed to them. This proves conclusively where the real grievance of the Indians lay. There was no occasion for the British to excite them to war. They were already excited and had only to await their opportunity for action.

The so-called machinations of the British appear to have had a more real existence in the Southeast than in the Northwest; but here, as there, were totally without governmental sanction. Moreover, the period of their activity came after war had actually been declared between Great Britain and the United States. From the Spanish dominions as a base, they operated upon the disaffected of the four great tribes, among whom the peculiar ideas of Tecumseh had been early disseminated.[b]   It is only in a very limited sense, nevertheless, that British or Spanish emissaries can be said to have instigated the Creek insurrection of 1813. The cause of that lay deeper than recent events; deeper even than the supernaturalism of Tecumseh, and was mainly territorial.[c]   Its interest for us rests, not upon the military exploits of General Jackson,[d] but upon the influence which it exerted

[a] Avery, I : 339.

[b] Circular letter from the Department of War to the Southern agents, June 20, 1805, " Indian Office Letter Books," Series I, B, p. 85.

[c] Letter of Governor Benigno Garzia to Governor Mitchell, of Georgia, December 12, 1812 ; Niles's Register, vol. III : p. 311.

[d] There are very few papers in the Indian Office that throw light upon Indian wars. The supposition is that all such records were, upon the creation of the Interior Department, retained by the War Office.

over the agitators of removal, the history of which falls more properly into the narrative of the next chapter.

The general attitude of Madison's Administration toward the Indians was well brought out during the progress of the peace negotiations at Ghent in connection with the proposed establishment of buffer State. The idea of erecting some such barrier between the United States and British dominions, though not entirely new in 1814,[a] seems to have been suggested by the Canadian authorities,[b] who fully appreciated the services that had been rendered their otherwise inadequate forces and therefore the debt that was due the disaffected tribes. More than that, they were in a position to know that land disputes were the real cause of bad feeling between those tribes and the United States. How better then could they repay the debt than by preventing encroachments and consequent dispossessions in the future?

Castlereagh, though familiar with the benefits to be derived from a country neutralized, since that was the very precaution being taken by the allied powers against the ambition of France, was hardly prepared to pose as an advocate of Indian sovereignty. Nevertheless, under the force of colonial public opinion, he advanced the buffer State idea as a possible means of adjusting Indian difficulties but did not intend it, as is commonly supposed, to constitute in itself a sine qua non of peace. His first instructions to the British commissioners,[c] which were preliminary only, devised as a working basis, were issued under date of July 28, 1814. From their examination it will be observed that, while an " adequate arrangement of Indian interests " was to be " considered " as an ultimatum, the specific details of that arrangement were not.[d] They were simply thrown out as suggestions upon which diplomatic conferences might commence. The position taken by Castlereagh was still more clearly defined in his letter of August 14, 1814.[e] The sine quâ non is there said to be 'the express inclusion of the Indians as allies in the treaty of peace, signifying that they were not to be ignored as in 1763 and 1783.

---

[a] Annual Report of the American Historical Association, 1894, p. 433, note.
[b] Henry Adams, IX : 7.
[c] " Castlereagh Correspondence," X : 67–72.
[d] " Upon the subject of the Indians, you will represent that an adequate arrangement of their interests is considered by your Government as a *sine quâ non* of peace ; and that they will, under this head, require not only that a full and express recognition of their limits shall take place : you will also throw out the importance of the two States entering into arrangements which may hereafter place their mutual relations with each other, as well as with the several Indian nations, upon a footing of less jealousy and irritation. This may be best effected by a mutual guarantee of the Indian possessions, as they shall be established upon the peace, against encroachment on the part of either State.

*   *   *   *   *   *

The best prospect of future peace appears to be that the two Governments should' regard the Indian territory as a useful barrier between both States, to prevent collision ; and that, having agreed mutually to respect the integrity of their territory, they have a common interest to render these people, as far as possible, peaceful neighbours to both States * * * ."

[e] " Castlereagh Correspondence," X : 90.

The misconception as to the real character of the buffer State proposition may be doubtless attributed to the unusual stress laid upon it in the course of the negotiations and, more than all, to the fact that both the British and American commissioners in turn seem to have considered the mere recognition of Indian boundaries, which Castlereagh had declared to be incidental to the sine quâ non proper, as identical with the erection of a neutral belt.[a] It was not necessarily so, and there is no authority for supposing that the British cabinet originally intended it to be. The recognition of a boundary was an integral part of the ultimatum, the establishment of a buffer State was a subject for discussion only.[b]

It is furthermore a misrepresentation of facts to accuse the British Government in the person of its foreign secretary of a willful design to create a neutral belt solely at the expense of the United States. Lord Liverpool's instructions of the 31st of August, issued after the American note [c] complaining of nonreciprocity had been received, were a strong repudiation of any such charge.[d]. The confusion arose doubtless from the fact that the British, in proposing the Greenville treaty as a starting point, neglected to state specifically, as they did later,[e] a corresponding contraction of Canadian territory. Very early they declared themselves averse to demanding anything by way of conquest; [f] and it was not until the Americans objected to a resignation of any of the territory ceded by the Indians since 1795 [g] that they went one step further and pronounced the war to have abrogated the treaty of Greenville.[h]

---

[a] J. Q. Adams's "Memoirs," III: 6, 19; American State Papers, "Foreign Relations," III: 708; "British and Foreign State Papers," I, part 2, pp. 1585–1586.

[b] J. Q. Adams's "Memoirs," III; entry in diary, August 10, 1814; British Note of September 4, 1814; "British and Foreign State Papers," I, part 2, pp. 1605.

[c] American State Papers, "Foreign Relations," vol. III: pp. 711–713.

[d] " On the subject of the Indians the Commissioners must repeat that an adequate provision for their interest is conceded by the British Government as a *sine quâ non* in any pacific arrangement between the two countries; but it has never been the intention of the British Government to propose to the Government of the United States any stipulation on this subject which they were not ready reciprocally to adopt. They have proposed for this purpose as the basis of an arrangement a treaty concluded by the Government of the United States with the same Indians; and, whatever restrictions are imposed on the subjects of the United States with respect to the Indians in the districts under the American Government, the British Government are ready to adopt with regard to those Indians who may reside in the districts under their power.

If the peculiar circumstances of the Indian tribes and natives render such an arrangement inconsistent, let it be fairly considered whether an allotment of territory at present uninhabited by either British or American subjects cannot be allotted to them, to which the respective Governments of Great Britain and America shall forego all right. The object of the British Government is to fulfil their engagements to the Indians, to secure them against encroachments, and to remove all cause of misunderstanding in future. * * * * " Yonge's "Liverpool," II: 66–67.

[e] " British and Foreign State Papers," I, part 2, p. 1605.

[f] J. Q. Adams's "Memoirs," III: 18.

[g] Ibid., pp. 11, 19.

[h] Bathurst to Goulburn, September 1, 1814, "Wellington Supplementary Despatches," IX: 245–249; "British and Foreign State Papers," I, part 2, pp. 1605, 1614,

The fate of the buffer-State proposal is instructive because of its bearing upon Indian removal. Had it been accepted, removal for the northwest tribes would never have been necessary. It might have brought about a similar arrangement on the southern frontier, or, failing that, have consolidated the tribes in the northern instead of in the western region. It is not quite clear from the documents just how comprehensive it was expected to be. Apparently its benefits were to be restricted to the northwest tribes, since they were the only ones finally included in the amnesty clause.[a] Perhaps, however, if the British commissioners had been a little more explicit as to what they meant and the American had been willing to meet them halfway, the matter might have had a discussion on its own merits and resulted in the collection of all the North American Indians in one place and their withdrawal from any territory occupied by citizens of Canada or of the United States. In content the proposition went very much further than removal ever did. It exceeded the most enthusiastic dreams of Isaac McCoy. He scarcely dared to hope for an Indian State in the Union. This was to be a State outside the Union, practically independent for all internal affairs. Its external affairs, we presume, were to be controlled by Great Britain and the United States conjointly. They were to exercise the authority of a suzerain, each against the unprovoked encroachments of the other, with the right of conquest, though not of purchase, remaining in the protectorate powers.[b]

Naturally enough the question arises, Was the plan feasible? Its rejection by the American commissioners can hardly be taken offhand as a sure criterion of its worth. They came to Ghent quite unprepared to include the Indians in the general pacification,[c] and, thus hampered, thought it useless to confer on the special topic of the buffer State. Clay was of the opinion that the American people would never accede to any such arrangement, and he was probably right. In the absence of instructions, the commissioners even hesitated to discuss the matter with a view to a provisional article.[d] The negotiations, notwithstanding, hinged for two months upon the Indian question. For a brief space, the British expected a compliance with their wishes;[e] but were soon undeceived. The Americans steadfastly refused to recede from the position that, in so far as the outside world was concerned, the Indians were the subjects of the country in which they resided, be it Canada or the

[a] "Treaties and Conventions," pp. 404–405.

[b] Goulburn to Bathurst, August 21, 1814, "Wellington Supplementary Despatches," IX : 188 ; Castlereagh to Liverpool. August 28, 1814 ; "Castlereagh Correspondence," X : 101 ; J. Q. Adams's " Memoirs," III : 9.

[c] J. Q. Adams's "Memoirs," III : 7.

[d] Ibid., p. 8.

[e] Castlereagh to Liverpool, August 28, 1814, " Castlereagh Correspondence," X : 100.

United States.[a] A change in their status through the intervention of a foreign power was not to be thought of. The British somewhat weakly attacked this position and referred to the practice of treaty-making as proof that the tribes were considered, on occasion, by the Americans as independent powers.[b]

So much at variance were the opposing diplomats on the Indian question that, toward the end of August, the rupture which J. Q. Adams had anticipated[c] became well-nigh an accomplished fact.[d] Castlereagh pretended to be much annoyed at Goulburn's insistance and complained[e] to Liverpool that one of two things remained to be done—either to continue the war by placing it " solely and avowedly on a territorial basis " or to recede somewhat from the earlier position and induce the Americans among other things " to sign a provisional article of Indian peace as distinct from limits." Gallatin had foreseen this predicament, but had prophesied a different way of withdrawing from it.[f] In his opinion, Great Britain would force an issue on the Canadian frontier so as to drive the Americans to prosecute a vigorous Indian war, in which the troublesome natives would be either exterminated or compelled to sue for peace. There would then be no occasion for defining limits, much less for erecting a buffer State.

Lord Liverpool more than acquiesced in the criticism of Goulburn. His motive was anything but worthy or his course fair. Knowing it to be incumbent upon the ministry to extricate itself from such an awkward dilemma, he was ready to charge the British commissioners with having exceeded their instructions and the American with having taken for ultimata points that were brought forward for discussion only and at their own suggestion.[g] Considering how unwilling the Americans had been to bring the Indians into the negotiations at all, the perversion of truth is self-evident. Goulburn tried to evade responsibility by insisting that the United States had never seriously wished for peace and that her commissioners had seized upon the Indian boundary question as an easy way of reconciling the nation to a continuance of the war[h]—an argument that found ready favor with British editors[i] against whose nation the charge of temporizing could have been more appropriately brought.[j]

---

[a] American Note, September 9, 1814, American State Papers, " Foreign Relations," III : 715–717.

[b] J. Q. Adams's " Memoirs," III : 9, 27 ; British Note, September 4, 1814 ; " British and Foreign State Papers," I, part 2, p. 1605.

[c] J. Q. Adams's " Memoirs," III : 20–21.

[d] Goulburn to Castlereagh, August 26, 1814, " Castlereagh Correspondence," X : 99.

[e] Ibid., pp. 100–102.

[f] " Writings," I : 637–640.

[g] Liverpool to Wellington, September 2, 1814, " Wellington's Supplementary Despatches," IX : 211–213 ; Liverpool to Castlereagh, September 2, 1814, ibid., p. 214.

[h] Goulburn to Bathurst, September 5, 1814, ibid., p. 221.

[i] "Annual Register," 1814, p. 192.

[j] Henry Adams, IX : 27.

16827—08——18

The determined attitude of the American commissioners finally brought about a modification of British demands. The instructions of September 16 [a] renewed the ultimatum of Indian pacification and restoration to ante bellum rights and privileges, but weakened the neutral belt position by making it conditional in time.[b] The note [c] prepared in accordance therewith reached the Americans on the 20th instant.[d] They were still dissatisfied. On the 27th they received letters and papers from home which apprised them of a treaty [e] that had been lately concluded with the refractory Indians—welcome news— which was, at Clay's suggestion, communicated to the British commission.[f] This had, undoubtedly, much to do with the final abandonment of the plan for an Indian neutralized State. It had proved so deeply offensive [g] to Adams and his colleagues that it is no wonder the British seized the first opportunity to surrender it with honor. Indeed, it is a question whether Parliament would have supported them in its enforcement.[h]

It has been sometimes intimated that Great Britain was not sincere in her advocacy of a neutral belt, and that it was only a ruse to gain time. There was certainly much to be hoped for from procrastination; but there is no shadow of a doubt that she wished for a permanent barrier between the United States and Canada.[i] The spirit of aggrandizement shown by the former in the direction of Louisiana and Florida, coupled with the intemperate speeches of Congressmen [j] and the proclamations of invading generals,[k] seemed to offer incontrovertible evidence that the acquisition of Canada had been the controlling motive in declaring war at a time when Great Britain was fighting for the liberties of Europe. Moreover, the Indians to be benefited were British allies, and by championing their cause the fur trade monopoly, which the Americans had frequently hinted at re-

---

[a] " Wellington's Supplementary Despatches," IX : 263–265.

[b] " They are further instructed to offer for discussion an article, by which the contracting parties shall reciprocally bind themselves not to purchase the lands occupied by the Indians within their respective territory, according to boundaries to be agreed upon ; this engagement, however, to be subject to revision at the expiration of a given period. It is hoped that, by making the engagement subject to revision, it may obviate the objection to the establishment of a boundary beyond which the settlements of the United States should be forever excluded." Ibid., p. 265.

[c] " British and Foreign State Papers," I, part 2, pp. 1613–1616.

[d] J. Q. Adams's " Memoirs," III : 36.

[e] 7 United States Statutes at Large, p. 118.

[f] J. Q. Adams's "Memoirs," III : 43, 44.

[g] Goulburn to Bathurst, September 16, 1814, " Wellington Supplementary Despatches," IX : 265–267.

[h] (1) Hansard's " Parliamentary Debates," XXIX : 367–387. (2) The British people were also probably not in sympathy with any measure recognizing to so great an extent Indian rights. (New Annual Register, LVI : 192.)

[i] J. Q. Adams's " Memoirs," III : 25 ; Protocol of August 8, 1814, American State Papers, " Foreign Relations," III : 708 ; British note, August 19, 1814 ; ibid., p. 710.

[j] Swain's " Clay," I : 16.

[k] Niles's Register, II : 357 ; Cruikshank, p. 193.

stricting by denying access to the western regions, might be confirmed to the Canadians. That the object of Great Britain was, in the main, a selfish one goes without saying, yet she deserves credit for the effort displayed to preserve the integrity, such as it was, of the northwest tribes. The Americans were equally selfish in refusing to grant the concession. They placed themselves on record as resorting to Indian treaty making as a temporary expedient only. They admitted that they had no intention of regarding such compacts as binding, not even though they were made by duly accredited commissioners and solemnly ratified by the Senate. The history of the contemplated buffer State is an interesting reflection upon the United States Indian policy. It is the best possible proof that the Indian war of 1811–12 was the outcome of territorial aggressions. When we come to consider J. Q. Adams as President and as the friend of the Georgia Creeks, a doubt will arise as to whether the man most instrumental in 1814 in refusing to the Indians " some spot where they might live in tranquillity " could conscientiously be the advocate of Indian removal on the John C. Calhoun plan.

Chapter IV.

THE PROGRESS OF INDIAN REMOVAL FROM 1812 TO 1820.

The war of 1812 marks a great change in Indian affairs. The agitation of the removal project, previously confined to individuals or at most to communities essentially local, extended itself to States. Jefferson's plan, exaggerated to the prejudice of the Indians, entered politics; and, although it never became what would be strictly called a party issue, joined forces, nevertheless, with the tariff and internal improvements to divide the sections. In point of fact, it figured in its later days as a purely Democratic measure, involving the doctrine of State rights, and on this, its constitutional side, became identified with the history of the Southern States. On its economic side it belonged equally to both South and West. There party lines were forgotten.

In reviewing the history of Monroe's Administration, the student is forcibly impressed with the apparent unanimity of opinion respecting the Indian policy of the Government. Monroe, Calhoun, and Jackson stood at the head of a coterie of men favoring vigorous measures. Jackson was the leading spirit and began to exercise a most weighty influence over the Indian policy of the Government as far back as the time when Monroe held the portfolio of War—an influence which, after Monroe became Secretary of State and presumptive heir to the Presidency, increased in character and amount, proportionate to the development of Jackson's own ideas. From 1817 the influence continued, working at times directly through personal correspondence with Monroe, but most often indirectly through Calhoun. Prominent as the President and his Secretary of War appear in those years to have been as revivalists and propagandists of the removal idea, they were not the soul of the movement, for that was Jackson. They simply fell in with his ideas, adopted them as far as their conservatism would permit, and gave official expression to them. Jackson was essentially a western man with western ideas, anxious for western development, no real friend of the Indians. It is true his influence over them was almost unbounded, owing partly to his military reputation, partly to the great show he made of justice. The enemies of the Indians were invariably to be found among his strongest supporters. As commander of the southern division, then as governor of the Floridas, his opinions carried weight with the War Department and, for ten long eventful years, he and his friends managed to secure most of the Indian patronage.

The economic results of the second war with Great Britain were more immediate than the political. They manifested themselves in the unprecedented growth of home industries. European trade being cut off, the nation fell back upon its own, as yet undeveloped, resources and the consequence was that a new impetus was given to all branches of economic life. This created a demand for labor, which, to a great extent, disorganized Europe supplied. Few foreigners ventured beyond the Alleghanies, but settlers from the older States, who had filed westward during the period of commercial depression, caused by the embargo and nonimportation acts, were less diffident.[a] Upon the cessation of hostilities they were joined by other pioneers, young men mostly, hardy and enterprising, who, having shared in the western campaigns, had become filled with enthusiasm to penetrate the solitudes of the upper Mississippi Valley.[b] Their eagerness was heightened by the expectation that the lands of the hostile tribes would be confiscated and thrown at nominal rates upon the market.[c] The Indians, discouraged by repeated failures, were powerless to make headway against the stream of immigration and it flowed on unobstructed. So fast did the population increase that two of the three Territories, Michigan, Illinois, and Indiana, that had in 1810 contained less than 42,000 inhabitants, were soon admitted to statehood, Indiana in April, 1816, and Illinois two years later. Nevertheless, settlers did not arrive so fast as the Indian country was vacated. Politicians seemed to think that an immense surplus acreage must always be held in reserve, cleared of Indians so as to swell the advertisement of public lands. The extinguishment of Indian titles became in truth almost a mania in the Northwest and that even before Madison's term had expired. Crawford was indignant and restrained as best he could an extinguishment that went too far in advance of settlement.[d]

The impulse to spread over new lands and to attract settlers was scarcely less active in the slaveholding communities, and everywhere growth came at the expense of the natives. The capitulation of the Hickory Ground,[e] secured by General Jackson from some of the Creek chiefs after the final defeat of the " hostiles " in the battle of the Horseshoe Bend, proved the nucleus of cessions in the South

---

[a] McMaster, IV : 382.
[b] Monette, II : 532.
[c] Niles's Register, IV : 315.
[d] Crawford to Clark, Edwards, and Chouteau, May 7, 27, and September 17, 1816, " Indian Office Letter Books," Series I, C, pp. 340–342, 363, 425.
[e] 7 United States Statutes at Large, 120–122.

vastly more extensive than those of the North, and was the first step in the direction of systematic removal. The circumstances of its exaction, added to the incompleteness and stringency of its terms, made it a fruitful source of trouble which came out when the commissioners,[a] appointed by act of Congress,[b] attempted to run the lines of its cession. They anticipated opposition from three distinct parties; namely, the friendly Creeks, who claimed that the ratified document was not the one they had sanctioned;[c] the hostile Creeks, who had Colonel Nicolls's assurance that the treaty of Ghent rendered Jackson's treaty nugatory,[d] and the bordering tribes, whose limits were likely to be encroached upon.

The twofold Creek opposition may be disposed of in a few words. It practically amounted to nothing. The commissioners, protected by the strong military guard detailed by Jackson for the purpose, began, after some preliminaries,[e] to mark the only line specified in the treaty, which was a broken line extending through central Alabama from a point on the Coosa (near where the Creek and Cherokee boundaries were supposed to intersect) to the Chattahoochee, and thence at right angles across the southern part of Georgia.[f] The friendly Indians followed them aimlessly,[g] their destitution precluding all possibility of resistance. When the commissioners first saw them at Fort Strother, they were reported as literally starving,[h] the United States having failed to supply them with the provisions promised by the seventh article of the treaty. And so the line proceeded unobstructed to Summochico Creek on the Georgia border. Not far away, at the junction of the Flint and Chattahoochee, the "hostiles" had assembled to bar its extension eastward. This was the first show of resistance by force, and it was only a show. The Indians were frightened at the sight of so many soldiers, and contented themselves with swearing that the land, though surveyed, should never be settled.[i]

The opposition of the neighboring Cherokees, Choctaws, and Chickasaws was a much more serious affair. It reached its climax when

[a] William Barnett, Benjamin Kershaw, and John Sevier were the men first appointed. Colonel Kershaw soon resigned and General Sevier died in October. Their places were respectively filled by Colonel Hawkins and General Gaines. "Jackson Papers."

[b] March 3, 1815, 3 United States Statutes at Large, 228.

[c] Macdonald to Gaines, October 5. "Jackson Papers," 1815.

[d] Protest of Nicolls, addressed to Hawkins, June 12, 1815. Ibid.

[e] Toulmin to Jackson, July 3, 1815; Hutchings to Jackson, July 7, 1815; Hawkins to Dallas, July 8, 1815; Hawkins to Jackson, July 17, 1815; Hawkins to the Commissioners, July 18, 1815. Ibid.

[f] John Donelson to Jackson, July 23, 1815. Ibid.

[g] Hawkins to Macdonald, September 22, 1815; Hawkins to Gaines, October 17, 1815. Ibid.

[h] Strother to Jackson, June 6 and 10, 1815; Gaines to Jackson, June 8, 1815. Ibid.

[i] Hawkins to Jackson, December 1, 1815. Ibid.

Gen. John Coffee [a] started an independent survey of the lines that would limit the Creek cession to the north and west—a most unwarranted proceeding and one not within the province of the Commission.[b] To quiet the Cherokees, he made a private contract with Richard Brown,[c] the chief of the village through which the line passed, an irregular course, to be sure, yet Jackson approved it [d] and otherwise seconded Coffee's efforts by personally remonstrating with the Chickasaws, threatening dire vengeance should any insult be offered to his lieutenant.[e] Ere long a Cherokee delegation obtained a hearing at Washington and entered complaint against the measures of the Commission. Colonel Meigs was present, and testified to the authenticity of a document by which, a year and a half before, Jackson had himself recognized the Cherokee claims.[f] As a consequence, the Department of War entered into a convention of limits, March 22, 1816,[g] from which Jackson's intense hatred for Crawford is said to date and to which he certainly took great exception.[h]

At about the same time the Department of War resolved upon other and similar conventions, the understanding being, that a preliminary inter-tribal conference, recommended by Barnett and his colleagues,[i] should first be held in the Chickasaw council house. That being done, Coffee, John Rhea, and Col. John McKee were to negotiate with the Choctaws; [j] Jackson,[k] Gen. David Meriwether, and Jesse Franklin with the Chickasaws.[l] Both commissions were successful; yet, judged by the white man's standard, the methods

---

[a] General Coffee was not a bona fide member of the Commission. Jackson had wished him to succeed Kershaw, but had been a little late in urging the appointment. (Graham to Jackson, July 28, 1815. "Jackson Papers.") The serious illness of Hawkins soon gave prospects of another opening, and Gaines was instructed, should anything happen, to fill in an accompanying blank commission with Coffee's name (Graham to Gaines, October 14, 1815, ibid.), which he straightway proceeded to do without waiting for the contingency to occur. There were then four men on the Commission, while Congress had provided for but three. The proper thing for Coffee to do was to withdraw, but apparently he had no such intention. Jackson and he now had the opportunity they had waited for so long and it was not to be lightly thrown away. A letter, found among the "Jackson Papers," bearing date December 27, 1815, would show that Jackson and Coffee were suspected of being personally interested in the new lands; but their eagerness may have been simply that of all Tennesseeans.

[b] Crawford to Jackson, May 20, 1816. "Indian Office Letter Books," Series I, C, p. 351.

[c] Coffee to Jackson, February 8, 1816. "Jackson Papers," 1816.

[d] Jackson to Coffee, February 13, 1816, ibid.

[e] Jackson to George Colbert, February 13, 1816, ibid.

[f] John Donelson to Jackson, July 23, 1815; Hawkins to Jackson, August 4, 1815; Jackson to Brown, a Cherokee, August 10, 1815, "Jackson Papers," 1815; Crawford to Jackson, June 19, 1816, "Indian Office Letter Books," Series I, C, pp. 382–384.

[g] 7 United States Statutes at Large, p. 139.

[h] Parton's "Jackson," II: 356; Schouler, III: 62, note.

[i] Resolve of February 9, 1816, "Jackson Papers."

[j] Letter of Instructions, "Indian Office Letter Books," Series I, C, pp. 353–355.

[k] Jackson had wished to serve on the Choctaw Commission, but there was no place for him. Coffee was appointed because he had already compromised himself with the tribe, Rhea because a political debt was owing to him for good work in the late session of Congress, and McKee because he was the resident Choctaw agent. (Crawford to Jackson, May 20, 1816, "Indian Office Letter Books," Series I, C, p. 351.)

[l] Letter of Instructions, "Indian Office Letter Books," Series I, C, pp. 395–403.

pursued were anything but honorable.[a] Intimidation and bribery have no legitimate place in civil or diplomatic contracts. Such practices were, however, so much a part of negotiations with the Indians that we can safely take them henceforth for granted.

While these conventions were in progress, removal was again brought to the notice of the southern Indians. Late in the preceding winter, the Tennessee contingent in Congress [b] urged Madison to rid their State of the Cherokees. The time seemed opportune, for local prejudice supported Jackson's construction of the Creek cession, so much so, indeed, that settlers appropriated the contested territory and declared that they would vacate it only upon the understanding that it was a part of the public domain.[c] Such quibbling was highly flattering to Jackson's vanity, and he hesitated to enforce the law against intruders until compelled thereto by a peremptory order from Crawford.[d] Negotiation, under such circumstances required either very delicate or very vigorous handling. It was first intrusted to Meigs; but, in the event of failure,[e] was to devolve upon Jackson, Meriwether, and Franklin. That was enough for Jackson. Soon we find him managing the whole business and acting in a double capacity as commissioner for Tennessee and for the United States.[f]

Jackson made a provisional arrangement with the Cherokees at the Chickasaw council house and a little later met them at Turkey Town, where, with Crawford's tacit approval,[g] the old proposition of exchanging lands was discussed. The matter came before the meeting in this wise: For some time past the Cherokees on the Arkansas had been much molested by the Osages and Quapaws and had appealed to the United States for protection. It will be remembered no definite tract of territory had ever been assigned to them in the West and none was ever likely to be, since the Federal Government deemed it inexpedient to treat with them except upon the principle of exchange. Concerning the purport of Jefferson's talk of 1809, the Eastern and Western Cherokees represented two widely differing schools of interpretation. Indeed, at the earlier March convention,[h]

[a] Journal of the Commissioners for holding Chickasaw treaty, "Jackson Papers," 1816.

[b] Crawford to Meigs, May 27, 1816, "Indian Office Letter Books," Series I, C, pp. 365–366.

[c] Crawford to Jackson, July 1, 1816, "Indian Office Letter Books," Series I, C, pp. 389–390.

[d] Ibid.

[e] Letter of Instructions, "Indian Office Letter Books," Series I, C, pp. 395–403.

[f] Commission from Governor McMinn, August 30, 1816, "Jackson Papers."

[g] "Should an arrangement be made founded upon the principle of exchange as Contemplated by Mr. Jefferson and the Cherokee emigrants, a cession adjoining the settlements of Georgia may possibly be obtained." (Extract from Instructions of September 12, 1816, "Indian Office Letter Books," Series I, C, p. 420.) American State Papers, "Indian Affairs," II : 104.

[h] Crawford to William Clark, Governor Ninian Edwards, Auguste Chouteau, September 17, 1816, "Indian Office Letter Books," Series I, C, p. 424.

delegates from the former took the stand that, as the national council had not been a party to the transaction of 1809, the tribe was under no obligation to surrender land proportionate to the number of emigrants. The matter was now referred to the assembled chiefs at Turkey Town, but with no other result than that it raised the question of the practicability of removal.[a] Jackson anticipated much from this discussion,[b] his enthusiasm spread abroad,[c] and even affected the War Department.[d]

Although Monroe seems not to have seen his way clear to outlining a policy of general removal in any official communication prior to 1824, there is no doubt that some such purpose was well defined in his own mind at the very commencement of his Presidency. The Fourteenth Congress had shown itself opposed to Indian emigrations on a large scale. Nevertheless, the Senate of the second session had managed, though with difficulty, to pass a bill for general exchange, but pressure of business had blocked it in the House. Monroe had therefore no recent Congressional sanction to work upon; but, not to be deterred in his object, he revived [e] the fifteenth section of the otherwise obsolete Louisiana Territorial act of 1804. At various times thereafter communications were opened with the Indian tribes north and south.

[a] " Oct. 4 * * *. It was intimated however to us by several of the chiefs that a strong disposition prevailed among many Individuals of the nation to emigrate to the West of the Mississippi & they wished to know whether in the event of a national removal it was practicable to effect an exchange with the General Government giving their Teritory in this neighbourhood for a like extent in the vicinity of White River. We encouraged a belief that it was feasible & advised that when the nation had come to a conclusion on the subject, that Delegates clothed with full authority to negotiate a Treaty of exchange should be sent to Washington * * * ." (" Journal of the Commissioners," " Jackson Papers," 1816.)

[b] Jackson to Crawford, October 18, 1816, American State Papers, " Indian Affairs," II : 102–103.

[c] " Fay E. Ville, 11th October, 1816.—Magr. Franklin returns compliments to Genl A. Jackson and acknowledges the rect of his polite note of the 9th instant * * * Magr. Franklin is happy to be informed that the Genl. believes that those tawny brothers of ours will shortly be disposed to exchange their present Domicile for lands on the Arkansaw or White river, and woud be highly gratified that in the course of the next year the Genl might be the organ of such exchange and while engaged in the business have better water to Drink than the Chickasaw old field affords * * * " (" Jackson Papers.")

" * * * I am sorry you could not prevail on the Cherokees to sell on the North Tennessee, tho. I have strong reasons to believe they will agree to an exchange of Territory as spoken of in your letter 16th Oct. inst. Nearly 20 of the cherokees of whom ar Major Walker, Major Ridge Juleskey and several other head men are here who have agreed to hold a Talk with me this afternoon on the subject of an exchange so that in my next I will be able to give you some information on that score * * * ." (Extract of letter from Joseph McMinn to Jackson, October 21, 1816; " Jackson Papers.")

[d] " Whenever the Cherokee nation shall be disposed to enter into a negotiation for an exchange of lands they now occupy, for lands on the West side' of the Miss'ippi, and shall appoint delegates, clothed with full authority to negotiate a treaty for such exchange, they will be received by the President and treated with on the most liberal terms." (Graham to the Commissioners, October 26, 1816, " Indian Office Letter Books," Series I, C, p. 437.)

[e] Graham to Jackson, May 14, 1817, " Indian Office Letter Books," Series I, D, p. 36.

Trusting to the information received respecting the Cherokees,[a] Monroe had great hopes of their willingness to emigrate. Jackson and Meriwether were again appointed commissioners. Associated with them was Governor McMinn, whose special agent had all the winter been among the Cherokees industriously campaigning for removal.[b] A conference was arranged for at the agency; but it was not able to begin, as planned, on the 20th of June, inasmuch as delegates from the Arkansas branch were the only ones to put in an appearance.[c] Evidently Jackson had overestimated the disposition to remove. The Cherokee women,[d] influential half-breeds,[e] and several white men, including one missionary,[f] were known to be working against it. Their influence was great and had to be counteracted.

When negotiations did finally begin, much time was lost in debating Jefferson's talk. Some of the older chiefs impeached its credibility.[g] Jackson was at his wit's end. Either the Indians were deliberately lying or, as is more probable, had failed, at the time, to understand what Jefferson meant. One poor fellow who did understand it said the Secretary of War had turned him out of doors because he opposed the plan.[h] As the days wore away, the Eastern Cherokees seemed less and less disposed to treat. The Western were of course graciously compliant, since they had everything to gain and nothing to lose by an exchange. The negotiations ended the 8th of July in a treaty, the best that could be expected. Its every clause revealed the influence of the emigrants, and it was they who were to profit by it. Comparatively few of the other party signed. Of those who did, some, like Richard Brown and John Walker, were notoriously self-interested, easily susceptible to Jackson's influence. The rumor that the commissioners had failed to secure " the unbiased sanction of the tribe " was certainly based upon fact, and was likely to jeopardize ratification,[i] especially as the false assumption had been " too strongly enforced " that vested rights had accrued to the United States in consequence of the transaction of 1809.

The inherent weakness of the treaty of 1817 [j] came to light prior to its legal execution. In the interval between July and December

---

[a] Meigs wrote to Crawford, November 8, 1816, saying that some of the Cherokees were already preparing to go to the Arkansas River and that he had drawn up a treaty of exchange for his "own satisfaction," a transcript of which he forwarded. (American State Papers, "Indian Affairs," II: 116.) This would indicate that the desire to emigrate was general enough to convince the agent of the practicability of exchanging eastern for western land.

[b] McMinn to Jackson, January 10, 1817, "Jackson Papers."

[c] Jackson to Monroe, June 23, 1817, "Jackson Papers."

[d] Copy of Nancy Ward's talk to the National Council at Amoiah, May 2, 1817, " Jackson Papers."

[e] Jackson to Robert Butler, June 21, 1817, "Jackson Papers."

[f] " Miscellaneous Files," Indian Office Manuscript Records.

[g] " Journal of the Proceedings," " Jackson Papers."

[h] Ibid.

[i] Graham to the Commissioners, August 1, 1817, " Indian Office Letter Books," Series I, D, p. 64.

[j] 7 United States Statutes at Large, 156–160.

(the earliest date at which ratification could take place) great preparations were set on foot to incline the Cherokees to removal, and in cases of refusal to impress upon them the wisdom of taking 640 acres and of becoming citizens of the United States,[a] according to the eighth article. A special agent [b] was employed to assist Meigs, but even that did not satisfy the zeal of McMinn, and it was not long before he assumed the self-appointed task of canvassing the nation for emigrants.[c] The treaty contemplated a voluntary enrollment, but McMinn's methods were different.[d] There was no longer any doubt that force and fraud had been instrumental in securing signatures. The national will was lacking. So pronounced was the opposition that Graham's hopeful note to Cass July 30, 1817,[e] seemed very ill-timed. No pains, however, were spared to remove obstacles. In advance of an appropriation, the Secretary of War furnished [f] all things needful for the journey and prepared to extinguish [g] the Quapaw claim in Arkansas, which was then believed to limit the Cherokee territory on the west. All this testified to the heartiness with which the Administration entered into the plan for removal.

The attitude of the Cherokees augured ill for the peaceful execution of the third article. In fact, long before June came, the Department was advised by Walker [h] not further to antagonize the tribe by proceeding to the census taking. It was therefore deferred until September, and meanwhile McMinn, who had, with the President's approval, come to reside within the tribe, used the balance of the $80,000 appropriated to carry the treaty into effect in the way " best calculated to remove prejudice." [i] He even called out the Tennessee militia to compel obedience.[j] It was all of no use. The Cherokees as a body

---

[a] Graham to Meigs, August 9, 1817, " Indian Office Letter Books," Series I, D, p. 72.

[b] The name of Nicholas Byers was at first suggested but, as his interest in the turnpike road (7 U. S. Stat. at L., p. 198) was thought to stand in the way of hearty cooperation, Sam Houston's, at the instance of Jackson, was substituted.

[c] Graham to McMinn, November 29, 1817, " Indian Office Letter Books," Series I, D, p. 101.

[d] Calhoun to McMinn, January 19, 1818, " Indian Office Letter Books," Series I, D, p. 114 ; same to same, May 11, 1818, " Jackson Papers ; " Calhoun to Forsyth, December 22, 1824, " Indian Office Letter Books," Series II, No. 1, p. 270.

[e] " Indian Office Letter Books," Series I, D, p. 62.

[f] Graham to Jackson, August 9, 1817, " Indian Office Letter Books," Series I, D, p. 70.

[g] Talk of Monroe to Arkansas Cherokee delegates, March, 1818, " Indian Office Letter Books," Series I, D, p. 124.

[h] Calhoun to McMinn, April 11, 1818, " Indian Office Letter Books," Series I, D, p. 135.

[i] In 1825, when Georgia was straining every nerve to force the hand of the Government in negotiating with the Creeks, documents were submitted by the Department of War to the House of Representatives which showed that McMinn had submitted to Calhoun some plan for extensive bribery ; Calhoun had accepted it, and resubmitted it to McMinn under the name of instructions, as though it had originated with the head of the Indian Office. (Calhoun to Forsyth, " Indian Office Letter Books," Series II, No. 1, pp. 34, 41, 270, 285 ; Calhoun to Henry Clay, January 10, 1825, p. 287, ibid.)

[j] Calhoun did not object to intimidation, and he connived at bribery, yet he seems to have taken exception to the use of militia when the regular recruits were available. (Letter to Governor McMinn, August 1, 1818, " Indian Office Letter Books," Series I, D, p. 198.)

were unalterably opposed to any radical change in their tribal relations, and met menace with menace.[a] The time never came when it was perfectly convenient and practicable to take the census; for a Cherokee delegation went to Washington and, by engaging to surrender a proportionate amount of land without it, secured the " Calhoun treaty "[b] of 1819, which, to the discomfiture of Southern politicians, effectually put an end to Cherokee removals for the time being. Not until 1828 did the tribe condescend to enter again into treaty relations with the United States Government.

Jackson's repeated successes with the Indians emboldened Monroe to send him, in the autumn of 1817, upon a mission among the Chickasaws,[c] the purpose being to sound them as to a relinquishment of territory in Kentucky and Tennessee covering, for the most part, Revolutionary war land grants to soldiers of the Virginia line. In the following May, under the recent appropriation act[d] "to defray the expenses incidental to Indian treaties," Generals Isaac Shelby and Andrew Jackson were commissioned to treat with them by sale or exchange.[e] Great latitude[f] was given in the expenditure of money and undoubtedly it was used to the best advantage.[g] It was only, however, after a very long time, that Jackson's " appeal to fear and

---

[a] " The conduct of part of the Cherokee nation, merits the severest censure. After the ratification of the treaty, resistance to its fair execution can be considered little short of hostility. The menaces offered to those who choose to emigrate or take reservations cannot be tolerated. It is an open violation of the treaty and will, in its final result, not avail them anything. The United States will not permit the treaty to be defeated by such means * * *." (Extract from letter of Calhoun to McMinn, July 20, 1818, ibid., p. 192.)

[b] 7 United States Statutes at Large, 195–198.

[c] Graham to Jackson, October 25, 1817, " Indian Office Letter Books," Series I, D, p. 88.

[d] 3 United States Statutes at Large, p. 463.

[e] " Indian Office Letter Books," Series I, D, p. 150.

[f] Calhoun to Shelby, July 30, 1818, " Jackson Papers."

[g] Jackson's actions in this negotiation were the occasion of a very bitter political controversy in later years, especially in connection with the salt lick (Article IV), which Col. John Williams accused him in the Senate of having caused to be leased to his particular friend, Maj. W. B. Lewis, " before the ink of the treaty was fairly dry." (" Jackson Papers," 1819–1831.)

A more disgraceful proceeding, well authenticated by the secret " Journal of the Commissioners " and by the evidence of Monroe's acquiescence (Message to Senate, November 30, 1818, " Monroe Papers," Vol. V) was the secret Government purchase of the Colbert reservations (Article V), for which Jackson gave his personal bond of $20,000. The deed of sale was not, for very obvious reasons, embodied in the treaty. The tribe, as it was, was very suspicious and would have been righteously incensed at the Colbert-Jackson duplicity.

While it may not be quite fair to ascribe mercenary motives to Jackson personally, as the Shelby family is said to have done later, this much is certain, he was the easy dupe of designing men, and was the devoted friend of land speculators. Upon his several Indian missions, he was invariably surrounded by a group of these, selfish and unscrupulous, who never lost a single opportunity to gain their own ends. The Indian records likewise show that the persons selected by him for clerical work and the like on the treaty ground were not above imposing upon the Government. Note, for instance, the case of Col. Robert Butler, who acted as secretary to this same Chickasaw treaty commission. His rates were so exorbitant that even Calhoun lost patience and refused to honor his bills. (" Indian Office Letter Books," Series I, D, p. 329.)

avarice " in a measure succeeded. As the agent had prophesied,[a] the tribe could not be induced to move.[b]

While these things were going on, Col. John McKee, Gen. William Carroll, and Daniel Burnett, esq., were similarly treating with the Choctaws; [c] but they failed utterly. Almost a year later, March 29, 1819, a new commission issued with Jackson in the place of Carroll; for it was believed that the people of Mississippi, who had pressed for a cession, would not be easy until an effort under his supervision had been made.[d] Another failure was the result. The Choctaws refused to treat under any conditions,[e] and their obstinacy called forth a loud protest from Jackson [f] against the practice of Indian treaty making.[g] His argument was, that Congress ought to be held competent to deal with all Indian concerns. Things had come to such a pass under the existing system that the corruption of the chiefs was a prime requisite in every negotiation. For his part he hoped he would never again be called upon to treat with the Indians. But that was not to be. Before long Jackson was again in the Choctaw country, this time in company with Gen. Thomas Hinds. He had reconsidered his decision out of deference to the wishes of the people of Mississippi,[h] who were still clamorous for land and had lately secured from Congress an appropriation of $20,000, over which Jackson was, with Monroe's consent,[i] to have unlimited control.

As usual, Jackson selected as secretary to the Commission one of his own most intimate friends; but, even with that excellent opportunity for having only such facts recorded as would not be too damaging to himself, he seems not to have cared to preserve a very full account of

[a] Sherburne to Jackson, July 28, 1818, " Jackson Papers."

[b] " Confidential Journal of the Commissioners," " Jackson Letter Books," vol. K.

[c] " * * * The time and place of holding the treaty, and the terms to be offered, are left to your judgment and discretion ; but if they can be brought to exchange lands on this side for that on the West of the Mississippi, the President would greatly prefer it * * * ." (Extract from instructions of May 2, 1818, " Indian Office Letter Books," Series I, D, p. 151).

[d] Senator T. H. Williams to Jackson, March 29, 1819, " Jackson Papers."

[e] Deliberations of the Choctaw Council, August 12, 1819, " Jackson Papers."

[f] Jackson to Calhoun, August 24, 1819, " Miscellaneous Files," Indian Office. It is well to remark that a letter of similar import and of almost the same phraseology is to be found in the Jackson Letter Books, Vol. L, under date of August 25, 1820. It must be a mistake in chronology, for, although Jackson was treating with the Choctaws at that time, he had no reason to despair of success.

[g] This letter was followed by others of the same tenor (Jackson to Calhoun, September 2, 1820, and January 18, 1821, " Jackson Letter Books," Vol. L), the immediate object of which was to get Congress, under a forced construction of the treaty of Hopewell, 1785 (7 U. S. Stat. at L., 18), to legislate for the removal of the Cherokees. There was some indication that could the power of the chiefs be thwarted, the rank and file would gladly emigrate. Undoubtedly, Jackson's was the common-sense view ; but it was impossible in 1819 to anticipate the measures of 1871.

[h] Jackson to Calhoun, June 19, 1820, " Jackson Letter Books," Vol. L.

[i] Christopher Rankin to Jackson, May 16, 1820, " Jackson Papers."

the inside history of the treaty of Doak's Stand.[a] In its absence, we are thrown back upon our own surmises as to the means employed to secure the cooperation of the Choctaw chiefs, especially as John Pitchlynn, the official interpreter, had made of himself an easy cat's-paw for Jackson. Internal evidence, furnished by the treaty, tells the same old story of perjured faith, yet the long array of signatures points to a more than ordinary compliance. We infer that the nation was well represented, and are surprised to learn that four years after-wards—when bitter passions had had ample time to cool—Puckshe-nubbe was soundly beaten for his subserviency to Jackson in 1820.[b]

By the first article of the treaty of Doak's Stand[c] the Choctaws ceded the coveted tract in western Mississippi, and obtained in exchange, by the second, a new territory between the Red and Arkansas rivers to which it was expected the more nomadic of the tribe would remove. If they went within one year the Government pledged itself to allow them the full value of their improvements,[d] Mississippi was delighted, and her legislature, sharing in the grati-tude of Governor Poindexter,[e] resolved upon a vote of thanks to Jackson.[f] Congress appropriated $65,000 to carry the treaty into effect,[g] and a new agent,[h] William Ward, was appointed to register the emigrants; but it soon developed that very few, if any, were inclined to remove.[i] The time was extended another year, but to no purpose. One reason for their unwillingness to go was the difficulty that arose over their territory in the West. Jackson had been care-fully instructed[j] to assign them an uninhabited portion of the Quapaw cession;[k] but scarcely was the treaty ratified before com-

---

[a] American State Papers, "Indian Affairs," II : 233–245.

[b] William Cocke to Jackson, July 10, 1824, "Jackson Papers."

[c] 7 United States Statutes at Large, 211.

[d] Article IX, ibid., p. 212.

[e] " * * * I beg you to accept the grateful acknowledgments of myself individually, and through me, as their executive magistrate, of the citizens at large. You will live in our affections to the latest period of time, and I trust our posterity will not be unmindful of the obligations, conferred on their ancestors * * * ." (Extract from letter of George Poindexter to Jackson, October 25, 1820, " Jackson Papers.")

[f] Resolution, approved February 9, 1821.

[g] 3 United States Statutes at Large, 634.

[h] In the appointment of Colonel Ward, we find one of the many proofs of the unwise selection of Indian agents. The character of the man seemed to count for almost nothing, apparently the more unscrupulous the better. Ward was appointed in March, and in October Calhoun had to call him to account for " vending whiskey " to the Choctaws and for applying to his own use their annuities. (" Indian Office Letter Books," Series I, E, p. 177.)

[i] " Indian Office Letter Books," Series I, E, p. 193.

[j] " Indian Office Letter Books," Series I, D, pp. 462–463.

[k] Monroe's method of procedure was more straightforward than Jefferson's. He did not tell the would-be emigrants that there were no red men in the West to dispute their entry ; but he acknowledged the indigenous occupancy claim and prepared to extinguish as much of it as was necessary to locate the eastern tribes. That accounts for the in-structions to William Clark and Auguste Chouteau, " to acquire lands on the west of the

plaints came in to the War Department that citizens of Arkansas had a prior claim to the land.[a] Thus ended another futile attempt to dispose of the southern Indians without their free consent.

If a shade of doubt exists as to Jefferson's intention to include the northwestern tribes in the plan of removal, there is none in the case of Monroe. Madison, too, seems to have had no pronounced partiality for his own section. In the instructions issued June 11, 1814, to Harrison and Cass for bringing Tecumseh's warriors to terms, this thought occurs,[b] explicitly or inferentially: Offer in exchange, for a cession that would please the people of Ohio, "a tract of equal dimensions lying between Lake Michigan and the Mississippi." Instructions sent later in the same day [c] withdrew the authority to exchange, so that a simple treaty of offensive and defensive alliance was all that was negotiated.[d] Some seventeen months afterwards the first signer of this treaty—Tarhe, the Crane, principal chief of the Wyandots—died, and his clan expressed a wish to leave Sandusky for western parts.[e] Thinking it a good time to connect the white settlements of Ohio and Michigan, but not caring to appear solicitous for removal, the Government temporized and the opportunity was lost.

If, in tracing the history of removal from 1815 to 1825, we draw any comparisons between the working out of the Government policy in the South and Northwest, respectively, we must not fail to make allowances for the widely differing conditions in the two localities, remembering first of all that only a small part of one great tribe in the South took issue against the United States during the war period, while the numerous bands of the Northwest were almost universally hostile. Their natural propensities were more of the roving, hunting, and fighting order. The thirteen treaties of amity negotiated in the

---

Mississippi in order to exchange with such of the Indians on this side as may choose to emigrate to the West * * * ." The result was the Quapaw treaty of August 24, 1818 (7 U. S. Stat. L., 176). A month later, Clark negotiated in a similar manner with the Osages (ibid., p. 183), it having been discovered that they and not the Quapaws obstructed the outlet of the Cherokees. (Calhoun to Reuben Lewis, July 22, 1819, "Indian Office Letter Books," Series I, D, p. 298.) Jefferson may have intended by the Osage treaty of 1808 (7 U. S. Stat. at L., p. 107), to prepare, in just the same way, for Indian emigration. This treaty was negotiated by Peter Chouteau under authority from Meriwether Lewis, governor of, and superintendent of Indian affairs in, Louisiana Territory, whose instructions (American State Papers, "Indian Affairs," I : 765,) state that the land was needed for white hunters and intimately friendly Indians. General Clark's communication to Secretary Eustis on the subject of the cession does not, however, indicate any such purpose as colonization.

[a] The Choctaws surrendered their claim January 20, 1825 (7 U. S. Stat. at L., 234) ; but not until they had thoroughly convinced the Government that the uncertainty respecting Indian tenure in the West was the main obstacle to general removal. How could it be otherwise when every group of emigrants thus far had had some such difficulty to contend with?

[b] " Indian Office Letter Books," Series I, C, p. 171.

[c] " Indian Office Letter Books," Series I, C, p. 172.

[d] 7 United States Statutes at Large, 118.

[e] General McArthur to John Graham, January 20, 1816, "Miscellaneous Files," Indian Office ; Crawford to McArthur, February 14, 1816, " Indian Office Letter Books," Series I, C, p. 302.

summer and early autumn of 1815 were not enough to insure peace.
To all appearances, the Kickapoos, the Pottawatomies, and the Sacs
and Foxes of Rock River continued unfeignedly hostile.[a] Removal,
moreover, was not likely to be such a radical measure to the northwest
tribes, inasmuch as some of them claimed hunting grounds on both
sides of the Mississippi River, and thought nothing of crossing the
stream at its narrower part to wage war against Sioux and Osages.
Besides, treating with small tribes, whose title to a particular piece
of land was always being disputed by other bands, was a very different matter from treating with the politically powerful Cherokees.
Less effort is required in persuading the few than the many. It was,
however, mainly owing to Governor Cass, of whose methods in dealing
with the Indians too much can not be said as a general thing, or at
least when we compare him with other Indian superintendents and
treaty negotiators, in commendation, that greater success attended
removal north of the Ohio River than was ever possible south.

The views of Monroe's Administration respecting exchange with
northern tribes were first communicated to Cass in a letter of March
23, 1817,[b] by which he was instructed to interview the Indians of
Ohio, and propose a negotiation on this basis: " that each head of a
family, who wished to remain within the limits ceded, should have
a life estate in a reservation of a certain number of acres, which should
descend to his children in fee, reserving to the Widow, if any, her
thirds; and that those who do not wish to remain on these terms
should have a body of land allotted to them on the west of the Mississippi." Gen. Duncan McArthur was associated with Cass on the
commission, and in deference to the wishes of Ohio Congressmen,[c]
who estimated aright the advantages to be derived " from connecting

---

[a] The reports of their warlike intentions came mostly from Ninian Edwards and William Clark, governors of Illinois and Missouri Territories respectively. Lewis Cass, governor of Michigan Territory, declared such reports exaggerated. (Cass to Dallas, July 2,
1815, " Jackson Papers.") The chief cause of difficulty seems to have been the location
of the 2,000,000 acres of military land designed for the soldiers of the late war. (Edwards to Jackson, August 9, 1815, " Jackson Papers.") The original plan of the Government was to select those lands in Michigan, but the country was falsely declared
unproductive (" American Historical Association Papers," III : 72), and the Illinois country preferred. (Crawford to Cass, "Indian Office Letter Books," Series I, C, p. 360.)
The change involved an encroachment upon the lands of the Sacs and Foxes, and it was
not until September 13, 1815, that Clark, Edwards, and Chouteau were able to negotiate a
cession. Even that was not sufficient to preserve peace, and in January, 1816, the
Illinois militia was irregularly called out to protect the surveyors.

[b] Graham to Governor Cass, March 23, 1817, " Indian Office Letter Books," Series I,
D, p. 22 ; American State Papers, " Indian Affairs," II : 136.

[c] (1) Graham to Cass and Gen. Duncan McArthur, May 19, 1817, " Indian Office
Letter Books," Series I, D, p. 42 ; same to same, March 23, 1817, American State Papers,
" Indian Affairs," II : 136.

(2) The time seemed propitious for extinguishing the Indian title in Ohio, inasmuch
as the death of the Wyandot chief, " The Crane," had " occasioned great commotion
among the Indians on the Sandusky " and the majority of them were desirous of
emigrating to the White River country or even farther west. (McArthur to Graham,
January 20, 1816, " Miscellaneous Files," Indian Office Manuscript Records ; Crawford
to McArthur, February 14, 1816, " Indian Office Letter Books," Series I, C, pp. 302–303.)

the population of the State of Ohio with that of the Territory of Michigan," they were told that they might offer a more liberal compensation than usual for a relinquishment of the land in the vicinity of Lake Erie.[a] Both sets of instructions were interpreted liberally, the former so liberally, indeed, that many of the Indian allottees received grants in fee simple. The Senate [b] refused to contemplate so radical a change in the red man's tenure, and the commissioners were ordered to reopen the negotiation. In neither instance was any arrangement made for removal,[c] and yet a step was taken that would

---

[a] The Connecticut Western Reserve comprehended the greater portion of Ohio land bordering upon Lake Erie, and had long since been disencumbered of the Indian title, the eastern part by the Greenville treaty of 1795 and the western part, including the Sufferers', or Fire Lands, by the Fort Industry treaty of 1805 (" Indian Land Cessions in the United States," pp. 667, 668 ; " The Firelands Pioneer," January, 1906).

[b] American State Papers, " Indian Affairs," II : 149,; Calhoun to Cass and McArthur, May 11, 1818, " Indian Office Letter Books," Series I, D, p. 160.

[c] Removal was, however, as is shown by the following letter, suggested :

ST. MARY'S, *Sept. 18, 1818.*

SIR.

Accompanying this we have the honor to transmit you a treaty yesterday concluded by us with the Wyandot, Shawnese, Seneca and Ottawa tribes of Indians.

The proposition to remove to the west of the Mississippi was made to the three former tribes and enforced as far as we believed it politick to enforce it. It was received by them with such strong symptoms of disapprobation, that we did not think it proper to urge them too far upon the subject. The time was not arrived for them voluntarily to abandon the land of their fathers and seek a new residence in a Country with which they are unacquainted and among powerful and hostile Indians. As our settlements gradually surround them, their minds will be better prepared to receive this proposition, and we do not doubt, but that a few years will accomplish, what could not now be accomplished, except at an expense greatly disproportioned to the object.

The treaty now concluded, requires few observation from us. We trust all its stipulations will be found in strict conformity to our instructions.

The Chippewa, Potawatamie and Delaware tribes of Indians are not parties to this treaty. None of the provisions in the treaty to which this is supplementary, which related to them, has now been affected, and their participation was therefore unnecessary, and might have been injurious.

We have promised to the tribes, parties hereunto, that they shall receive a quantity of goods equal in value to the twelve thousand dollars. These goods cannot now be distributed, because such distribution would provoke the jealousies of the other tribes, who are waiting the result of the treaty to be negotiated for a cession of land in Indiana. It is thought politick to make a general distribution to all the tribes at the same time, and it is certainly proper that these tribes should receive as much in proportion to their numbers as any others. At the conclusion therefore of that treaty bills will be drawn upon the War Dept. for the amount of goods, which we think it correct to purchase, payable after the ratification of the treaty, and we trust they will be duly honoured.

We transmit an extract from the speech of the Ottawas in relation to the grant made by them to Doct[r] William Brown by the treaty concluded last year at the foot of the Rapids. We cannot but hope, that the claims will be confirmed. Doctor Brown's professional services to these Indians have been long continued and gratuitous, equally uncommon in their occurrences and honourable to him.

Very respectfully Sir
We have the honour to be

Yr. obt. servts

LEW CASS
DUNCAN McARTHUR.

Hon. JOHN C. CALHOUN,
Secy. of War.

(" Treaty Files," 1802–1853, Indian Office Manuscript Records.)

inevitably lead to it.   Indian lands in Ohio [a] were apportioned in reservations,[b] some so comparatively small that community life was imperiled.

The first treaty of exchange [c] successfully negotiated in the Northwest was entered into with the Delawares of Indiana, October 3, 1818.   Presumably they were the Indians reported two years before [d] to be contemplating removal on their own account, something not at all surprising, considering how much and how far they had wandered since the days of William Penn.   They had been approached, late in 1817,[e] for a cession on the Wabash and White rivers; but not for one whole year did anything result.   Finally, Jennings, Cass, and Parke, under strong suspicions of compulsion,[f] stipulated for their removal to an unspecified country west of the Mississippi.   As soon as possible, Governors Clark of Missouri and Miller of Arkansas were consulted [g] as to the best place to locate them.   The tract agreed upon was that in southwestern Missouri [h] upon which the Cape Girardeau Delawares had encamped.[i]   The emigrants were invited [j] to send out a reconnoitering party to pass judgment upon it; but they neglected [k] to and lingered [l] themselves so long on the road that the Government became impatient.[m]   When they did at length reach the spot it fell so short of their expectations that they addressed a lengthy

[a] The Miami Indians lived partly in Ohio and did not relinquish their title until October 3, 1818.   Monroe personally importuned them, May 5, 1818, and they pitifully told him that they had many times asked for a civilized life, but their speeches had been lost in the woods.   (" Indian Office Letter Books," Series I, D, pp. 156–158.)

[b] The supplementary treaty of September 17, 1818 (7 U. S. Stat. at L., 178) changed the tenure of and in some cases enlarged the area of the allotments of the treaty of September 29, 1817 (7 U. S. Stat. at L., 160).   It also created additional allotments. There were then twelve territorially distinct tracts, one Delaware, two Seneca, three Shawnee, three Ottawa, and three Wyandot, in Ohio.

[c] 7 United States Statutes at Large, 188.

[d] Graham to Governor Jonathan Jennings, December 31, 1816, " Indian Office Letter Books," Series I, C, p. 451.

[e] Graham to Gen. Thos. Posey and Benjamin Parke, October 25, 1817, " Indian Office Letter Books," Series I, D, p. 87.

[f] " We have had direct information of the Treaty with the Indians, and it is reported, that ' the Delawares were *forced* to sell, and to sign the Treaty ; ' and that ' the poor Delawares had not a friend to support their cause ! ! ' * * * ."   (John Sergeant to Rev. J. Morse, December 15, 1818, Morse's Report, Appendix, p. 116.

[g] Calhoun to Cass, August 24, 1819, " Indian Office Letter Books," Series I, D, p. 313.

[h] The memory of John Johnston, agent to the Delawares, must have played him false when he wrote, " I removed the whole Delaware tribe, consisting of 2,400 souls, to their new home southwest of Missouri River, near the mouth of the Kansas, in the years 1822 and 1823."   (Cist's " Cincinnati Miscellany," December, 1845, II : 241.)   The Delawares were not transferred to the fork of the Kansas and Missouri rivers until the early thirties.   (Adams, p. 154.)

[i] " Indian Land Cessions in the United States," p. 725.

[j] Calhoun to John Johnston, January 6, 1820, " Indian Office Letter Books," Series I, D, p. 354.

[k] Calhoun to Clark, June 27, 1821, " Indian Office Letter Books," Series I, E, p. 125.

[l] Calhoun to Pierre Menard, August 8, 1821, " Indian Office Letter Books," Series I, E, pp. 141–142.

[m] Calhoun to Clark, August 30, 1822, " Indian Office Letter Books," Series I, E, p. 320.

complaint to Monroe,[a] their principal grievance being the ridiculously small acreage given in exchange [b] for all their valuable [c] possessions in Indiana.

It was not to be supposed for one moment that Illinois[d] could watch these proceedings in behalf of sister States with equanimity and leave her own Indians in peace. In November, 1817, therefore, Clark and Edwards were commissioned to treat [e] for an exchange with the Kickapoos and Pottawatomies, but they met with no success.[f] Indeed, no further progress was made in removal until the treaty of Edwardsville, July 30, 1819,[g] provided for the emigration of the Kickapoos,* exclusive of those on the Vermillion,[h] to that part

---

[a] " Father : We know you have fulfilled your promise to us as furnishing provisions untill we get to our land. We have got in a Country where we do not find as was stated to us when we was asked to swap lands with you and we do not get as much as was promised to us at the Treaty of St. Marys neither.

Father : We did not think that big man would tell us things that was not true. We have found a poor hilly stony Country and the worst of all no game to be found on it to live on *   *   * ." (Extract from address of Delaware Chiefs on White River to Monroe, February 29, 1824, " Miscellaneous Files," Indian Office MS. Records.)

[b] Calhoun to Clark, March 3, 1824, " Indian Office Letter Books," Series I, F, p. 58.

[c] The Stockbridge Indians had a joint claim with the Delawares to the land in Indiana, but, as we shall afterwards see, their rights were totally ignored by the treaty of St. Marys.

[d] Illinois profited, though only in a very slight degree, by the treaty of St. Marys, 1818. ("Indian Land Cessions, p. 692.) She received an enormous tract, however, from the Peoria-Kaskaskia cession of September 25, 1818 (7 U. S. Stat. at L., 181), but still she was not satisfied, especially as the Kickapoos contested the right to the northern part.

[e] " If either of the tribes who have a claim to the land is desirous of exchanging their claim for lands on the West of the Mississippi, you are authorized to make the exchange, and your extensive local knowledge of the country will enable you to designate that part of it, where it would be most desirable to locate the lands to be given as an equivalent *   *   * " (Extract from letter of Graham to Governors William Clark and Ninian Edwards, November 1, 1817, " Indian Office Letter Books," Series I, D, p. 94.)

[f] This must have been a great disappointment, for the Government hoped, by accurately fixing the boundaries and by reporting the quality of the land in detail, to facilitate emigration " from New England and the State of New York " to the country " lying between the Illinois River and Lake Michigan." (Graham to Edwards, November 8, 1817, " Indian Office Letter Books," Series 1, D, pp. 96–97.

[g] 7 United States Statutes at Large, 200.

[h] The Vermillion Kickapoos surrendered their land on the Wabash by the treaty of Fort Harrison, 1819. (7 U. S. Stat. at L., 202.) The cession was covered, unauthoritatively, by that of the main body done at Edwardsville the same year. (" Indian Land Cessions," p. 697.)

*By the letter of their instructions, March 25, 1819 (" Indian Office Letter Books," Series I, D, p. 272), the commissioners, Auguste Chouteau and Benjamin Stephenson, were ordered to extinguish the conflicting claims to the Peoria-Kaskaskia cession of September 25, 1818, but were not specifically empowered to suggest exchange to the various Illinois tribes. That they did so and immediately is evidenced by their correspondence with the War Department. There were probably other instructions, semi-official in character, since this same correspondence indicates a clear compliance with the Secretary's wishes : " In compliance with your instructions we have held a council at this place [Edwardsville, Illinois] with the Kickapoo Tribe of Indians—upon whose minds, impressions very unfavorable to the propositions we were authorised to make to them, had been produced by the artful and insidious representations of certain Traders who were amongst them last winter—and whose object evidently was, from interested motives, to prevent their removal to the west side of the Mississippi. We, however, have been so fortunate in removing those impressions as to render them not only willing but anxious to make the proposed exchange. And for the purpose of consummating the arrangement they have promised to meet us at this place in eight or ten weeks.

" But we feel it our duty to apprize you, of a difficulty that will probably occur which

of Missouri lying immediately north of what was to constitute the
Delaware Reservation.   Their departure was much delayed by the

---

will be much more within yours, than our control—and which may, indeed, require efficient
interposition on the part of the Government.

"The Pottowatomies who are neighbours to the Kickapoos, instigated, no doubt, by
white men, and unwilling to see our settlements approximate theirs, as they think they
will soon do, if the latter cede their land, have by every kind of menace endeavoured to
deter the Kickapoos from entering into any agreement with us and they openly declare
that the moment the Kickapoos commence their removal to the west side of the Mississippi,
they will waylay, attack, plunder, and murder them.   And we are not without some
apprehensions that they may attempt to carry their threats into execution.   We shall
endeavor to conciliate them, and earnestly warn them of the danger of opposing the views
of our Government in this particular.

"But if all this should prove insufficient, what next is to be done is for you to decide."   (Letter from Aug. Chouteau, and Ben. Stephenson to Calhoun, June 7, 1819,
"Miscellaneous Files," Indian Office.)

"I have rec'd your letter of the 7th ult.   It is gratifying that you have so far succeeded in accomplishing the object of your Commission, as to obtain the consent of the
Kickapoos to remove West of the Mississippi.

"It is to be hoped that the Potawatamies will not be so indiscreet as to attempt to
execute the threats upon the Kickapoos on their removal across the Mississippi.   Should
they, however, oppose the movement in that way, it will be considered an act highly
unfriendly to the United States, and will be noticed accordingly."   (Calhoun to Aug.
Chouteau and Benj. Stephenson, " Indian Office Letter Books," Series I, D, p. 293.)

ST. LOUIS, *the 20th August, 1819*.

SIR.

We are happy to inform you, that we have at length been fortunate enough, to bring
to a successfull issue, the negotiations that have been so long depending with the Kickapoo Tribe of Indians, by a treaty, which we have the honor herewith to transmit to
you, and which we flatter ourselves will meet with the President's entire approbation.

None could regret, more than we ourselves have done, the delays that have prevented
an earlier consummation of so desirable, and important an Object, but it is but Justice
to ourselves to state, that they have been unavoidably the result of the artifices, in-
trigues, and false reports of certain Indian traders, who left no effort untried—with
either the Kickapoos themselves, or with the neighbouring Tribes, to dissuade, & deter
the former, from treating with us, which added to a repugnance that they very strongly
manifested, to leaving the place of their nativity, for a distant land, kept them almost
to the last moment, in a constant state of oxillation upon the subject.   The chiefs
themselves, when made willing to accede to the terms we proposed, hesitated to con-
sumate a treaty till the apprehensions, prejudices, and predilections of their Tribe could
be overcome, and several times, when we thought we were upon the point of concluding
the negotiations successfully ; occurances presented themselves, that rendered it necessary to suspend the business, and vary our propositions, particularly with regard to
the limits of the land proposed to be given them in exchange.   And even at the moment
of signing the treaty ; we were compelled to promise an equivalent in lieu of one of the
stipulations, which previous to that time, they had seemed to make a sine qua non,
which we prefered doing, rather than risque the further delay, that would have been
necessary in preparing a new treaty.

The stipulation alluded to, is that which provided, that they should be furnished with
two boats well manned, for the transportation of their property, from their present, to
their intended residence.   The subsequent agreement upon that subject, which is herewith transmitted, is however much to the advantage of the United States, as the amount
given as an equivalent for that stipulation, is less than it would have cost, to have
furnished the transportation agreed upon.   And we have no doubt that the exchange
was insisted upon, by the chiefs merely, for the purpose of enabling them by an additional quantity of goods, to give more satisfaction to a portion of their Tribe.

By the Treaty it will be seen that they have relinquished all their lands on the southeast of the Wabash river, where it is known to one of the Undersigned, they many
years ago, held undisputed possession, and he believes, from the best information which
his long residence in this country, and his intimate knowledge of the Indians thereof,
have enabled him to obtain, that they had an incontrovertable right to a large extent
of Country on both sides of the Wabash river, which they heretofore, had neither
abandoned, or relinquished.

Claiming the most, if not the whole of the land which was ceded by the Pottawatamies, by the treaty of St. Mary's, on the second October 1818, they have relinquished all

Senate refusal to ratify the treaty until an obnoxious clause which

their right to the same, and have released the United States from all obligations imposed upon them, by virtue of the second article of that treaty.

They have also ceded & relinquished a tract of land specially described in the treaty, which contains between thirteen and fourteen millions of acres, including the whole of their claim to the Sangamo country (a large portion of which they have long claimed and inhabited) and all the land lying between the eastern boundary of the cession made by the Illinois-nation, and the line that divides the States of Illinois & Indiana. And that no pretense of right except what was given them in exchange might remain to them, they have expressly relinquished their right & title to all lands on the east side of the Mississipi river. And thus is settled, some very important, and embarrassing disputes in adverse Indian titles. completing the extinguishment of all Indian claims west of the dividing line between the States of Illinois & Indiana, and south of the Kankakee and Illinois rivers, thereby placing at the disposal of our government, a vast extent of land of unrivalled fertility which seemed to be necessary for the purpose of connecting the different settlements in the State of Illinois, & particularly those now formed, with those which are commencing on the military bounty lands.

They have also relinquished their right to a perpetual annuity of one thousand dollars, & their proportion of 150 bushels of salt per annum which they were entitled to in consideration of their former cessions, and by virtue of former treaties.

And they have agreed to take in lieu of all former stipulations, and for the cessions made by the present treaty, the merchandize which we paid them, an annuity of two thousand dollars, for fifteen years ; and the tract of land described in the treaty, which is greatly inferior in quality, and less in quantity than that portion of the lands which they have ceded, to which, their right was exclusive and indisputable.

It was our intentions to have transmitted to you a map of the lands ceded by the Kickapoos, taken from a map of the State of Illinois, that Mr Daniel D. Smith is now preparing to publish which will be infinitely more correct than any that has yet been given to the public, but after having made out the map for us, he became apprehensive that copies of it might be taken to his injury, and therefore he refused to let us have it, but has sent it on to Washington City as a present to the Cabinet, where you of course will have an opportunity of refering to it.

We believe we hazard nothing in saying that a more important, and advantageous Indian treaty, has never been concluded on the N. West side of the Ohio river. None could have been more ardently desired, or more highly approved by the State of Illinois, whose interest & prosperity will be greatly promoted by it, not only as it affords the means of bringing into market the most desirable portion of the State and of connecting its different settlements, but in removing from its borders and out of the reach of British influence one of the most warlike and enterprising tribes of Indians in North America ; whose incursions during the late war (exceeding those of any other tribe) will be long remembered, and deeply deplored.

In fulfilling the duty assigned to us, we assure you, that we have not for one moment, lost sight of your injunction, to observe as much economy as possible, and for an object as important, and at the same time so difficult as we have found it, requiring several formal councils, at different times, We do not expect that less expense has ever been incurred under similar circumstances.

In a few days we shall transmit our account and shall draw upon you for the amount of the expenditures, dividing that amount into different bills, so as to enable us to negotiate them with the greatest facility.

A report of our proceedings would have been made at an earlier day, but for the necessary attendance of Mr Stephenson on the public sales at Edwardsville, which allowed him no time, since the conclusion of the treaty, to devote to this subject.

We flatter ourselves, that the measures we have adopted for that purpose, will prevent any further attempt on the part of the Pottawatamies of Illinois, to oppose the removal of the Kickapoos ; and we have now little doubt, but that the Pottawatamies themselves could be easily prevailed upon to remove to the West side of the Mississipi river, whereby the Indian title to the whole of the lands in Illinois could be extinguished, and the Government obtain possession of a Vast extent of Mineral Country pretty accurately described by Mr Jefferson in his Notes on Virginia, and of great value.

We have the honor to be very respectfully

Sir

Your Most Obediant
& humble servts
Augte Chouteau
Ben Stephenson.

The honorable J. C. Calhoun,
Secretary of War.
("Treaty Files," 1802–1853, Indian Office Manuscript Records.)

it contained,[a] providing for a change in Indian tenure, had been removed. Some of them did not want to leave Illinois,[b] and many who did were apprehensive of Osage aggressions.[c]

Momentarily deterred as the emigrant Indians were by fear of their own fellows, they were not suffered to falter in their original enterprise. So energetically [d] was the removal project carried for-

---

[a] Calhoun to Auguste Chouteau and Benjamin Stephenson, June 10, 1820, "Indian Office Letter Books," Series I, D, p. 441; same to same, October 4, 1820, ibid., E, p. 14.

[b] Calhoun to Clark, May 18, 1820, "Indian Office Letter Books," Series I, D, p. 429.

[c] Calhoun to Clark, February 10, 1820, "Indian Office Letter Books," Series I, D, p. 367.

[d] The following letter will indicate that if it had been practicable the General Government would even have removed the Chippewas from Michigan in 1819.

DETROIT, *Sept. 30, 1819.*

SIR,

Accompanying this I have the honour to transmit to you a treaty, concluded by me on the part of the United States with the Chippewa Indians, for the cession of a considerable portion of their Country within this Territory. I trust the general provisions of the treaty will meet with your approbation.

The boundaries of the tract ceded may be easily traced upon any good Map of the United States. But owing to our ignorance of the topography of the interior of this Territory, it may eventually be found, when the lines are run, that the South eastern corner of the tract ceded is in the possession of the Grand River Indians. If so there will be no difficulty, and very little expense in quieting their claims.

That portion of the Chippewa Indians, which owned this land, have not made the necessary advances in civilization to appreciate the importance of education for their youth. It was therefore hopeless to expect from them any reservations for this object, or to offer it as an inducement for a cession of their Country.

Some consideration more obvious in its effects, and more congenial to their habits was necessary to ensure a successful termination to the negociation.

In acceding to the propositions, which they made upon this subject, I endeavoured to give such form to the stipulations on the part of the United States for the payment of annuities, as would be permanently useful and at the same time satisfactory to them.

Their own wishes unquestionably were, that the whole sum stipulated to be annually paid to them, should be paid in specie. With the habitual improvidence of Savages they were anxious to receive what they could speedily dissipate in childish and useless purchases, at the expense of stipulations, which would be permanently useful to them. * * *.

Although I am firmly persuaded, that it would be better for us and for these Indians, that they should migrate to the Country west of the Mississippi, or at any rate west of Lake Michigan, yet it was impossible to give effect to that part of your instructions which relates to this subject, without hazarding the success of the negociation. An indisposition to abandon the Country so long occupied by their tribe, a hereditary enmity to many of the Western Indians, and a suspicion of our motives are the prominent causes, which for the present, defeat this plan. When they are surrounded by our settlements, and brought into contact with our people, they will be more disposed to migrate.

In the mean time we may teach them those useful arts, which are connected with agriculture, and which will prepare them by gradual progress for the reception of such institutions, as may be fitted for their character, customs & situation.

Reservations have been made for them to occupy. * * * Reservations have also been made for a few half breeds. It was absolutely necessary to our success, that these should be admitted into the treaty. Being only reservations, and the fee of the land remaining in the United States, I trust it will not be thought improper, that I admitted them. * * *. It was my object to insert in the supplementary article every provision, which was demanded by the Indians, respecting the principle of which I felt doubtful, so that the President and Senate might avoid the establishment of a precedent, the effect of which may be dangerous.

A large portion of the Country ceded is of the first character for soil and situation. It will vie with any land I have seen North of the Ohio River. The cession probably contains more than six millions of acres.

I shall be anxious to learn, that you approve the result of this negociation.

Very respectfully, Sir, I have the honour to be Yr. obt. Servt.

LEW CASS.

Hon. JOHN C. CALHOUN,
    Secretary of War,
      Washington City.

(" Treaty Files, 1802–1853," Indian Office Manuscript Records.)

ward both by national and local endeavor that by 1820 the three large States of the Northwest could almost foretell the time when they would be altogether cleared of the native incumbrance.[a] It is true they were not relieved so soon as might have been expected, but that was probably because during the next ten years their personal grievances against the Indians were so slight that they could not well offer them in contrast to those of Georgia. In these earlier years they had one decided advantage over the South in the greater pressure of population. Indiana professed to feel this in 1811, and in the years following she certainly spared no efforts, for one reason or another, to oust the Indians. Ohio succeeded with considerably less solicitation in reducing her incumbrance to a minimum, for the Indians, once forced to be content with tiny reservations, were on a sure road to removal. In Illinois, after the idea of exchange had been fairly introduced, the rapidity of extinguishment, owing to the extraordinary zeal of Ninian Edwards, was even more marked; but here we meet with more instances of small bands wandering westward without troubling about negotiations or going because, being homeless, they felt obliged to, stronger factions having ceded the land they claimed as their own. The influx of Indians into Missouri was very noticeable.[b] Statehood was near at hand and already there were faint glimmerings of trouble over Indian possessions.[c] In the very nature of things, it would be but a few years before the Federal Government, following a mistaken policy and neglecting to meet an important issue squarely, would have all its work to do over again.

[a] The Rev. Jedidiah Morse, speaking of Indiana and Illinois Indians, says: "Not many years since, we could point to the populous villages of these Indians, and knew where to direct our efforts for their benefit. Now we may ask the question, 'Where are they?' and there is no one among us who is able to give an answer. The most of them, however, are already gone, or are going, beyond the Mississippi, to some spot selected, or to be selected, for their future 'permanent' residence * * * ." Morse's Report, pp. 29, 30.)

[b] (1) " * * * between the Missouri river, north, and Red river, south, and the Mississippi, east, and the Rocky Mountains, west; a number of the tribes lately residing on the east of the Mississippi, having sold all their lands to the U. States, are replanted, or to be re-planted, on lands selected; or to be selected, and such as shall be approved by the tribes concerned. Some of these tribes are satisfactorily settled: others have had lands assigned them, with which they have been dissatisfied, and have refused to accept them; and others still linger on the lands of their fathers' sepulchres, which they have sold, and the places which are to be their future home are unknown to them. Not a few of the tribes lately rich in valuable lands, have now no spot to which they can point, and say, 'that is my land; there is my home.'" (Morse's Report, Appendix, pp. 202–203.)

(2) Menard to Calhoun, August 27, 1819, "Miscellaneous Files," Indian Office Manuscript Records.

[c] Duff Green to Calhoun, December 9, 1821, ibid.

CHAPTER V.

THE NORTH AND INDIAN REMOVAL, 1820-1825.

Calvin Colton, reflecting upon the United States Indian policy at a moment when its worst effects were prominent, when the labors of ten long years were being ruthlessly undone, when the red man was being forced again into the wilderness and back to savagery, and when Georgia was protesting against the work of the missionary because it tended to make the Indian a fixture in the land, bitterly declared that the white people had habitually neglected the moral well-being of the aborigines."[a] "No *efficient State* measures," said he, " have ever yet been instituted for their preservation and improvement." [b] The careful wording of this sweeping criticism, its verbal limitations, as one might say, save it from being utterly untrue. Admittedly the State in its political capacity had never up to that time done very much for the Indian, its methods had never been efficient, its policy had been fluctuating; but religious organizations and benevolent individuals, included within that State, had done a great deal. Beginning with John Eliot and coming down to and beyond John Heckewelder and David Zeisberger, these agents of civilization had put forth many a brave effort to reclaim the red men of the forest and even, though to his shame be it said, to counteract the evil example of the frontiersman. They had gone forth to the North and to the South, not only to build churches and schools, but to toil side by side with the natives and, by daily intercourse and actual experience, to discover their needs. As a result, the instruction imparted had been both theoretical and practical, both religious and industrial. Once in a while, too, we find men in public office interesting themselves in the Indian's material and spiritual welfare. Instance the case of Governor Rabun of Georgia who, probably seeing the good effects of Baptist teaching among the Cherokees, begged the foreign board of that denomination to labor similarly with the Creeks.[c] Such solicitude was, however, very rarely exhibited in the youthful days of the Republic; for the rapid growth of a particular Territory or State upon which a public man's reputation so often depended seemed frequently to be enhanced, not so much by the elevation as by the suppression of the native inhabitants. Yea, more, it had been known actually to be injured by a too pronounced humanitarianism.

When Monroe became President and the country was full of enthusiasm concerning its future and interested in everything that offered an outlet for its energies, the Indian was not neglected. He too had his possibilities, and the missionary with recovered zeal

---

[a] " Tour of the Lakes," II : 217.

[b] Ibid., p. 219.

[c] Rev. Doctor Staughton to Calhoun, August 3, 1819, Morse's Report, Appendix, p. 166.

started out once more to investigate them. Two obscure missionaries, the Reverend Messrs. Mills and Schermerhorn, had traveled [a] some years before among the tribes west of the Alleghenies and had come back with glowing reports that so fired the imagination of others in the same walk of life that they desired to go and do likewise. The Rev. Elias Cornelius, corresponding secretary of the American Board,[b] was one of these. He made his expedition in 1817, going first on a tour through New England to raise funds for the enterprise and then down through the Southwest, where he fell in with the Cherokees. From this trip came important consequences in the successful establishment of mission stations [c] that worked for so great a change in the mode of living of the southern Indians that their eventual expulsion from the scene of their birth and of their development was nothing short of a crime, and thus posterity has come to regard it.

In the following year or thereabouts, the Rev. Jedidiah Morse, another Connecticut divine, but one of an even broader mental horizon than Elias Cornelius, though influenced, perhaps, by the same reports of prospective Indian advancement, began by interviews and a wide correspondence to collect data on the present inclinations and advantages of the eastern tribes. At that time he may not have defined even for himself his own real purpose, but before a very great while he was able to outline it to the Government. The moment was auspicious; for the new interest in the Indian was more general than one would have supposed, and Congress had just passed a law creating a civilization fund in the shape of an annual appropriation of $10,000 to be distributed among organizations concerned or willing to be concerned with the object for which it was intended. On the 3d of September, 1819, Calhoun sent out a circular letter calling for infor-

---

[a] Mass. Hist. Soc. Colls., 2nd Series, II : 1–45.

[b] The American Board of Commissioners for Foreign Missions (Congregational in the main, but in its very early years partly Presbyterian), was organized in 1810 and incorporated two years afterwards. It numbered among its members, corporate, corresponding, or honorary, some of the best educated and most enlightened men of the country ; and, after 1820, became more closely identified with Indian interests than any other single religious organization. (This is said with all due regard for the noble work of the Baptists among the Ottawas and Pottowatomies, of the Episcopalians among the Oneidas, and of the Quakers among the Senecas.) Its best work, in fact, almost its entire work, was done among the southern tribes, either in their original home or in that to which they were removed west of the Mississippi. At the latter place the first school established under its auspices was begun in the autumn of 1820, and named "Dwight" in "affectionate remembrance" of President Timothy Dwight, of Yale College.

[c] The Congregational Indian school at Brainerd, established in 1817, and named after the Rev. David Brainerd, was not a pioneer in the furtherance of Indian education. Doctor Moore's Indian school, for the erection of which England and Scotland sent donations, antedated it by more than half a century. There were less progressive, less ambitious, if you please, but yet similar institutions in the South. The Moravian Brethren had had one at Springplace, 3 miles east of the Connesaga River, since 1801, and the Presbyterians one at Marysville, Tennessee, since 1804. The school at Cornwall, Connecticut, on the east bank of the Housatonic River, which was established in the autumn of 1816, with the Rev. Doctor Daggett as its principal, was seemingly more freely patronized by prominent Indians than any other North or South. Elias Boudinot, John Ridge, John Vann, McKee, and Folsom were all educated there.

mation as to the work already accomplished along the line of Indian philanthropy, together with suggestions as to the best method of continuing it under Government supervision.[a] Eager responses came in from all over the land, showing that theretofore poverty of funds and not poverty of zeal had put a constraint upon missionary labors.[b] The result of this official patronage was marvelous. New civilizing agencies were set in motion, and by a sort of reflex action the Indians were animated by new desires for their own improvement.[c]

Doctor Morse was an independent enthusiast on this same subject, but he was not slow to seize the opportunity offered for advancing a project of his own. This project was a peculiar and at the same time a very laudable one. It proposed to gather the Indians into a number of small communities, under the care of " Education Families," [d] as Morse called them, and, by evolving an ideal out of a primitive communism, prepare for individualism. It was not removal [e] in the

---

[a] Calhoun wrote to the Right Rev. J. H. Hobart, New York; to the Rev. John Gambold, Cherokee Country; to Thomas Eddy, New York; to John Johnston, Indian agent; to the Rev. Samuel Worcester, corresponding secretary of the American Board for Foreign Missions, Cornwall, Connecticut; to the Rev. Philip Milledoler, corresponding secretary of the United Foreign Mission Society, New York, and to the Rev. William Staughton, corresponding secretary of the American Baptist Board, Philadelphia. The circular letter is to be found in the " Indian Office Letter Books," Series I, D, p. 318.

[b] The outgoing correspondence of the War Department, to be found in " Indian Office Letter Books," Series I, D, for 1820, shows there was a lively interest all over the country in Indian civilization.

[c] " There is evidently a great and important revolution in the state of our Indian population already commenced, and now rapidly going forward, affecting immediately the tribes among us and on our borders and which will ultimately and speedily be felt by those at the remotest distance. The evidence of this revolution exists in the *peculiar* interest which is felt and manifested for the general improvement and welfare of Indians, and in the peculiar corresponding feelings and movements among the Indians themselves *   *   * ." (Morse's Report, p. 84.)

Isaac McCoy, laboring among the tribes in central Illinois, also remarked upon the " perceptible change " that had taken place in the Indians themselves since 1820. " Considerable and continually increasing numbers," said he to Morse, " are already inclined or becoming so, to quit their Indian habits, and to adopt those of civilized life *   *   * ." (Morse's Report, Appendix, p. 120.)

[d] " I give this name [Education Families] to those bodies which have been commonly denominated *Mission Families,* because it seems better to describe their character, and may less offend the opposers of Missions. By an *Education Family,* I mean, an association of individual families, formed of one or more men regularly qualified to preach the Gospel, to be at the head of such a family; of school-masters and mistresses; of farmers, blacksmiths, carpenters, cabinet-makers, mill-wrights, and other mechanics—of women capable of teaching the use of the needle, the spinning wheel, the loom, and all kinds of domestic manufactures, cookery, &c. common in civilzed families. This family to consist of men and women in a married state, with their children, all possessing talents for their respective offices, with a missonary spirit, devoted to their work; contented to labor without salary, receiving simply support *   *   *. These bodies are to be the great instruments in the hands of the government, for educating and civilizing the Indians." (Morse's Report, pp. 78–79.)

[e] Morse strongly discountenanced a removal that meant isolation; for he said, " On the subject of the removal of the Indians, who now dwell within our settlements, there are different opinions among wise and good men. The point on which they divide is, whether it be best to let these Indians quietly remain on their present Reservations, and to use our endeavors to civilize them where they are; or for the Government to take their Reservations, and give them an equivalent in lands to be purchased of other tribes beyond our present settlements. The Indians themselves too, are divided in opinion on this subject; a part are for removing, and a part for remaining, as in the case of the Cherokees, Delawares, Senecas, Oneidas, Shawanees, and indeed, most of the other tribes

technical sense; for it was intended to take the place of that and to avoid its disadvantages. It planned no gigantic colony of more or less unwilling emigrants in some remote part of the country, but rather the gathering together of scattered bands in a fertile spot, or, if that were not possible, then a series of little settlements in the most favorable localities that could be found. Of course segregation of any kind was sure to necessitate removal for some of the Indians. Economy was to be a prime consideration. Consequently, to avoid unnecessary outlay and a disintegration of resources, the Indians were to be placed in as large groups as could be managed, perhaps in a single group. Some of them would therefore have to be removed from their native haunts. The scheme in broad outline was a sort of reminder of the old Spanish mission system, except that the life lived was to be too energetic to admit of ultimate reduction to helpless childishness. The Indians were to be excluded from too free an intercourse with the questionable characters that are always to be found on the outskirts of civilization, but they were not to be shielded absolutely from temptation as though their preceptors were Dominican friars. On the contrary, they were to be prepared for a nineteenth century world. Each community was to have its own equipment of teachers, its own school, its own church. After a time there was to be a great central college for all.[a] Politically, Morse thought

living among us. Difficulties in deciding this question present themselves, on which side soever it be viewed. To remove these Indians, far away from their present homes, from ' the bones of their fathers,' into a wilderness, among strangers, possibly hostile, to live as their new neighbors live, by hunting, a state to which they have not lately been accustomed, and which is incompatible with civilization, can hardly be reconciled with the professed views and objects of the Government in civilizing them. This would not be deemed by the world a wise course, nor one which would very probably lead to the desired end. Should that part of the tribes only, remove, who are willing to go, and the remainder be permitted to stay—this division of already enfeebled *remnants* of tribes, would still more weaken their strength, diminish their influence, and hasten their destruction. Nor would this partial removal satisfy those who are for removing the whole ; nor those either, who are for retaining the whole. The latter wish them to remain for the benevolent purpose of educating them all where they now are, urging, that they are now among us, in view of examples of civilized life ; and where necessary instruction can be conveniently, and with little expense, imparted to them. On the other hand there is much to be said in favor of the removal of the *smaller* tribes, and remnants of tribes— not, however, into the wilderness to return again to the savage life, but to some suitable, *prepared* portion of our country, where, collected in one body, they may be made comfortable, and with advantage be educated together, as has already been mentioned, in the manner in which we educate our own children. Some such course as this, I apprehend, will satisfy a great majority of the reflecting part of those who interest themselves at all in this subject, and is, in my belief, the only practicable course which can be pursued, consistently, with the professed object of the Government." (Report, pp. 82–83.)

[a] Morse suggests " the expediency of establishing, in some suitable situation, a College, for the education of such Indian youth, as shall have passed through the primary Indian schools with reputation and promise. Here, under competent instructors, let them be prepared to teach their brethren of the wilderness, all, even the higher branches of useful knowledge. Let this College be liberally endowed out of the avails of those public lands, which have been purchased of the Indians * * * . Such an Institution * * * was early established, and nobly endowed in India. * * *" The school at Cornwall, in Connecticut, could be very easily raised into such an Institution * * * ." (Report, pp. 76, 77, 78.) Again he says : " Should the expectations raised in regard to this project, be realized in any good degree, I should think this [Wisconsin] the place for the ultimate es-

that if these various communities were not too widely scattered they might eventually develop into an Indian State. The idea was new to him, but he afterwards [a] found that it was not so new to others since it had been loosely spoken of in the treaty of Fort Pitt,[b] negotiated with the Delawares in 1778.

To collect information that would bear upon the feasibility of the plan for establishing " Education Families " Doctor Morse [c] prepared, in the summer of 1820, to make an extended tour of the Northwest. He left New Haven on the 10th of May, bearing with him a commission [d] from the Government with instructions to report upon four main topics; viz, the number of Indian tribes within reach, whether actually visited on the trip or not, their present condition in point of civilization and territorial possessions, Indian trade, and personal reflections or suggestions. On the way, while crossing Lake Erie, he fell in with Charles Stuart, of Malden, Upper Canada, and the two men discussed the practicability of a general plan upon which Great Britain and the United States could amicably unite for civilizing and for safeguarding the interests of the Indian. Other British gentlemen at Detroit and Mackinaw conversed intelligently on the same subject. Had they all forgotten the failure of the early Ghent negotiations? Probably they had or else thought that their own ideas were an improvement upon those advanced by others, less disinterested, in 1814. At all events Doctor Morse thought the scheme was worth following up and the next summer made a special trip to Canada in its interests. At York he talked with Governor Maitland, who manifested great readiness to cooperate and felt confident of the support of his colleague in the lower Province; but Governor Dalhousie was not at Quebec and, the responsibility being shifted, Morse had to return home with his efforts unrewarded.[e]

---

tablishment of the Indian College, which might,in time be furnished with Indian officers and instructors, as well as students, and have their own Trustees to manage its concerns. The funds belonging to Moor's Indian School, which is connected at present with Dartmouth College, deposited with the other funds, consecrated to the benefit of American Indians, in the Treasury of the Society in Scotland for propagating Christian Knowledge ; together with funds in the Treasury of Harvard College, and of the Society for propagating the gospel among the Indians and others in North America, should the colonization plan succeed, might be appropriated, in whole, or in part, to this Institution. And if our brethren in Canada shall be disposed to unite with us in this great and desirable object, and make the Institution common for the benefit of Indians on both sides of the line which separates us * * * large funds * * * exist in England, designed expressly for an object of this kind * * * the annual interest of the funds granted in the reign of George II for civilizing and christianizing *the Indians in New England* * * * ." (Report, Appendix, pp. 315–316.)

[a] " The idea of an *Indian State,* though suggested to the President in my Report, as new, [it was so at the time] had been suggested, it seems, many years ago, in a treaty with the Delaware Indians * * * ." (Report, Appendix, p. 313, note.)

[b] 7 United States Statutes at Large, p. 14.

[c] Calhoun to Dr. Jedidiah Morse, February 7, 1820, "Indian Office Letter Books," Series I, D, pp. 362–364.

[d] Report, pp. 11–13.

[e] Report, pp. 17, 19, 20.

By that time he must surely have despaired of his whole project, for nothing had as yet resulted from the trip of the preceding year. He had reached Detroit to find Cass, the man who could and would have helped him most, absent on an expedition to the headwaters of Lake Superior.[a] Colonel Visger, a Wyandot interpreter,[b] gave him some facts that seemed encouraging; so did the Miami chief, Jean Baptiste Richardville,[c] but a prosperous old Wyandot farmer-chief from the Huron River district [d] rejected his every idea with scorn. From Detroit, Morse went around Lake Mackinaw to Little Traverse Bay and there met Col. George Boyd, who had come to L'Arbre Croche to negotiate with the Ottawas for the purchase of the St. Martins Islands.[e] Here was a good opportunity for speaking before an assemblage of Indians, and Morse took advantage of it, but only to advise their settling down and following agricultural pursuits. His whole impression of Michigan and of the country to the immediate westward was that it was just the locality for his Indian settlement.[f] But before going into the subject of his suggestions to the Government let us consider the way in which the Morse plan was likely to affect the tribes not included within the visitation of 1820.

The southern tribes may be disposed of in a few words, for they seem not to have been reported upon at all in 1820, with special reference to "Education Families;" but before Morse published his book in 1822 he had heard from Capt. John Bell, Indian agent in Florida, that the Seminoles, though "unwilling to leave their country," "make no objection to quitting their present scattered villages, and dwelling together in some suitable part of Florida." "Here, then," commented Morse, "is a station well prepared and ready for the immediate establishment of an Education Family."[g] John Ross,[h]

---

[a] The final destination of this expedition was left to the discretion of General Cass, who had among his companions Henry R. Schoolcraft and James D. Doty, the latter as official secretary. ("Doty's Journal," Wis. Hist. Colls. XIII : 163–220.) The objects of the expedition as they appeared on paper were not so very dissimilar from those given Morse; but Cass's personal reason for going was the investigation of mineral resources, while Morse's was the ultimate foundation of "Education Families."

[b] Morse's Report, Appendix, p. 18.

[c] Ibid., p. 96.

[d] Ibid., p. 16.

[e] Report, p. 14.

[f] "The whole of these Territories constitute one great field for moral cultivation; and when Education Families shall have been planted at the different military posts, a plan seriously contemplated, of immense importance; and which it is hoped will shortly be carried into effect, a channel, through them, will be opened to many large tribes W. of the Mississippi, to the Council Bluffs. Here again a military post is established, and a large Education Family are ready to occupy this commanding station. All the tribes within the United States, N. of the Missouri, as far .W. as the Council Bluffs, and beyond them, placed between these posts and these families, may be made to feel, in a greater or less degree, their combined, controlling, civilizing, and reforming influence * * * ." (Morse's Report, p. 29.)

[g] Report, Appendix, p. 310.

[h] John Ross to David Brown, July 13, 1822, Morse's Report, Appendix, pp. 399–400.

writing of his own people, the Cherokees, about the same time drew happy conclusions from the unprecedented interest shown on all sides in Indian civilization; but, while deploring the disastrous results of removal to Arkansas, never even hinted at concentration after the Morse pattern. In Connecticut there were only a very few Mohicans and Pequods, degenerate and decreasing, left in 1820, too few, thought Morse, to deserve notice.[a] In Rhode Island there were scarcely more than four hundred and twenty-five natives, and they were nearly all of mixed blood. They were not badly off, though, for they owned jointly about 3,000 acres of land. They expressed themselves negatively on removal as follows: " We wish not to be removed into a wild country. We have here farms and homes of our own. Those who will work, may here get a comfortable living; and those who will not work here, would not probably in a wilderness. We have land enough, and wood enough, and living on the salt water, and having boats of our own, have plenty of fish." [b] Of the Maine Indians the Rev. E. Kellogg wrote: " None of these tribes have made other than incipient improvements in anything which pertains to civilized life. It is not probable, such is the religious influence under which they act, combined with their natural attachment to their native places, and to the sepulchres of their fathers, that a proposal to remove, and join a larger community of Indians, should it be made to them, would be accepted." [c] The report on the Massachusetts Indians was even more decisive adversely. "As to the plan of removing them, *were they in favor of the measure*, it would scarcely be an object. They are of public utility *here*, as expert whalemen and manufacturers of various light articles; have lost their sympathy with their brethren of the forest; are in possession of many privileges, peculiar to a coast indented by the sea; their local attachments are strong; they are tenacious of their lands; of course, the idea of alienating them and removing to a distance, would be very unpopular." [d] This was all very true, and Doctor Morse was satisfied that the New England Indians were not fit subjects for colonization. They " are all provided for," said he, " both as to instruction and comfort, by the governments and religious associations, of the several states in which they reside * * *. Should the Government of the United States provide an Asylum for the remnants of these depressed and wretched people * * * a portion of them might be persuaded to take shelter * * *. The body of them, however, would doubtless prefer to remain where they are, for this prominent reason, among others, that very few of them are of unmixed blood. The others, having intermarried with the lowest classes of white people and negroes, and feeling no sympathy with Indians

---

a Report, Appendix, pp. 74, 75.   c Ibid., p. 66.
b Ibid., p. 74.   d Ibid., p. 70.

of pure blood, would not be comfortable, or happy, or of wholesome influence, if removed and planted among them * * *." [a]

The suggestions that Doctor Morse had to offer to the Government were born, in part, of his observations during the trip and, in part, of his reflections upon events occurring within a few months after his return home. In the first place, he recommended the formation of a society "for promoting the general welfare of the Indian tribes in the United States " [b] and such an one seems to have been soon afterwards organized or projected with John Jay, C. C. Pinckney, Thomas Pinckney, Andrew Jackson, Henry Clay, James Hillhouse, Jedidiah Morse, and others, less well known, as honorary members. William Wirt and Col. Thomas L. McKenney were to serve on a committee of ways and means. [c] In the second place, Morse submitted, as though himself indorsing, the plans of other men. The following may be cited in illustration: George Sibley, factor at Fort Osage, reporting for the Osages, Kanzas, and Ioway Indians, October 1, 1820, advised that the government should distinctly survey and mark the Indian country and "whenever an Indian evinced a serious disposition to settle himself permanently, and to pursue civilized habits, a portion of this land, from 160 to 640 acres, as might be proper, should be allotted to him, patented to him by the Government, and secured to him and (to his) family forever * * *." [d]

In the third place, Doctor Morse considered the suitability of various tracts of land for the establishment of " Education Families." Generally speaking, since he was not bent upon forcing emigration, he was inclined to provide for a corps of teachers wherever there was a sufficiently large concourse of Indians to justify it. For instance, he thought one could settle on L'Arbre Croche territory " which is abundantly large enough for the accommodation of several thousands " " and scattered villages of this [Ottawa] nation, and of the Chippawas, who intermarry with the Ottawas, and in various ways are connected with them, might probably be induced to remove " thither; [e] another on the eastern shore of the lower Michigan peninsula, say on Flint River near Saginaw, where Jacob Smith, a man appointed by the Government in 1819 to be a sort of guardian for the Chippewas and who had lived among them several years and knew them well, thought that the United States could very easily gather together the numerous bands then dwelling upon detached reservations and so make an exchange that " would be reciprocally advantageous " to the red and white people. It might even be possible to accommodate not only all the Indians from that part of Michigan Territory, but also all the remnants of tribes in Ohio, New York and

---

[a] Report, pp. 23–24.
[b] Report, pp. 75–76.
[c] Report, Appendix, p. 284–290.

[d] Ibid., p. 208.
[e] Ibid., p. 26.

New England " who might be inclined to remove; a body of from twenty-five to thirty thousand." [a]

These suggestions were all very good, but they were none the less all secondary to the grand scheme of making one vast Indian Territory out of the present State of Wisconsin and of the upper Michigan peninsula. We shall have more to say of the origin of this idea later in connection with the removal of the New York Indians. At present let us consider Morse's advocacy. " In the treaty with the Choctaws of October, 1820, it is stipulated," wrote he, " that ' the boundaries ' of the territory of this nation shall ' remain without alteration, until the period at which said nation shall become so civilized and enlightened, as to be made citizens of the United States, and Congress shall lay off a limited parcel of land for the benefit of each family, or individual in the nation.' Let similiar regulations be made relative to the proposed colony, [in the North] with such variations and additions as shall suit their peculiar circumstances; one particularly, which shall prohibit the introduction of white settlers within· the limits of the territory assigned for the proposed colony; i. e. within the limits bounded south by Illinois, east by lake Michigan, north by lake Superior, and west by the Mississippi: Let this territory be reserved, exclusively for Indians, in which to make the proposed experiment of gathering into one body, as many of the scattered and other Indians, as choose to settle here, to be educated, become citizens, and, in due time, to be admitted to all the privileges common to other territories and States, in the Union. Such a course would probably save the Indians * * * . Within its limits, are more than twenty thousand souls, exclusive of the new colony [New York Indian] to be planted on the late purchase [from the Menominees and Winnebagoes]. Half of these are Menominees and Winnebagoes; the rest, Chippawas, Sioux, Sauks and Foxes. If the whole of these tribes last mentioned be reckoned, as belonging to the Territory, (though a great part of them are now west of the Mississippi,) the whole number would exceed sixty thousand; enough, when educated, to form a separate Territory, and to have a representative in Congress * * * ." [b]

Doctor Morse's reference to the New York Indian purchase from the Menominees and Winnebagoes of Green Bay calls vividly to mind the unique position of the Iroquois bands. Under colonial grant, as extending from sea to sea, Massachusetts claimed a large share of the Empire State.[c] To settle the pretension, commissioners on her part and commissioners in behalf of New York met at Hartford toward the close of 1786 and agreed, with the sanction of the Con-

---

[a] Report, Appendix, p. 20.
[b] Ibid., pp. 313–315.
[c] Report of New York Assembly, 1889, p. 16.

federate Congress,[a] that, while New York should continue to exercise governmental jurisdiction over the whole of the land within her prescribed limits, Massachusetts should hold the preemptive right to the western part (except a strip 1 mile wide along the Niagara River), lying beyond a meridian line drawn southward from Lake Ontario through Seneca Lake to the Pennsylvania boundary, and also to a tract, equal to ten townships, between the Oswego and Chenango rivers. The preemptive right constituted the privilege of buying the land, as a private person or corporation, from the Indian occupants whenever they might choose to sell. Within a comparatively short time, the Bay State sold this privilege, as applicable to the smaller tract, to Samuel Brown and fifty-nine associates; and, as applicable to the larger, to Oliver Phelps, of Connecticut, and Nathaniel Gorham, of Boston; [b] but she retained the authority of superintending all subsequent negotiations with the Indian owners. Before long, Phelps and Gorham, owing to financial embarrassments, were obliged to reconvey to Massachusetts the preemptive right to most of the land; and, in 1791, a new contract was formed, whereby Robert Morris became the beneficiary. He, in turn, sold out to William Willink and eleven associates in Holland. From them it passed to David A. Ogden [c] who, in 1821, transferred his rights to a trust composed of his brother, Thomas L. Ogden, Robert Troup, and Benjamin W. Rogers—the germ of the notorious Ogden Land Company. Between any two of these successive changes in ownership, the preemptive privilege had been variously exercised and the lands covered by it had steadily contracted.

Upon the authority of Wilson Lumpkin,[d] it is sometimes asserted that, in 1810, the New York Indians held a council and resolved to ask permission of the Federal Government for them to emigrate westward. It is doubtful whether we can fix the date quite so early; but, in June of 1815, Governor Tompkins wrote to Washington advocating removal and received from the Acting Secretary of War a summary of the difficulties that would confront the project.[e] A little later the

---

[a] " Journals of Congress," IV : 788.

[b] W. H. Sampson in his consideration of the "Claim of the Ogden Land Co." says, "Massachusetts sold this (preemptive) right to Phelps and Gorham; they bought some of the land; then failed, and their right to buy the remainder reverted to Mass., which sold the right to Robt. Morris * * * ."

[c] The Ogden brothers were at one time law partners of Alexander Hamilton, Report of New York Assembly, 1889, p. 22.

[d] " Congressional Globe," Twenty-sixth Congress, 1st sess., Appendix, p. 286.

[e] " Sir, I have submitted your letter of the 28th of June last to the consideration of the President of the United States; and I am instructed to inform you, that there is a great desire, on his part, to accomodate your wishes, and the interest of the state of New York, in relation to the proposed removal of the Senecas from the territory which they at present inhabit, to lands on the Western frontier of the United States. · There are, however, national views of the subject, which must be combined with such a movement, on motives of state policy. All transactions with the Indians relative to their lands, are more, or less, delicate; and a removal of them from one region of country to another, is critically so, as relates to the effect on the Indians themselves, and on the white neighbors to their new abode. You do not designate any particular part of the Western country, to which it is intended by you, or desired by the Indians, that they

sachems of the Six Nations memorialized Madison to the effect that it was their desire to sell out and join their friends in or west of the State of Ohio. They were told that they might leave New York if they wished to, but might not locate in Ohio or in its immediate neighborhood for the reason,[a] already stated to Governor Tompkins,[b] that

should be transferred; nor can it be ascertained from the general expression of a transfer to lands within the territories of the United States, on the Western frontier, you mean lands where the Indian titles have been extinguished, as well as lands, which are still in Indian occupancy. If the latter only be meant, the arrangement will essentially be between the Senecas and the state of New York on the one part, and the Indian occupants, on the other; but if it be contemplated to transfer the Senecas to lands, which have been purchased from other Indians, the government seems bound to take into view, the effect of such an arrangement, 1st in shutting the lands against the sales and settlements contemplated by the purchase, or involving the expense of a repurchase from the Senecas. 2d in giving Indian neighbours to white settlements which might be averse to such an arrangement. When it was proposed to transfer the Indians on the North frontier of Ohio, to a new abode on the Illinois &c, the neighbouring territories of Illinois and Missouri protested against the measure.

"Having briefly suggested these difficulties, I am instructed to request those explanations which will enable the President to decide upon the subject of your letter, with the requisite attention to the national interests under his charge. If, however, a removal of the Indians should take place, I am authorized to add, that it will not affect the annuities, which have been granted to them, provided they conform, in other respects, to the terms of the grant.

"I am very respectfully &c."

(Letter from Alexander J. Dallas, Acting Secretary of War, to Daniel D. Tompkins, governor of New York, August 5, 1815, "Indian Office Letter Books," Series I, C, pp. 271–272.)

[a] W. H. Crawford to the Six Nations of New York Indians, February 12, 1816, "Indian Office Letter Books," Series I, C, pp. 299–301.

[b] "Sir, Your letter and the memorial of the Sachems of the six nations of Indians, communicating the desire of the latter to sell the reservations of lands upon which they at present reside, in the state of New York, and to remove and settle upon lands in or West of the state of Ohio, have been regularly received, and submitted to the consideration of the President.

"The greatest difficulty in deciding the case, is the uncertainty of the spot, which will be selected for the future residence of these Indians, after they shall have disposed of their present possessions. It is an object of the first importance to the nation, with a view to any future war which may occur with the British Empire, that the settlements of the state of Ohio should be connected with those of the Michigan Territory, with the least possible delay. It is also important that our settlements should be extended to Southern margin of lake Michigan. This may be done, either by extending the settlements from Ohio Westwardly, or by obtaining a cession of the lands lying between the Illinois purchase, and the South Western margin of the Lake. The settlement of the six nations, in the districts which must be ceded in order to accomplish these desirable objects, cannot fail to protract the time of obtaining those cessions. The extent of the country also, which may be set apart for their use, is of some importance in the consideration of this subject. Having approximated more to the habits of civilized man than their Western brethren, and accustomed to attach a higher value to land, cessions will be obtained from them with more difficulty and at a greater expense. At the same time it is believed that the settlement of a friendly tribe of Indians in that part of the country, bound by the ties of interest and friendship to the United States, will have a beneficial influence upon the conduct of their savage friends in the event of another war with England.

".The interest which the state of New York takes in this transaction, and the influence which the cession may have upon its happiness and prosperity, have induced the President to determine that a treaty shall be held, with a view to accomplish the wishes of your excellency, and to gratify the desires of the Indian tribes in question. If your excellency is informed of the particular district in which the settlement is contemplated, and the extent of the grant which is intended to be made, a prompt communication of it may facilitate the conclusion of the business.

"I have the honor to be &c.

"Wm. H. Crawford."

(Letter from W. H. Crawford to Daniel D. Tompkins, governor of New York, January 22, 1816, "Indian Office Letter Books," Series I, C, pp. 294–295.)

the Government was even then contemplating a consolidation of settlements this side of Michigan as a safeguard should another war break out with Great Britain. Barred from Ohio, the Indians lost all desire to emigrate; but land speculators, especially the proprietor of the Massachusetts preemptive right, began, or dare we say continued, to harass them with that object in view.

A little before this time there arrived among the New York Indians an Episcopal missionary in the person of Eleazer Williams—Bishop Hobart, of the New York diocese, having licensed him as a catechist and lay reader[a] "at the earnest request of the Oneida chiefs."[b] This man, the same who figured later on in fact and fiction as a pretender to the French throne, was himself of Indian extraction, also a lineal descendant of the survivor of the Deerfield massacre. In character he was wild and visionary, full of vagaries that would account in part for his easy seduction by the New York speculators. In 1817 he seems to have been opposed to removal and to have resisted the blandishments of De Witt Clinton, who wanted him to advocate that measure before a general council of the tribes. By the next year his opinions had undergone a radical change,[c] but in the interval he had been entertained by and had, perhaps, succumbed to the influence of David A. Ogden.[d] New pressure was then being brought to bear upon the Government to have the Iroquois sent westward, but without, as yet, much success. The profits of title extinguishment in that particular part of the East occupied by the Six Nations would accrue, not to the Government, but to the proprietor of the preemptive right; consequently there was no motive for pushing matters, although conversely there were valuable interests at stake for the rich capitalist since the market value of land in western New York depended, as Calvin Colton remarked years afterwards, " entirely upon the nearer or more remote prospects of the removal of the Indians— in other words, of their ejectment."[e]

The official correspondence of 1818 is very interesting as bearing upon New York Indian emigration; for it shows clearly how Calhoun came to be concerned in the scheme for erecting a part of the Northwest into an Indian Territory, and also to what lengths politicians and speculators were willing to go in order to accomplish their purposes. An effort was made to deceive the Indians into thinking that if they obtained any land in the West it would be in exchange for an equal amount in New York. Calhoun was inclined to be angry at this.[f] Furthermore, he was annoyed that people persisted in holding

---

[a] " Wis. Hist. Colls.," II : 419.
[b] Schroeder's " Memoirs of Bishop Hobart."
[c] " Wis. Hist. Colls., II : 421.
[d] Hanson, " The Lost Prince," p. 282.
[e] " Tour of the Lakes," I : 99.
[f] Calhoun to Jasper Parish, sub-agent to the Six Nations, May 14, 1818, " Indian Office Letter Books," Series I, D, pp. 165–166.

out to the Indians the hope of going west of Ohio and in prejudicing them against Arkansas,[a] whither the Government would have wished to have them go,[b] the Arkansas Cherokees being very ready to receive them.[c] Calhoun knew that the people of Indiana and Illinois would never permit an immigration of Indians into their territory. Meanwhile Cass was becoming interested in the Ogden plans.[d] Indeed, he

---

[a] " SIR.

It is certainly much to be regretted, that the Six Nations should, by the arts of officious and designing men, be induced to hesitate in changing their present residence, for one more congenial to their habits, and better calculated, by its remoteness from the settlements of the Whites, permanently to secure their interest and happiness. The country on the Arkansaw was designated, as combining every advantage most likely to render the change agreeable to them and to produce these results; while it would, at the same time, promote the views of the government, with which it is a desirable object to induce, as many of the tribes of Indians as may be disposed to change their residence, to emigrate to the West of the Mississippi. The objection to the Arkansaw on account of its unhealthiness is an erroneous one. It is believed that no section of the country is more healthy. However, should they adhere to the determination not to remove to that country, Gov[r] Cass will be requested to consult with the Indians on Fox river and its vicinity, or with the tribes inhabiting the country lying North of the state of Indiana and the Illinois territory, and ascertain whether they are willing to make a cession of land to the six nations and receive them among them ; and, in the event of any of them assenting to the proposition, he will be instructed to make the arrangements necessary for their reception and to facilitate their removal : provided the portion of country so selected for their new residence, receives their approbation * * *." (Extract of letter from J. C. Calhoun to David A. Ogden, August 19, 1818, " Indian Office Letter Books," Series I, D, pp. 204–205.)

[b] " SIR. M[r]. Graham transmitted your letter to him of the 8th inst. yesterday. The subject to which it refers had previously attracted my attention. Governor Cass in his letter to you states, that it will be necessary as a preliminary step, that this department should designate the place to be assigned to the six nations. I think there are almost insuperable difficulties in assigning a place between the Lakes, Ohio, and Mississippi. It is certain that, should it be selected in Ohio, Indiana, or Illinois, great discontent and complaints would be justly excited ; and beyond the limits of those states, no position presents itself to me to which the Indians in New York could be tempted to emigrate. I am, of opinion, that the Arkansaw, in every point of view, presents much the most advantageous site for their new residence. I have already presented my views to you on this subject in conversation and will not now repeat them. Should the Six nations be induced to emigrate thither, every facility will be presented by this department. I will direct M[r]. Lewis, the agent at the Arkansaw, to bring the subject before the Chiefs of the Cherokees, who live West of the Mississippi, and tho' I do not think it proper to make a formal address, in reply to the letter written by the Missionary Schoolmaster, yet M[r]. Parish, the sub-agent, will be made acquainted with the views of this Department, on the points referred to in your letter." (Calhoun to Hon. David A. Ogden, Madrid, N. Y., May 14, 1818, " Indian Office Letter Books," Series I, D, pp. 164–165.)

[c] Calhoun to Reuben Lewis, agent to the Cherokees on the Arkansaw, May 16, 1818, " Indian Office Letter Books," Series I, D, p. 168.

[d] The best documentary evidence forthcoming in proof of the willingness of Cass to have the New York Indians settle in the West is the following letter :

WASHINGTON, *October 22d, 1821.*

SIR.

I have the honour to submit to you a copy of the treaty, executed at Green Bay between the Winnebagos and Menominies forming one party, and the delegation of the Six Nations of the Munsees, of the Stockbridge, and of the St. Regis Indians forming the other party. I intended to transmit the original instrument, but some accident has prevented it. I shall do it however immediately on my return.

I submit also a copy of the report of the person, authorized by me, at the expense of the persons holding the reversion of the lands owned by these Indians in New York, to visit Green Bay in company with the delegation and to conduct the negotiation. It is due to him to say, that this duty was zealously and ably performed.

A copy of my instructions to him should have accompanied this report, but I find on examination, that I have it not with me. It shall be transmitted, as speedily as possibly.

seems already to have been in correspondence for some months on the subject, first with Granger, the Indian agent at Buffalo, and later with the proprietor himself. When it became evident that the Indians disliked the thought of Arkansas as a home, Calhoun agreed to let them go to the vicinity of Fox River, or, if that region were not suitable, then to the lower peninsula of Michigan. At the time he had an impression that the Fox River intended flowed entirely outside of Illinois.[a] Finding that it did not and probably not knowing of the Fox River in Wisconsin he countermanded the first part of his permission; for " I wish it understood," said he, " that the Indians are not to receive lands in exchange for those they have in New York, within the State of Indiana or Illinois."[b]

It was not likely that the Federal Government would cumber one State with Indians in order to please a private individual even though that individual were supported, as it was well known Ogden was, by the strongest of local politics, and it was particularly unlikely that it would cumber Indiana at this time; for it was about to relieve her of the Delawares. Nevertheless, as events turned out, it was an incident occasioned by this very Delaware removal that finally helped to commit the Government to the scheme for placing the New York Indians in Wisconsin.

Among the remnants of the Iroquois was a small group of Stockbridges, exiles from Massachusetts, who, in one way or another, but in a way that President Jefferson approved, had become possessed, by deed of gift from the Delawares, of a joint claim to the land on White River;[c] yet it was not until 1817 that any of their families had an inclination to respond to the request of the resident Miamis and Delawares that they should remove thither, although their obstinacy was much deplored by Solomon Hendricks, one of their number and " a strong advocate of the policy of emigration."[d] In that year, 1817, two families went West and more prepared to follow, but

My apology for the omission will be found in the little time afforded me for the arrangement of my papers, after the conclusion of the treaty of Chicago.

The result of this negotiation I consider important to the parties and to the United States. If no improper influence be excited, these Indians will gradually withdraw from New York, and establish themselves upon the land thus ceded. They will there form a barrier, which may be highly useful in the event of any difficulties in that remote quarter.

    Very Respectfully Sir
        I have the honour to be
            y[r] obt. serv[t]

                      LEW CASS.

Hon. J. C. CALHOUN,
    Secretary of War.

(" Treaty Files," 1802–1853, Indian Office Manuscript Records.)

[a] Calhoun to David A. Ogden, August 28, 1818, " Indian Office Letter Books," Series I, D, p. 208.

[b] Calhoun to Cass, September 2, 1818, " Indian Office Letter Books," Series I, D, p. 208.

[c] Marsh's Scottish Report for 1833, " Wis. Hist. Colls.," XV : 86.

[d] Davidson, " The Coming of the New York Indians," " Wis. Hist. Soc. Proc.," 1899, p. 160.

were deterred by a report in a Boston newspaper that the Delawares had sold out to the United States Government. The Stockbridges at once wrote to the Delawares to have the report either confirmed or denied, and were assured by the Indians that it was utterly false, and by the agent that "there would be no attempt at present, to buy out and remove the said Indians."[a] Taking courage, therefore, the Stockbridges prepared a second party, which left New York under the leadership of John Metoxen. "They did not get away so soon by a month, as they had intended;" wrote Sergeant to Morse, "and on that account they did not arrive at their place of destination *before the country was all sold:*"[b] During the winter following, they stayed with the Shawnees in Ohio and applied, though unsuccessfully, to Congress for a redress of their grievance. Morse championed their cause, as they had requested him, for he was their friend, and their disappointment was his also; inasmuch as, trusting to the prophecies of Hendrick and Sergeant, he had hoped to establish an "Education Family" with them as a center on White River.[c] Indiana being now out of the question, he made a personal appeal to President Monroe.[d]

---

[a] Hendrick to Sergeant, March 30, 1818, Morse's Report, Appendix, p. 112.

[b] Sergeant to Morse, December 15, 1818, Morse's Report, Appendix, p. 116.

[c] (1) "If nothing takes place unfavourable, I judge the Stockbridge Indians will *all* remove into that country [on White River] in the course of eight or ten years. They say they must send a few families there this summer, to take possession of the country, and satisfy the Delawares. As soon as this takes place, there will be an agreeable home at once, for a missionary, and a most excellent stand for the establishment you propose. It is altogether probable, that in the course of a few years, the Delawares from Upper Canada, and the Munsees from various parts, will remove to White river, probably making upwards of two thousand souls. The Brotherton Indians, so-called, are about to remove to this place * * *."

(Hendrick to Sergeant, March, 1818, Morse's Report, Appendix, pp. 112–114.)

(2) "It is *reported* that the Indiana Government, this season, intend to purchase the lands on the White river. It is my opinion, that they will not be able to do it, by fair means. If they should be able to do it by a stretch of unlawful power, the proposed plan will be at an end [i. e. of a mission establishment.] Partly on this account, I would recommend that your Society employ some missionary, visiting the Ohio, or Indiana Territory, or some minister in the vicinity, to spend a few weeks among my people, and from the Chief, who is going, the Missionary will be able to report to your Society all necessary information respecting your missionary establishment * * *. I am well informed that the Tuscaroras, living near Buffalo, are about to remove to White river; and by a late letter from Buffalo, I understand a number of Munsees will go on with my people. All these will be friendly to a religious establishment * * *."

(John Sergeant to Morse, June 29, 1818, Morse's Report, Appendix, p. 115.)

(3) To this letter of Sergeant's Morse added the following editorial comment: "If these Indians were disposed to settle together in this place, why not, I ask, in some other eligible spot?" (Report, Appendix, p. 116.)

[d] "I take the liberty here respectfully to suggest to the President, whether it would not be expedient, and have a conciliatory and good effect on the Stockbridge Indians, and on others also, white people as well as Indians, to consider the *hard case* of these Indians, and to grant them a portion of the lands which they claim on White river, with an understanding, that they shall exchange them for a tract somewhere in the N. W. Territory, which shall be agreeable to them, and which the Government might purchase of the present owners for this specific purpose? Or make them a grant in the first instance, in some part of the N. W. Territory?

"I have conversed with Mr. Sergeant on this subject, and he has suggested to me, that some course like this would satisfy the Stockbridge Indians. This, I think, might lead ultimately to the gathering together of many of the scattered remnants of tribes, in this Territory, so peculiarly adapted to this purpose." (Morse's Report, Appendix, p. 117.)

urging that a tract in the Northwest Territory be given to the Stock-bridges in compensation for the one they had lost; and, as we shall see, in following his advice, the Government was ready to accede to the wishes of David A. Ogden.

During the summer of 1819 the proprietor of the Massachusetts pre-emptive right made a most desperate effort to induce the Senecas to emigrate westward; but, led by Red Jacket, they stood out like ada-mant against all proposition having removal as their burden.[a] The Oneidas were more pliable, owing to a division in their ranks on the score of religion. Dating from a period soon after the coming of Missionary Williams into their midst (for their tribe was his special field), they had been divided into two parties, the Pagan and the Christian. The latter, made up of Williams's supposed proselytes, was inclined to place implicit confidence in his advice on matters material as well as spiritual. This was but natural. More impres-sionable than their fellows of the Pagan party, as evidenced by the effect that the beautiful Anglican Church ritual had had upon them, they were allured by a most Utopian dream of an Indian Empire. Just when Williams began to argue this before them or just when he first indulged in it himself is matter for conjecture. He always claimed it as an original idea, but it looks very much like an exaggera-tion of Morse's Indian State, which Morse may have projected as he had projected the " Education Families " even before his trip to the Northwest.

Be that as it may, we know for certain that in the winter of 1819 and 1820 Eleazer Williams went to Washington and represented to the Government that the Oneidas and other New York Indians were anxious to move West. The War Department was just beginning to take efficient measures toward a compromise with the Stock-bridges [b] and, perhaps, with that partly in view was commissioning their advocate, Doctor Morse, to investigate northern Indian condi-tions; so Calhoun agreed to help bear the expenses of a delegation of ten Iroquois, desirous of exploring " certain parts of the north-western territory and " of making " arrangements with the Indians residing there, for a portion of their country to be " thereafter " in-habited by such of the Six Nations as " might " choose to emigrate." [c]

The expedition set out under favorable auspices. Calhoun was

---

[a] "At the meeting [of the Council "at Pollard's Village, about five miles from Buffalo"] on the 9th the Chief Red Jacket, on behalf of the Senecas, rejected the proposition to re-move or to contract their limits, or dispose of any part of their lands ; the rejection was so unqualified and so peremptory, as to forbid all reasonable expectation, that any good purpose could be effected by adjourning the Council : it was therefore finally closed * * *" (Extract from Report of Morris S. Miller to Calhoun, July 25, 1819, " Miscellaneous Files," Indian Office Manuscript Records.)

[b] Report of the Commission of 1830.

[c] Calhoun to Eleazer Williams, February 9, 1820, " Indian Office Letter Books," Series I, D, p. 364. Calhoun to Cass and to Gen. Alex. Macomb, February 9, 1820, " Indian Office Letter Books," Series I, D, p. 366.

compliant, Bishop Hobart [a] benignly encouraging, to say nothing of De Witt Clinton and David A. Ogden. Both were active, the latter securing from Schoolcraft a ready promise to render all the assistance that lay in his power.[b] But there were breakers ahead. When the delegates reached Detroit they heard news that caused them to turn back disappointed.[c] The land they thought they wanted was reported gone. In the absence of Governor Cass and, as it afterwards proved, with his strong disapprobation,[d] Colonel Bowyer, the Indian agent at

---

[a] The Rev. Joseph Hooper, of Durham, Connecticut, who helped to make a most minute examination of the Hobart Papers for Doctor Dix's "History of Trinity Church," reports : "From any documents that I have seen it does not appear that Bishop Hobart had any especial influence over the Indians concerning their removal * * *." Hanson, however, furnishes extracts from a letter purporting to have been written by Bishop Hobart at this time to the Oneidas, which indicates a certain measure of sympathy with Williams's undertaking : "My Children—It is expedient that he [Williams] should go on a journey to the west, to see if he can find some territory, where the Stockbridge Indians and others, who are disposed to go, may reside ; and particularly to ascertain whether your western brethren are inclined to embrace the Gospel of our Lord and Saviour, Jesus Christ * * *." ("The Lost Prince," p. 290.)

[b] "I shall pass through that country [Green Bay] some time in August. If Mr. Williams, with the delegation from the six nations could be there at that time, I might be able, more effectually than in any other way, to aid him in the accomplishment of his object * * *.

"The plan of locating these Indians in the country, to which you refer, is the most practicable, which has yet been proposed. There are none of our citizens interest in that country to oppose the measure. There will be no political prejudices to encounter, and no misrepresentations to correct. I believe the soil, climate, and other advantages of the country will be found to equal any expectations which these Indians may have indulged respecting them * * *." (Henry R. Schoolcraft to Hon. David A. Ogden, May 5, 1820, "Schoolcraft Unbound Correspondence," Smithsonian Institution.)

[c] "Rev. E. Williams who has for several years past been officiating as a preacher for the Oneida Indians, in the State of New York, arrived here in the steamboat Walk-in-the-water last Saturday. He is accompanied by some of the men of the tribe, who constitute a delegation to visit the Indians in this Territory, for the purpose of ascertaining the prospect of success in the endeavor to christianize them. We learn that it is a further object with the delegation to find a suitable tract of country within the Territory, to which the Oneida Indians, or a part of them, will remove—for this purpose the country in the vicinity of Green Bay will be visited. No doubt can be entertained of the importance of this project. The influence which the example of Indians who are in a great measure civilized, will have over the habits of their more unfortunate brethren, will, perhaps, have much more effect in weaning them from their savage modes of living than all the theoretical lessons which can be given them by white men." ("Detroit Gazette," Friday, July 28, 1820.)

[d] DETROIT, *November 11, 1820.*

SIR,

While I was at Green Bay I understood from Col. Bowyer that he had obtained a cession from the Indians of the country extending forty miles up the Fox River and twenty-five or thirty miles on each side of that River. I presume he transmitted to you the instrument of cession, which he obtained.

I do not know the instructions which he received nor what were the views of the Government upon the subject. But I take the liberty of expressing to you my doubt respecting the policy of the measure. A purchase of the land in the immediate vicinity of Green Bay, and including all the settlements upon the Fox River is certainly proper. It is proper with a view to the undisputed operation of the laws, and to relieve the Inhabitants from the disagreeable & anomalous situation, in which they are placed. But more than this is not now required, and I presume an immediate increase of the population in that Country by emigration is not anticipated————

The effect therefore of extinguishing the Indian title to this large tract of land, independent of the pecuniary stipulations, which may be made, is, that it is thrown open to every adventurer, who may choose to enter it.

The laws of the United States respecting the intercourse of our Citizens with the Indians will cease to operate, and no restraints however wholesome can be imposed.

Green Bay, surmising that Indian immigration into Wisconsin upon such an extensive scale as was rumored to take place would embarrass if it did not utterly preclude white settlement, negotiated upon his own responsibility [a] a treaty of cession with the Menominees for land on Fox River. Morse, who came to Detroit at the same or about the same time as Williams,[b] heard of the transaction and subsequently interviewed the Menominees concerning it. He found them feeling sad, for only a part had sanctioned the relinquishment.[c] He then talked with them of his own plans and of the prospective coming of the Iroquois, but they were not elated. Their dissatisfaction with the Bowyer treaty, however, enabled Morse and Williams to present a strong case against its ratification. Governor Cass's objections were an added weight with the War Department; so Monroe decided not even to submit it to the Senate.[d]

The news of the rejection of the Bowyer treaty emboldened Williams to make a second trip to the Northwest, for which he had of late been gathering pecuniary reenforcements.[e] By this time Thomas

---

A large portion of this land must be inhabited by the Indians for many years, and any measure, should be deprecated, which would prevent the laws of the United States and the regulations of the Government from extending to them.

But there is another consideration of much weight upon this subject. I have reason to believe that the Six Nations from New York would select a part of this Country for their residence, and the policy of permitting them to do it, cannot be doubted. They reached this place last summer on their way to Green Bay, but having heard that a purchase had been made of the land to which their attention had been directed they returned without accomplishing the object of their mission & without my having seen them. It is very desirable to place them in that Country. Their habits & the strong pecuniary ties which bind them to the United States would ensure their fidelity, and they would act as a check upon the Winnebagoes, the worst affected of any Indians upon our borders.

Under these circumstances I would respectfully suggest whether it would not be expedient to delay acting upon the purchase made by Col. Bowyer and to direct his successor to procure a cession better suited to the objects, which the Government have in view.

Respectfully Sir, I have the honour to be, Yr obt Servt

LEWIS CASS.

Hon. JOHN C. CALHOUN, *Secy. of War.*

("Miscellaneous Files," Indian Office Manuscript Records.)

[a] Calhoun to Cornelius Bard, Jno. Anth⁰ Brandt, and Dan'l Tegawerateron of the Oneida Nation of Indians, April 14, 1821, "Indian Office Letter Books," Series I, E, p. 91.

[b] Davidson in "Wis. Hist. Soc. Proc.," 1899, p. 171, Morse's Report, Appendix, pp. 54–55.

[c] Morse's Report, Appendix, p. 53, note.

[d] Calhoun to Cass, April 4, 1821, "Indian Office Letter Books," Series I, E, p. 81.

[e] General Ellis writes: "In the spring of 1821, I accompanied Williams on a visit to New York and Philadelphia. At New York he was in long consultation with Thos. L. Ogden, Esq., chief man of a New York Land Company, * * * Mr. Ogden conceived that Williams would be a powerful agent in effecting the removal of the Senecas, and from him Mr. Williams received a good sum, several hundred dollars, in money. These largesses were repeated by Mr. Ogden many times after. At Philadelphia the conferences were with the executive committee of the Domestic and Foreign Missionary Society of the Protestant Episcopal church, and from whom Williams solicited aid for the establishment of a mission of that church among the Indians at Green Bay. Those gentlemen, Rev. Mr. Boyd, Rev. J. Kemper, and Dr. Milnor treated us courteously, but with evident caution. No money was obtained at this visit, though small sums were supplied Mr. Williams from that source for two or three years after." ("Recollections of Rev. E. Williams," Wis. Hist. Colls., VIII : 333.)

L. Ogden had become the chief proprietor of the Massachusetts preemptive right and was trying to oust the Indians by surveying their
lands prior to a sale.[a] This he did [b] in spite of an adverse opinion
as to its legality from Attorney-General Wirt.[c] His vigorous
methods may have had something to do with making the second delegation to the Northwest larger and more general in character than
the first.[d] There were fourteen in the troop, representing the Onedia,
St. Regis, Stockbridge,[e] Onondaga, Seneca, and Tuscarora Indians.[f]
Eleazer Williams was the special representative of the St. Regis, who

[a] Calhoun to William Wirt, United States Attorney-General, April 17, 1821, "Indian
Office Letter Books," Series I, E, p. 92.

[b] Calhoun to Jasper Parrish, "Indian Office Letter Books," Series I, E, p. 386.

[c] Calhoun to David A. Ogden, April 28, 1821, "Indian Office Letter Books," Series I,
E, p. 96.

[d] "Excepting those of the first Christian party of the Oneidas, and the Stockbridges, all
these delegates, to-wit : one from Onondaga, one from Tuscarora, one from the Senecas and
one, Williams himself, from St. Regis, went on their own private responsibility, without
any authority from their tribes. If any exception should be made in case of Williams, as
for the St. Regis, it never appeared, so far as I could discover, in any authentic form. In
fact, with the exception of the first Christian party of the Oneidas, and the Stockbridges,
the sentiment was universal, and most emphatically expressed against removal from their
homes in New York." (Ellis, "Recollections of Rev. E. Williams," "Wis. Hist. Colls.,"
VIII : 335.)

[e] The Stockbridges seem to have been a unit in their desire to remove. Note their
letter to Bishop Hobart quoted in Doctor Dix's "History of Trinity Church," p. 193.

NEW STOCKBRIDGE
June 9th, 1821.

Right Rev. Sir,

This is particularly to state to you that our tribe have all agreed to send messengers
to meet with the Tribes in the Northwest Territory agreeable to an arrangement made
with those Tribes last summer by Mr. Williams and his Oneida friends.

We would further inform you that we as a tribe united with our brethren in a
speach to those Tribes and received a friendly answer, brought by Mr. Williams.

We would further inform you that we are expected by those heathen Tribes to visit
and hold a general Council with them this season in union with our Brothers the Oneidas.

Our object is to recommend perpetual peace among themselves and among both Red
and White people.

Also to recommend Civilization and the Christian Religion among that heathen people.

We well know that those Tribes will expect us with a few of our brethren the Oneidas.
We have good reason to believe that Oneidas will not send unless your missionary Mr.
Williams goes as a leader.

We have reason to expect that we may obtain from those tribes a fine place or Country which will be beneficial to our tribes.

We are now nearly ready to send four of our principal young men on this great and
important business.

We have reason to hope we shall meet the blessings of Heaven, and by our Council
be able to do much good for the glory and honour of our Common Saviour to a numerous
population of Red people. Now, Right Rev. Sir, our request is that for the above-men-
tioned reasons you give your consent and approbation that your Missionary, Mr. Williams, go with us.

Remain Rev. Sir, your friends and children.

We shall expect an answer as soon as is convenient.

HENDRICK AUPAUMENT,
JACOB KONKAPOT,
ABNER W. HENDRICK,
SOLOMON W. HENDRICK.

Right Rev. Bishop.

[f] The Munsees also sent a delegate, who, by the special permission of the Government,
was included in the Stockbridge contingent. (Calhoun to Cass, June 21, 1821, "Indian
Office Letter Books," Series I, E, p. 121.)

were his own people, and he carried with him a letter[a] of introduction from De Witt Clinton. The delegation arrived at Detroit on the 12th of July, 1821,[b] and were met by Governor Cass, who added Charles C. Trowbridge[c] to their party, a representative of the General Government. When they reached Green Bay in August, they found no Indian agent in attendance; for Bowyer had died and his successor was temporarily absent. Cass had warned them that they would meet with interference from the French settlers and they certainly did;[d] but, after considerable delay, the Menominees and Winnebagoes of-

---

[a] " The Lost Prince," p. 291.

[b] " Detroit Gazette," July 13, 1821.

[c] Ellis, " Recollections of Rev. Eleazer Williams," in " Wis. Hist. Colls.," VIII : 335–336.

[d] The following letter from Trowbridge to Cass is confirmatory of this :

DETROIT, 7th Sept^{r}., 1821.

SIR.

The deputation from the Six Nations and Stockbridge and Munsee nations of Indians having returned to this place, I have the honor to report to you the proceedings and the result of their mission to Green Bay.

Soon after your departure from this place in July last, I learned that Maj. Biddle, the Indian agent at Green Bay, (whose advice and assistance, I was instructed, would be afforded the deputies) was about to leave that place for the purpose of attending the treaty to be held at Chicago.

I communicated this information to the deputies on their arrival here, and at their request I addressed a letter to your Excellency at Chicago, requesting that such instructions as would be most likely to secure the object in view, might be immediately forwarded to me at Green Bay. On our arrival at the place of our destination, we found the Agent absent, as was anticipated, and learned also, to our very great mortification, that his Interpreter had accompanied him. Upon consultation it was thought advisable to proceed in our business without delay, although we were sensible that we should meet with many difficulties ; and with this view we procured a commodious house in the vicinity of Fort Howard, where we were visited on the seventh of August, by a Menomini Chief and a few of his warriors. We informed these men that we should be pleased to hold a council with such Menomini Chiefs as were at the place, and requested them to attend us, accompanied by those chiefs, on the following day.

On the eighth a few of the Menomini Chiefs called at our house, and were soon followed by some Winnebagoes, who took seats with them in the council room, when the deputies addressed a short speech to the former, stating that they had an important communication to make to them, if their principal chiefs could be collected. This speech was, thro' mistake interpreted to them as addressed to both nations, which fact we did not learn until they gave their answer, when it was too late to correct the error, as they all professed themselves gratified with the invitation, and engaged to send immediately for the Chiefs of both nations.

Knowing that an enmity existed between the two parties, and that the Winnebagoes had refused to listen to propositions for the purchase of their lands, we were not a little displeased at this mistake of our Interpreter ; but, as will appear to you, it eventuated in the accomplishment of our object.

On the sixteenth, the Chiefs of the two nations assembled, and we immediately commenced business. The Deputies opened the object of their missions in a very handsome manner, taking care to set forth in a proper light, the advantages which would result to their brethren the Menominies and Winnebagoes, from a cession as proposed ; and after delivering a belt of wampum according to the Indian custom, the opposite parties replied in very flattering terms, and begged leave to consult each other, promising to give an answer on the following day.

On the 17th the Menominies opened the council with a positive refusal to accept the proposals made to them, alledging as a reason the limited quantity of lands possessed by them, and the difficulty they therefore experienced in gaining a livelihood. The Winnebagoes expressed a great deal of sorrow at this answer, and proposed to give their brethren of the east, the lands on the Fox river, from the Grand Chute to the Winnebago Lake, a distance of four and a half miles. Percieving that the Menominies were astonished at this reply, it was thought advisable to adjourn the council with a view

fered to sell them a strip of land on the Fox River.[a] The price was

to give them time for reflection. On the following day they met the deputies again, and having stated that their minds had changed, proposed to join the Winnebagoes in a cession of the lands from the foot of the Grand Kaccalin to the rapids at the Winnebago Lake. Immediately the articles of the treaty were prepared, but before being finished the Menominies received a message from some person without the house, in consequence of which some of the Chiefs left the room, and a bustle commenced among those who remained. We percieved at once the cause of the confusion, and began seriously to fear the influence of the french inhabitants, some of whom had exerted themselves in opposition to our measures from the time of our arrival.

After some time had elapsed, the Chiefs who had left us, returned, and it was then difficult to procure a decisive answer to our question, " whether they would sign a grant, the terms of which had been proposed by themselves alone "? After a good deal of hesitation between their own inclination and that of their advisers, they told us, that their speaker had not expressed their true sentiments, but that their first determination on our proposition was unchanged and unchangeable. All hopes of effecting a purchase of the Menominies were now at an end ; for we felt sensible, as well from experience as from information, that they were guided in everything by the advice and instruction of a few of the principal Frenchmen at the place, who have ever opposed with zeal, the progress of settlement and improvement in their country.

Upon reflection it was thought advisable to make another attempt, and the council was declared adjourned until the morning of the nineteenth, at which time the Winnebagoes were invited to attend and sign the grant which they had first proposed : The Menominies were told, that if they should feel disposed to join in the cession, we should be pleased to see them also.

In the evening the two nations held a consultation at their encampment, and on the following morning they all assembled and signed the treaty, of which I have the honor to enclose you a copy, together with a sketch of a part of Fox river, exhibiting the breadth and course of the tract.

The grant is not so wide as was wished for and expected by the deputies, but when it is considered that we were obliged to encounter serious obstacles, unaided and alone, it cannot be denied that the result has been favorable.

Some of the deputies have visited the lands on and adjacent to the river, and are much pleased with the apearance of the soil, timber and local advantages : Indeed it is pronounced by the inhabitants to be the most valuable tract in that country. The boundaries, as expressed in the articles of the treaty are rather indefinite, but under the existing circumstancs it was difficult to make them less so. The grantors claim to the northwest as far as the Chippeway lands ; sometimes they say three, at others, four, five and six days march. On the southeast their claims extend to Lake Michigan.

Should it be thought advisable, I have little doubt that a purchase may be effected, of the lands from the Rapid of the Fathers, four and a half miles above Fort Howard, and near the upper extremity of the French settlement, to the Grand Kaccalin, a distance of thirteen and a half miles ; which added to the present cession would make a breadth of upwards of thirty miles.

I cannot forbear expressing to your Excellency how highly I have been gratified with the correct moral deportment and statesmanlike conduct of the deputies from the Six Nations, under the direction of Mr. Williams, whose personal exertions in this business have been very great. With respect to the deputation from the Stockbridge nation, I cannot speak so favourably. Some of them, it is true, have genius and energy, but they have been more addicted to intemperance than becomes men on business of this importance ; and I fear that some part of their conduct has left an unfavourable impression on the minds of the inhabitants at the Bay.

I am aware that I have been prolix in this report, but a desire to give your Excellency a detailed statement of the facts attending the mission, has been the cause, and I offer no other apology ; not doubting, that when you shall take into consideration its imperfections, your goodness will prompt you to excuse them, under the belief that they do not arise from a want of inclination to make it more satisfactory.

With the highest respect, I have the honor to be Your Excellency's very humble and much obliged servant,

CHARLES C. TROWBRIDGE.

His Excellency LEWIS CASS,
    Governor of the Territory of Michigan.
(" Treaty Files," 1802–1853, Indian Office MS. Records.)
    [a] " Beginning at the foot of the rapids, usually called the Grand Kaccalin, on the Fox river, thence running up the said river to the rapids at the Winnebago Lake, and

$2,000, $500 to be paid in cash immediately and $1,500 in goods a year hence. Hendrick advised the acceptance of the offer and Trowbridge drew up a formal agreement to which the white men present subscribed as witnesses.

Williams thereupon returned to New York to receive the congratulations of De Witt Clinton [a] and the execrations of the pagan Oneidas,[b] who begged the Rev. William B. Lacey, of Albany, to intercede for them with Bishop Hobart to have Williams deprived of his office as missionary teacher. Other New York bands shared this sentiment of disapproval. Even those who had before shown a disposition to emigrate were now opposed, for they felt that the land just bought was quite inadequate. Nevertheless, Monroe unhesitatingly

---

from the river extending in this width from each side of the same, to the northwest and to the southeast, equidistant to the Lands claimed by the said Menomonee & Winnebago nations of Indians." ("Miscellaneous Files," Indian Office MS. Records. See also "Treaty Files," 1802–1853, ibid.)

[a] Hanson, "The Lost Prince," p. 292.

[b] ONEIDA, *Feby. 25th, 1822.*

(1) Rev[d]. & dear Brother,

We are sorry to intrude ourselves upon you at this time by letter, but we have so often addressed our father the Bishop, upon the subject of our grievances without having any answer to our complaints, petitions, that we are induced to solicit your assistance & advice.

From M[r]. Dana our interpreter, you learn'd something respecting our situation with regard to M[r]. Williams, as long as he remains with us we shall continue disunited, our affections for him are changed; we cannot reverence or respect him as we once did, he has tried every means in his power to draw us away from *our own lands,* he wishes us to leave the possessions we inherit from our fathers, to our white brethren, but *we cannot* sacrifice our *houses* & our *Church* & go to the land of strangers,—while he continued faithful to our spiritual interests & remained with us a teacher of good things we loved him & endeavour'd to assist him, but when he became discontented with his situation, neglected us & often left us we became jealous of our rights, & enquir'd into the motives that actuated him. Ambition appears to be the ruling passion in his breast, the humble cottages of the natives illy suits the dignity of his mind, we however forbear personal reflections,—& solicit relief—

Dear brother we are sorry to learn that M[r]. W. has insinuated that we have become disaffected with the *Church* & wished a change on that account but this is not the *case* we are still attached to our service & consider *our* Church as the true Church of Christ, we consider the Bishop our father & look to him for a teacher.

We have long looked for an answer to our letters but he has not written to us & we fear he has forgotten his red children.

Will you not intercede for us, dear brother? We desire a young man of piety & disinterested benevolence, one who is willing to conform to our modes & customs, & capable of learning our language. Our wishes center in M[r]. Davis, the young gentleman who acted in the capacity of reader during M[r]. W's absence last summer.

Dear brother we wish you to send us an immediate answer as we feel as if we were forgotten by our father the bishop. One circumstance ought not to be omitted in our communication to you. We learn that a petition has been sent to the Bishop (signed by a great number of Indians) requesting him to continue M[r]. W. with them in the capacity of a reader. This petition was signed by *some of them* in consequence of *a threat* that when *he went the Prayer Book* & the Bishop's support would be withdrawn & the petition was signed by several excommunicated members from the episcopal & also the presbyterian Church,— Dear Brother we think that if we should leave this place & go to the West among the Indians we should lose our Church service, we being few in number should be obliged to conform to them in their mode of worship here we have a Church & here we desire to die & be buried by the side of our fathers.

In January last we sent a letter to our father the Bishop requesting him to send M[r]. Davis among us as our reader this was signed by the chiefs & separately by the members

gave his personal sanction to the agreement.[a] He did not think it necessary to apply to the Senate, since it was only a contract between two sets of Indians;[b] but was soon called upon to consent [c] to a third

of the Church. We mention him in particular because he appears devoted to our Church & we are pleased with the mildness of his disposition & his easy familiar manners.

Dear Brother, we remain

Your friends & Brothers of the Oneida Church.

his
Nicolas X Garmigontaya
mark
his
Hendrik X Schuyler
mark
Peter Yaramynear
his
John X Cornelius
mark
his
Moses X Schuyler
mark
his
Christopher X Schuyler
mark
Martin Quiney
his
Abraham X Schuyler
mark

P. S. We intended to have obtained a greater number of subscribers to this but the inclemency of the weather; & a wish to send it immediately prevent our giving this a free circulation.

("Hobart Papers.")

(2) The Right Rev. Bishop Hobart.

Dear Sir,

Early in the winter Cap. Dana, and several chiefs of the Oneida Tribe, called on me, and requested that I would join with them in recommending Mr. Solomon Davis— a member of St. Peter's Church—to you, as a suitable person to succeed Mr. Williams; but not having sufficient information on the subject, I declined complying with their request. This morning I received the enclosed communication, urging me again to write you on the same subject; and not wishing to offend them by totally disregarding their request—I have taken the liberty to address you on a subject, with which you will have good reason to think I have no concern.

Although I have a high opinion of Mr. Williams zeal and fidelity in our cause, I am afraid, that owing to a concurrence of circumstances—a part of which undoubtedly is unfounded suspicion—he has lost his influence over the Oneidas, and that a removal as speedy as is consistent with his reputation, will contribute to the interest of the Church—Prejudice founded in invincible ignorance is often unconquerable, and the best way to avoid its consequences, is generally—in the case of clergymen—to flee from it. Under this impression I am inclined to think, that the sooner Mr. Williams enters on his mission to Green Bay, the better it will be for him and the Church.

As to the person the Oneidas has designated for his successor, I can at present only say, that about two years since he came recommended to me as a worthy communicant in our Church by the Rev. Mr. Butler; that he has resided about eighteen months in this place as a journeyman printer; is generally spoken of by those who know him, as a sober, moral, and pious man; and that he appears to possess much mildness of temper and suavity of manner. He was with the Oneidas last summer, and in the absence of Mr. Williams read sermons for them in the Church, and appears to have gained their esteem.

It is needless on the present occasion to be more particular, but should a communication subsequently be necessary, I will endeavor to answer all the queries you may propose.

I am Right Rev. and dear Sir, with very great respect and esteem, your humble obt servt.   WM. B. LACEY.

Albany 28th Feb. 1822.

("Hobart Papers.")

[a] Calhoun to Cass, November 22, 1821, "Indian Office Letter Books," Series I, E, p. 194, Treaty Files, 1802–1853, Indian Office MS. Records.

[b] Calhoun to Solomon U. Hendricks, November 22, 1821, "Indian Office Letter Books," Series I, E, p. 195.

[c] Same to same, February 13, 1822, "Indian Office Letter Books," Series I, E, p. 215.

expedition in quest of satisfaction. Meanwhile the Indians were in a very excited state, for the speculators in New York were trying to convince them that the Government was going to force them to go West. Calhoun [a] comforted them as best he could, for compulsory measures were the very farthest from the President's intentions.[b]

The third New York expedition to the Northwest [c] had no official leader, although Solomon Hendricks and Eleazer Williams [a] accompanied it as before, and Cass asked Sergeant to look after the interests of of the United States. On the 16th of September, 1822,[e] it

---

[a] Talk of April 15, 1822, to Chiefs of the First Christian Party of the Oneida Indians, " Indian Office Letter Books," Series I, E, pp. 234–235.

[b] " Your ideas as to the views of the Government in relation to lands claimed by Indians, are very correct, and the assurance you have given to the Oneida and Onondago nations, that the government will never permit them to be deprived of their lands without their consent, is in perfect accordance with them.ʳ It is my impression however that it would be for their advantage to remove beyond ⸢the whits settlements. ⁎ ⁎ ⁎ It was with this impression that the deputation referred to, was upon application signed by three chiefs of the Oneida nation, encouraged to visit the Indians in the neighbourhood of Green Bay, with a view to obtain a portion of their Country for the future residence of such Indians of the Six Nations as might *choose* to emigrate thither. A deputation of the Stockbridge nation was also, upon application of the chiefs, encouraged to visit that country for the same purpose. But it never was intended to *compel* any to emigrate, or to deprive them of their lands without their consent. In fact, the government can have no inducement to take any measure to remove the Indians, or even to assent to their removal ; but for their own interest as the Country occupied by them does not belong to the U. States but to individuals. ⁎ ⁎ ⁎ " (Extract of letter from Calhoun to Rev. O. B. Brown, September 27, 1821, " Indian Office Letter Books," Series I, E, p. 155.)

" For the information of Mr. Troup I herewith enclose copies and extracts of letters which indicate the views and measures of the gov't in relation to the removal of the Six Nations from the State of New York. By these it will be seen that the Government has endeavored to impress upon the Indians the advantages of changing their present residence for one further West, and it will continue to do so upon every suitable occasion, but no steps for their removal can be taken without their consent. ⁎ ⁎ ⁎ " (Extract of letter from Calhoun to Hon. W. D. Rochester, House of Representatives, April 15, 1822, " Indian Office Letter Books," Series I, E, p. 233.)

[c] Calhoun to Solomon U. Hendricks, February 16, 1822, " Indian Office Letter Books," Series I, E, p. 218.

[d] Calhoun to Rev. Eleazer Williams, May 8, 1822, " Indian Office Letter Books," Series I, E, p. 253.

[e] GREEN BAY, *Oct. 16ᵗʰ, 1822.*

(1) Dear Sir,

With respect to the commission with which your Excellency was pleased to honor me, I beg leave to submit the following report.

I left Detroit on the 19ᵗʰ of August in company with the New York Indians and arrived at Green Bay on the first day of Septʳ. Messengers were immediately dispatched to the different lodges of Menominie and Winnebagoe Indians who returned and collected of both Tribes about Eight Hundred people old & young. They assembled on the 16ᵗʰ Septʳ. and received from the New York Indians the amount of goods stipulated in the third Article of the Treaty made last year. The Winnebagoes then returned to their homes. The Menominies were then invited to treat with the N. York Indians for an extension of the purchase made last year. They were particularly informed through their interpreter that the purchase, if made, would be approbated by the Government of the United States and that I, as a commissioner under Government, was directed to make the statement to them. The French and other inhabitants in this place, who were interested in the subject also received the same notice. The Menominies after deliberating on the subject met on the 23ʳᵈ day of Sept and as far as I could learn, without a dissenting voice, agreed to the proposals made by the N. York Indians which were put in the form of a Treaty, which Treaty is herewith transmitted to your Excellency reference being had to the same particulars will more fully appear. I have been credibly informed that some of the French people at this place have taken much pains to create a party among [the] Menominies to frustrate the designs of Government and the N. York Indians in the aforesaid purchase and have been entirely unsuccessful in their attempts

managed to assemble the Menominees and Winnebagoes in council, and the latter stayed until after the payment for the joint cession had been completed. A serious deliberation then followed, in which the French settlers joined. The upshot of it was, that on the 23d the Menominees [a] agreed to an extension of the grant of 1821,[b] but soon

---

and I have the pleasure further to state that the Menominies appear to be much pleased with the bargain and their new neighbors.

The subject of any former purchase having been made by the French, British, or American Government has been particularly inquired into & that no transfer has ever been made to either, except a piece of land immediately in the vicinity of Fort Howard which the Indians acknowledge though it has never been reduced to writing.

All of which is respectfully submitted by, dear Sire,

Your Excellency's most obedient Servant,

JOHN SERGEANT, Jun[r].

To his Excellency LEWIS CASS, Esqr
  Governor of the Territory of Michigan
(True Copy of the 1st Copy.)
(" Miscellaneous Files," Indian Office MS. Records.)

(2) We arrived at Green Bay on the 1st day S[ep]t[r] where messengers were immediately sent on to different encampments or towns of the Menominies & Winnebagoes to notify them of our arrival.

In a few days after the Indians from the two Nations began to arrive & collect near where we had our quarters, accompanied by their Chiefs & Head Warriors. On the 16th September a council was held with the Chiefs & warriors of the two nations, when a short talk was delivered to them renewing the covenant of our friendship and the agreement we had made with them last year.

I had the gratification to find by their reply that they were all satisfied with the Treaty. ' No one, as they say, is against it.' They were much pleased to see a number [of] families from our Tribe had come, with a view to live near them. The goods were then delivered to them & the amount each Nation paid receipted on the back of the Treaty.

A few days after a council was again held with the Menominies with a view to endeavor to have an extension made to the cession of last year, and I have now the satisfaction to inform you that the Deputies succeeded in obtaining from the Menominies the cession of all the lands owned by them situated from the lower line of the Territory ceded to us last year including all islands in the Bay. The treaty was signed on the 23rd day of Sept. and I was requested by my Chiefs to carry the same to our father the President for his approbation and ratification and which I have the honor to present the Hon[ble] the Sec[y] of War, Together with a letter from John Sergeant Jr. Esq[r]. originally directed to his Excellency Lewis Cass who was absent having, as I understood, started for the seat of Government four days before our arrival at Detroit. i. e. Deputies from the Oneida, Tuscarora, St Regis, Munsee, & Stockbridge Tribe of Indians. (N. Y.)

True Extract from the 1st Copy.

Per J. W. ———

(Extract of a communication from S. U. Hendricks to Calhoun, " made at Washington City the 20th. of Feb. 1823," " Miscellaneous Files," Indian Office MS. Records.)

[a] In the summer of 1824, J. D. Doty submitted to Cass the depositions (" Miscellaneous Files," Indian Office Manuscript Records) of certain of the French settlers at Green Bay ; viz, Paul Grignon, Pierre Grignon, and Lewis Rouse, to the effect that the Menominees present at the treaty council of 1821 were not chiefs or headmen, but really persons of small consideration and of no authority. The deponents had nothing apparently to say against the personel of the later council of 1822. Are we then to infer that bona fide chiefs agreed to the larger grant?

[b] " Beginning at the foot of the rapids on Fox river, usually called the Grand Kaccalin, thence southeast (or on the lower line of the lands last season ceded by the Menominee and Winnebago Nations of Indians, to the six Nations, St. Regis, Stockbridge, and Munsee nations,) to or equidistant with the Manawohkink river emptying into Lake Michigan, thence an easterly course to and down said river to its mouth, thence northerly on the borders of Lake Michigan to and across the mouth of Green Bay, so as to include all the Islands of the Grande Traverse, thence from the mouth of Green Bay aforesaid a northwesterly course to a place on the Northwest shore of Lake Michigan, generally known and distinguished by the name of Weyohquatonk by the Indians ; and Bay de Noque by the French, thence a westerly course, on the height of land seperating the waters running into Lake Superior & running [into] Lake Michigan,

repented of their genorosity, the trading interests of the bay being all opposed to the coming of the New Yorkers. The proprietors now redoubled their efforts to induce emigration, and especially to overcome the prejudices of Red Jacket and his Senecas,[a] but to no purpose. Gradually Indians from the other bands did emigrate,[b] but met with constant interference[c] from the French settlers, who did their best to impeach the validity of the Menominee contract. Final sanction[d] by the Department was therefore necessarily delayed.[e] Meanwhile the white population steadily increased, so that as the years went on the New York proprietors found it more and more difficult to prevail upon the Senecas to emigrate.[f] Morse's grand scheme for the establishment of an Indian State had come to nothing. It had vanished before the spectre of James Duane Doty's " Territory of Huron." [g]

to the head of the Menomonee river, thence continuing nearly the same course until it strikes the northeastern boundary line of the lands ceded as aforesaid by the Menomonee and Winnebago Nations to the Six Nations, St. Regis, Stockbridge, and Munsee nations of Indians in 1821, thence southeasterly to the place of beginning." (" Miscellaneous Files," Indian Office Manuscript Records.)

[a] (1) Talk of Calhoun to Red Jacket, Major Berry, and Cornplanter, chiefs and deputies of the Seneca Nation of Indians, March 14, 1823, " Indian Office Letter Books," Series I, E, pp. 404–406. (2) Calhoun to T. L. Ogden, March 15, 1823, ibid., p. 406.

[b] Eleazer Williams to Right Reverend Father Bishop Hobart, May 15, 1823.

[c] J. Sergeant to Rev. J. Morse, February 16, 1824, " Miscellaneous Files," Indian Office MS. Records; New York Indians to Morse, November 6, 1824, ibid.; Solomon U. Hendricks to Calhoun, February 11, 1825, ibid.; McKenney to Maj. Henry B. Brevoort, Indian agent at Green Bay, March 8, 1825, " Indian Office Letter Books," Series II, No. I, p. 393.

[d] The President did almost immediately sanction the New York Indian Menominee agreement, but only in part; i. e., for as much land as he felt was amply sufficient for the needs of the emigrants. (Calhoun to T. L. Ogden and B. W. Rogers, August 21, 1823, " Indian Office Letter Books," Series I, E, p. 480.) Later, however, in deference to the wishes of the preemptive right proprietors he modified his decision, but still did not sanction the transfer of the whole of the grant. (Calhoun to T. L. Ogden and B. W. Rogers, October 13, 1823, ibid., p. 496; Calhoun to Rev. Eleazer Williams, October 18, 1823, ibid., p. 499.) This did not imply that the lands not included in the sanction were to revert to the grantors (Calhoun to T. L. Ogden and B. W. Rogers, October 23, 1823, ibid., p. 501) ; but, simply, that anything beyond a transfer of about 2,000,000 acres to which the governmental sanction was given, though reluctantly, would have to be a matter of arrangement among the Indians alone. The New York tribes were greatly dissatisfied and appealed to the War Department through A. G. Ellis, but to no purpose. (Calhoun to the chiefs and headmen of the Onondaga, Seneca, Tuscarora, Oneida, and Stockbridge tribes of New York, October 27, 1823, ibid., pp. 503–504.) The Ogden Land Company then tried to secure an entire change in the grant, but was told that nothing of the kind could be done until the President was " possessed of some unequivocal evidence " that it would be acceptable to the Indians. (" Indian Office Letter Books," Series I, F, p. 3, letter from Calhoun to T. L. Ogden, October 31, 1823.)

[e] McKenney to Cass, April 16, 1825, " Indian Office Letter Books," Series II, No. 1, p. 449.

[f] Their unwillingness was undoubtedly fortified by the repeated assurances of the Government that force would never be used to compel them to go. (McKenney to the chiefs of the Onondagas, Senecas, and Oneida tribes, April 20, 1824, " Indian Office Letter Books," Series II, No. 1, p. 44.) After the appearance of Monroe's special message on Indian emigration of January 27, 1825, the Six Nations sent a delegation to the southwestern tribes to consult about removal to that region, but the delegation reported unfavorably. (Jasper Parrish to Barbour, September 21, 1825, " Miscellaneous Files," Indian Office MS. Records.)

[g] (1) " Doty Papers," " Wis. Hist. Colls.," XIII : 221–226, 227–237. (2) " Wis. Hist. Colls.," XV : 401, note.

16827—08——21

Chapter VI.

THE SOUTH AND INDIAN REMOVAL, 1820-1825.

Toward the close of Monroe's first Administration the State of Georgia began to take a lively interest in Indian removal. The cause was not far to seek; for it had so happenéd that, of all the vast cessions secured from the natives since 1812 or earlier, a comparatively small portion only had fallen within her limits. It was of no use for the United States to urge in self-extenuation that expediency or Indian willingness had conditioned such a state of affairs. Georgia could attribute it to nothing but national selfishness. Ordinarily, land, as soon as it was disencumbered of the occupancy title, became a part of the public domain. It was not so in Georgia. There, as a result of the compact of 1802, it became outright the property of the State; and, in consequence, the Federal Government derived no pecuniary advantage from its sale.

The first expression of dissatisfaction came with the capitulation of Fort Jackson, 1814, by which two cessions of strategic importance were demanded—one in Alabama, throwing a white population into the very midst of the four great tribes, and the other, very much smaller, in southern Georgia, separating the Creek from the Florida Indians. The difference in size of the two cessions, whatever Georgia might say to the contrary, was based mainly upon ideas of indemnity, since the Alabama country was inhabited by the hostile Creeks and the Georgian by the friendly. Indeed, the only justification for taking any of the latter was the fact that the title to its southern portion was disputed by the Seminoles.

Georgia constantly intimated her desire to have the Creek line of 1814 changed, and, in 1817, while Monroe was absent on his eastern tour, Graham instructed the new Creek agent, D. B. Mitchell, to hold an interview with the chiefs for that purpose. The result was the treaty of 1818, and still Georgia was dissatisfied; for Wilson Lumpkin, who ran the western line of one of the two ceded tracts, reported the land unexpectedly small in quantity and poor in quality.[a] There was nothing to do but to try again. Great difficulty occurred, however, in securing suitable commissioners. Jackson, who could have

---

[a] Calhoun to Lumpkin, October 26, 1818, " Indian Office Letter Books," Series I, D, p. 224.

best pleased Governor Clarke, was not disposed to serve.[a] Four men in turn declined the honor, one of them, Gen. Thomas Flournoy, because the Georgia commissioners, whom the President had permitted to be associated in the conferences, assumed too much authority to themselves. As usual, an exchange of territory was offered to the Creeks,[b] but they refused to consider it, and made instead a cession upon a money basis highly discreditable to Georgia.[c]

It was subsequent to this Creek treaty of 1821 and, in part, growing out of it, that the compact of 1802 became the most prominent feature of all discussions bearing upon the Indian question. By that compact the United States, in consideration of a cession by Georgia of the territory now comprised within the States of Alabama and Mississippi, undertook to extinguish the Indian title within the reserved limits of Georgia as soon as it could be done " peaceably and on reasonable terms." It is well to note the date of the compact and also the two conditions of extinguishment. In 1802 neither Georgia nor the United States could have contemplated removal. Some other way of disposing of the Indians must therefore have been intended; but everything was to be done " peaceably and on reasonable terms." There was no intimation of a resort to force anywhere in the document. The United States was given its own time in which to execute the contract, providing it took advantage of every favorable opportunity. The action of Georgia in placing conditions upon her cession was entirely in line with that of other States claiming western lands; but the inclusion of the Indians was a novelty. Practically, though, they were the cause of the cession.

The constitutional significance of Indian removal may be said to date from the report[d] that a select committee (of which George R. Gilmer, a member of the Troup, or State Rights, party in Georgia politics, was chairman) submitted to the House of Representatives, January 7, 1822, on the question whether or not the United States was keeping her part of the Georgia compact. The report is highly interesting as affording a clear exposition of the grounds for complaint before race animosity and political acrimony had quite dulled the sense of justice. As regards the question at issue, it was an answer in the negative; and its argument resolves itself into a criticism of recent treaties by which the United States was held to have violated

---

[a] J. Q. Adams to Clarke, June 1, 1820, American State Papers, " Indian Affairs," II : 257.

[b] " Miscellaneous Files," Indian Office, MS Records.

[c] The Georgia agents presented claims against the Creeks for which, as was afterwards reported by the War Department to Congress, there was strong presumptive evidence of prior settlement. (American State Papers, " Indian Affairs," II : 254–257.) The United States commissioners were much embarrassed by the matter, yet framed a treaty that overruled the Creek repudiation. The history of the Preston commission, which was appointed to investigate the claims, furnishes abundant evidence of the unfair advantage which Georgia and her citizens were ready to take, not only of the Creeks, but also of the United States Government.

[d] American State Papers, " Indian Affairs," II : 259.

both the spirit and the text of the compact—the preference shown for other States in the matter of cessions and the supposed discouragement of Indian emigration being a noncompliance with the one, guaranties of integrity and fee-simple titles in contravention of the other. Going a little beyond its positive instructions, and taking, perhaps, its cue from the Louisiana case, the committee next ventured' to assert that citizenship promised by an Indian treaty was an infringement of the powers of Congress, and that, in so far as one treaty affected vested rights that had accrued under another, it was void. Have we not here an anticipation of the great Indian Springs controversy?

In due season, at the importunity of the legislature and by the advice of Monroe,[a] Congress acted upon a suggestion of the Gilmer committee and appropriated $30,000 toward extinguishing the Indian title within the limits of Georgia.[b] The President, considering the sum too small for effective negotiation with both Creeks and Cherokees, applied it exclusively to the latter and intrusted its disbursement to two Georgia citizens—Duncan Campbell and James Meriwether.[c] Their prospect of success was very slight; for, although the Creek Path towns were reported favorable to a cession, the majority of the Cherokees were opposed, and, in national council, decided to hold fast to the remainder of the tribal land. Of this decision the War Department was apprised in the fall of 1822.[d] Yet it allowed the commission to proceed, hoping that the aversion to a cession might be " conquered by a little perseverance and judicious management." [e] Georgia agents were again in evidence with their list of claims demanding settlement. It is no wonder the Indians continued obstinate, particularly as Joseph McMinn, their old enemy, was now their agent, and Congress, deferential to Georgia, had authorized [f] the purchase of all reservations taken in fee under the Creek treaties of 1814 and 1821 and the Cherokee of 1817 and 1819.

The official negotiations with the Cherokees did not begin until October, 1823, and were remarkable for the able rebuttal of all the arguments advanced by the United States commissioners, whose preliminary " talk," [g] taken in connection with later events, might well be cited as an illustration of the inconsistency to which white men were so often reduced in their dealings with the natives. This " talk " paid a high compliment to Cherokee civilization, and then proceeded to define the Indian political status as excluding interference by the

[a] Message, February 25, 1822, Richardson, II : 115.
[b] Act of May 7, 1822, 3 United States Statutes at Large, 688.
[c] Such was the commission as confirmed by the Senate. General Floyd, Maj. Freeman Walker, and Hon. J. A. Cuthbert had been asked to serve. Two of them declined. Floyd accepted, but soon resigned.
[d] Cherokee Files, Indian Office MS. Records.
[e] Calhoun to Campbell, March 17, 1823, " Indian Office Letter Books," Series I, E, p. 408.
[f] 3 United States Statutes at Large, 750.
[g] American State Papers, " Indian Affairs," II ; 467.

State. Finally, it urged removal on the plea that the white people were so crowded "that they were driven from friends and connections to foreign lands." The Great Father of the Universe had intended the earth "equally to be the inheritance of his white and red children;" but in Georgia the latter had a much larger share than the former. The Cherokees replied that they did not know as to the intention of the Supreme Father,[a] but it was quite evident that neither individuals nor nations had ever respected the principle; and, as experience had taught them that a small cession would never satisfy the white men, they were determined to make none at all. Love of country impelled them to stay where they were, where their ancestors had lived and died. Those who had gone West had suffered great hardships, and their numbers had been much lessened by sickness, war, and other fatalities.

The subsequent "talks" of the commissioners gained in harshness as the conviction strengthened that the Cherokees were not to be persuaded, cajoled, or intimidated. Campbell reported the failure to Calhoun with the information that the Creeks were likely to be more compliant.[b] At the beginning of the new year, for Cherokee chiefs— Ross, Lowry, Ridge, and Hicks—appeared in Washington, deputized by their nation to plead with the President personally against further requests for land; but Calhoun coolly informed them that all communications would have to pass through the War Department.[c]

Meanwhile, a change had taken place in the executive office of Georgia which was destined to have important consequences for the Indians. At the fall elections, the radical party triumphed over the conservative, and George McIntosh Troup became governor. He was supposed, in general, to stand for State sovereignty and, in particular, to represent the interests of the more aristocratic planter community, while his opponents of the Clarke variety found their adherents among the frontiersmen. Both factions were interested in Indian removal, but differed as to the means which they would employ to accomplish it. As we shall see, Troup was a veritable "Hotspur," impatient of restraint, possessed of an ungovernable temper, and determined to impress the world with his own forced construction of the compact of 1802.

His first display of arrogance toward the Federal Government came out as a result of the Cherokee visit to Washington in 1824. That visit was unusually prolonged by reason of the fact that Calhoun could come to no terms with Hicks and his colleagues. Replying, on the 30th of January, to their note of the 19th instant,[d] he

---

[a] American State Papers, "Indian Affairs," II : pp. 468–469.
[b] November 28, 1823, "Cherokee Files," Indian Office Manuscript Records.
[c] "Indian Office Letter Books," Series I, F, p. 32.
[d] American State Papers, "Indian Affairs," II : 473.

placed great stress upon the obligations of the Georgia compact, to which they rejoined that a full compliance with the terms of that agreement was conditional upon the consent of the Cherokee Nation.[a] This decision, at the instance of Monroe, was communicated to Governor Troup and also to the Georgia Congressmen.[b] Troup, in violent, dictatorial language, retaliated, that the Cherokees were only tenants in possession and that their opposition had been instigated by men in the employ of the Federal Government.[c] The Congressmen went even further; for, striking at the whole Indian policy, they remonstrated against the diplomatic courtesy shown to the delegates and declared, in conclusion, that if the Cherokees would not peaceably remove, it was the duty of the United States to order them.[d]

This formal protest of the 10th of March found its answer in the President's message of the 30th,[e] which reviewed the history of the Georgia compact, emphasizing its limitation of " peaceably " and insisting, from documentary and statistical proofs, that the United States had done its duty. On the whole, it was a very creditable state paper, complimented by Madison for its fairness,[f] and, from the viewpoint of abstract justice, much in contrast with a memorial of the Georgia legislature, which was transmitted to Congress early in April.[g] In the House of Representatives a select committee, with John Forsyth as chairman,[h] reported upon the message and accompanying papers the middle of the month. After exploiting the doctrine that the compact of 1802 did not affect the sovereignty of Georgia, but merely threw upon the General Government the burden of expense, the committee resolved, " That the United States are bound by their obligations to Georgia, to take, immediately, the necessary measures for the removal of the Cherokee Indians beyond the limits of that State." They further advised an appropriation looking toward the extinguishment of both the Creek and Cherokee titles. Monroe's message and the discussions which it aroused in Congress provoked another protest from Governor Troup as inflammatory as the first;[i] but a new appropriation put a temporary quietus upon the whole affair.[j]

The opinion seems to have prevailed in Congress that the Federal Government could as arbitrarily dispose of the Cherokees as it had

---

[a] American State Papers, " Indian Affairs," II : p. 474.

[b] Harden's " Troup," p. 201.

[c] Harden's " Troup," pp. 203–207 ; American State Papers, " Indian Affairs," II ; 475–476.

[d] Niles' Register, XXVI : 103–104 ; Harden's " Troup," pp. 216–218.

[e] Richardson, II : 234–237.

[f] " Writings," III : 434.

[g] It seems probable that Judge Berrien drew up the memorial and remonstrance of the legislature to the President. Harden's " Troup," p. 199, note.

[h] Annals of Congress, Eighteenth Congress, First Session, vol. II : p. 2349.

[i] Niles' Register, XXVI : 275–277 ; Troup to Calhoun, April 24, 1824, Harden's " Troup," pp. 210–216.

[j] Act of May 26, 1824, 4 United States Statutes at Large, p. 36.

disposed of the Seminoles; but the cases were a little different. While Ferdinand of Spain was hesitating to ratify the Florida treaty, fearful lest the United States, its object once secured and its hands free, would recognize the independence of the South American Republics, preparations were begun extra-legally to administer the province, and the Indians came in for a share of the premature handling. Andrew Jackson's attitude toward them was almost vindictive, and well it might be, for it was still politically necessary to propagate the belief that their aggressions alone and no ulterior design of conquest had provoked his unauthorized invasion of a foreign State. Consequently Monroe's January offer to him of the governor-generalship boded ill for Seminole integrity.[a]

During the progress of the Florida campaign, Jackson ordered the renegade Creeks to return to their own tribe,[b] and this seems to have suggested itself to the War Department as an easy way of disposing of all the hostile Indians, Seminoles included.[c] Unfortunately the obstacles proved insurmountable. The only valid excuse for consolidating Creeks and Seminoles was that the two tribes were originally of the same stock. If that be so, argued the Creek chiefs to the indignant Calhoun, and you unite the Seminoles with us upon that basis, then we have a claim to their country and a voice in its disposal.[d] Georgia took advantage of the same dilemma just a little later. It was when the Preston Commission was passing upon the validity of claims preferred for settlement under the Creek treaty of 1821. The State government asked that damages against the Seminoles be grouped with those against the Creeks and all be paid out of the Creek funds. Monroe pronounced against the injustice, and Calhoun denied that the Seminoles had ever been officially recognized as anything but a distinct tribe. As a matter of fact, however, these can hardly be called obstacles. At any rate they were not insuperable,[e] neither was the Seminole resistance, but the Georgian was; for the compact of 1802 gave the casting vote in the negative, since its

---

[a] " Jackson's Papers," January 24, 1821. Jackson, in a memorandum to be found among his papers, labeled " January 24, 1822," says the appointment was first offered in 1819.

[b] Jackson to J. Q. Adams, April 2, 1821, " Jackson Letter Books," Vol. M.

[c] (1) " He (the President) directs that should they [the Seminoles] offer to treat for peace it will be given them on condition that they should remove to the Upper Creeks, with the consent of the latter, whenever the President may direct such removal. The President entertains no doubt of the policy of removing them from Florida; but it might be improper at this moment to cause such removal. The more dangerous among them, however, should be removed immediately." (Extract from letter of Calhoun to D. B. Mitchell, October 26, 1818, " Indian Office Letter Books," Series I, D, p. 223.)

(2) " You are authorized to take such steps as may be necessary to effect the object [the removal of the Florida Indians up into the body of the Creek Nation] in the most expeditious and economical manner. The Government will furnish the provisions that may be required for the support of the Seminoles during the removal and until they are in a situation to provide for themselves." (Same to same, March 11, 1819, ibid., p. 263.)

[d] " Indian Office Letter Books," Series I, D, pp. 278, 312, 352.

[e] Calhoun to William P. Duval, August 19, 1822, " Indian Office Letter Books," Series I, E, p. 310; Gadsden to Jackson, April 9, 1823, " Jackson Papers."

purpose, inferentially, was not to increase but to decrease the number of Indians within the State limits.

Immediately upon the enactment of the law for carrying into effect the Spanish treaty, Monroe took measures to acquaint himself with the real condition of the Florida Indians by appointing as their sub-agent, under the general superintendency of Governor Jackson, a French political refugee, J. A. Penieres,[a] whose nationality and familiarity with the Spanish language were deemed special qualifications for the work. Penieres was instructed [b] to explore the country, to ascertain the number of the Indians and their tribal divisions, and to prepare them either for concentration within the peninsula or for removal to some other part of the United States.

The alternative proposition was the beginning of the end for the Florida Indians. More circumstances than one conspired at their undoing. A difference of opinion arose as to whether they owned any land at all and, even if they did, whether it might not be declared confiscated under the rules of war. Politicians of the Jackson stamp, eager to see Florida well populated before the next presidential election, argued first one thing and then another. They insisted that long ago the Indians had sold all their land to the British Government and had since been living in Florida on sufferance—an easy thing to do under the Spanish system. There was a germ of truth in all this. The Indians had, indeed, made a treaty with the British, after the French and Indian war, but it was one of limits only, a sale of the northeast corner, and not of entire surrender.[c] When the argument of nonpossession failed, that of forfeiture through conquest was advanced, then came that of expediency. It would never do to leave the Indians on the seaboard, accessible to smugglers and foreign emissaries, or scattered over the country, offering a safe harbor to fugitive slaves. To clinch the whole matter, Jackson wrote to Calhoun, September 17, 1821: [d] " Unless the Indians be consolidated at one point, where is the country that can be brought into market, from which the five millions are to be raised, to meet the claims of our citizens under the late treaty with Spain? "

Jackson's administration of the Floridas did not last long. Before the Christmas holidays he was back again at the Hermitage, a weary, disappointed man; but his influence continued. Unsuccessful in everything else as a governor, he managed to shape the destiny of the Seminoles for all time. Meeting some of them accidentally in

---

[a] " He was a foreigner of education and refinement, attached to his adopted country, particularly to Indians, for whose civilization and happiness he suggested many good plans, and devoted several years of his life." (Morse's " Report," Appendix, p. 151.)

[b] Calhoun to Penieres, March 31, 1821, " Jackson Papers"; " Indian Office Letter Books," Series I. E. p. 75.

[c] Horatio Dexter's " Observations on the Seminole Indians in 1823," " Miscellaneous Files," Indian Office MS. Records.

[d] " Jackson Letter Books," Vol. M.

September, he stated [a] plainly what they had to expect, and then left the actual negotiation to his friends. Could he have had entirely his own way no treaty at all would have been made; for if Congress were ever going to assert, as it ought to do, its power of legislation over Indian affairs, it could not do better than begin with the "conquered" Seminoles.[b] The acting governor, Walton, a Georgian, was of Jackson's own way of thinking and severely criticized the more humane secretary, Worthington, for suggesting to the Indians that the United States would buy their land.[c] Speculators had already frightened them by making them believe that the Government intended to despoil them of it.[d]

Having decided upon concentration, the Government considered the question of where? Jackson's choice was, first, the Creek reserved lands; [e] next, the region of the Appalachicola; [f] and the Government ordered Captain Bell [g] to propose it to the Indians, but they would not give him the chance, and so lost their own [h] of selecting a desirable locality. Somehow they got the idea that Jackson, in his talk of September 18, had promised them their own choice of a location.[i] They therefore selected Choctawhatchee Bay, which aroused the wrath of Samuel Overton.[j] Such audacity was never heard of before. It could not be permitted; for that was "one of the finest bodies of land in the Territory." Eventually, some one proposed the neighborhood of the Everglades, south of Charlotte Harbor, and there the matter rested.

Two years passed away in this dilatory fashion. The warm season of 1822 threatened before Congress had made an appropriation,[k] consequently nothing could even be attempted until the autumn, then came the yellow-fever epidemic, so bad in New Orleans and

---

[a] Talk, September 18 and 19, 1821, "Jackson Papers."

[b] Jackson to Calhoun, September 17, 1821, "Jackson Papers;" Jackson to J. Q. Adams, October 6, 1821, "Jackson Papers."

[c] " * * * Mr. Worthington seems to have misunderstood entirely the sense and object of your talk. There was surely no intention that any Treaty should be entered into with them, much less such a one as is contemplated by the draft accompanying M[r]. Worthington's communication. The idea is a cession on the part of the Indians of all their right and title to East and West Florida, which we neither ask nor want, for the simple reason that we do not admit that they have any right whatever—they then reserve and we acquiesce in the reservation of the very Country which you are most desirous we should reserve to ourselves; and then comes the project of a purchase of this Country from the Indians, excepting &c., which, in all probability there will be no disposition to sell, when it is once admitted to be theirs." (Extract of letter from G. Walton to Jackson February 4, 1822, "Jackson Papers.")

[d] Letter from J. A. Penieres to "My very dear and perfect friend." ("Miscellaneous Files," Indian Office Manuscript Records.)

[e] Jackson to Calhoun, September 2, 1821, "Jackson Letter Books," Vol. L; Jackson to Worthington, September 18, 1821, "Jackson Letter Books," Vol. M.

[f] Jackson to Calhoun, September 20, 1821, "Jackson Letter Books," Vol. M.

[g] Captain Bell seems to have been really kindly disposed toward the Indians.

[h] Calhoun to Duval, August 19, 1822, "Indian Office Letter Books," Series I, E, p. 310.

[i] Walton to Jackson, December 17, 1821, "Jackson Papers."

[j] Overton to Jackson, January 9, 1822, "Jackson Papers."

[k] Calhoun to Duval, August 19, 1822, "Indian Office Letter Books," Series I, E, p. 310.

Pensacola that no provisions could arrive at St. Marks, where Governor Duval had planned to hold his meeting with the Indians. It was therefore postponed from November 20 to a more convenient time.[a] Meanwhile the Indians were growing more and more anxious. They saw the white people pressing on and knew not what to think. Governor Coppinger had given them so little satisfaction as to the provisions made for them by the Spanish Government and they had everything to dread. The new agent, Col. Gad Humphreys, of New York, did his best to reassure [b] them, but the long waiting was irksome.

As it happened, the War Department had even then decided upon a definite action, and Monroe had appointed commissioners [c] to negotiate a treaty upon the basis of concentration " on the Country South of Charlotte Harbor, if there be a sufficient quantity of good land . . . ; if not, take in a part of the Country between that and Tampa Bay." [d] Jackson's great friend, Col. James Gadsden, was one of the commissioners and Bernardo Segui the other. Gadsden, feeling that his political reputation was at stake, spared no efforts to achieve success and wrote to Jackson for advice.[c] A despotic treatment of the Indians was not likely to be criticized in that faraway region if only the authorities in control were satisfied.[f]

The treaty of Camp Moultrie, which the United States commissioners negotiated with the Florida Indians in September of 1823,[g] is, without question, one of the worst in all history. It is not so characterized because of any bribery used to effect it, though that was not absent,[h] but for the misery that it caused, dare we say intentionally? to over four thousand hapless human beings. When Agent Humphreys interviewed the Seminoles, preparatory to the treaty, they professed themselves ready and willing to begin an agricultural existence,[i] which theoretically was what the Government most desired for

---

[a] Calhoun to Col. Abraham Eustis, October 23, 1822, " Indian Office Letter Books," Series I, E, p. 347.

[b] Talk, March 20, 1823, " Miscellaneous Files," Indian Office MS. Records.

[c] At first there were only two, for the sake of economy (Calhoun to Hernandez, the delegate from Florida Territory, April 3, 1823, " Indian Office Letter Books," Series I, E, p. 422), but later the number was increased to three by the appointment of Governor William P. Duval. (Calhoun to Duval, June 30, 1823, " Indian Office Letter Books," Series I, E, p. 459.)

[d] Calhoun to Hernandez, March 19, 1823, " Indian Office Letter Books," Series I, E. p. 410–411; Calhoun to Gadsden and Segui, April 7, 1823, Manuscript Journal of the Commissioners, Indian Office.

[e] Gadsden to Jackson, April 9, 1823, " Jackson Papers."

[f] Gadsden to Jackson, June 8, 1823, " Jackson Papers."

[g] 7 United States Statutes at Large, 224.

[h] " Minutes of the Proceedings," American State Papers, " Indian Affairs," II : 431; MS. Journal of the Commissioners, Indian Office Records.

[i] " I must not omit at this time, to state as a fact of apparent interest which may have influence on the measures hereafter to be adopted in relation to these people, that keeping in mind your Instructions of the 21st January, I made it a consideration of primary importance to ascertain the disposition and views of the Indians in relation to the cultivation of the soil, and the adoption of the habits of civilized life, and I am

them. Yet it deliberately [a] placed them in a region where subsistence by that means was absolutely impossible.[b] Moreover, intimidation was, by Gadsden's own confession,[c] and at Jackson's sugges-

---

happy to be enabled to say, that my inquiries have resulted in a seemingly well founded belief, that very little more is necessary to bring them into the measure, than to furnish them with the proper Implements of Husbandry, and locate them upon a tract of land sufficiently fertile to reward and encourage their labours. Although the settled practice of hunting for a living appears almost inseparable from their nature, yet the sensible and reflecting among them begin, even at this period, to look upon it as a precarious and uncertain means of subsistence, and urge with reasonable but unyielding pertinacity, the necessity of providing other and more stable sources of support. They declared themselves satisfied with what they heard at the Talk, and said that notwithstanding they felt great solicitude to know their destiny, yet they were resolved to wait patiently the determination and orders of the Government on the subject, in the belief that strict justice would be done them.

" They appear in general well disposed and not inclined to be troublesome ; yet there is a manifest impatience felt to be informed of the Intentions of the United States towards them, which they cannot disguise if they would ; they assert with much plausibility, that the incertitude of their condition, precludes the possibility of their making those permanent arrangements so essential to their comfort and well being. How long their present docility of temper may continue it is impossible to say, and I beg leave to take the present occasion to suggest, that the sooner they are attended to, and provided for the better. * * * ." (Extract from letter of G. Humphreys to George Walton, April 19, 1823, " Miscellaneous Files," Indian Office MS. Records.)

[a] Gadsden to Jackson, June 12, 1823, " Jackson Papers."

[b] The greater blame for this attaches itself to Gadsden ; for the Government was willing even as late as July 31, 1823 (" Indian Office Letter Books," Series I, E, p. 473), to place them on the Appalachicola, a plan that did not commend itself, however, to the commissioner ; because he was afraid it would intensify and prolong the sectional feeling between East and West Florida.

[c] (1.) Gadsden to Jackson, July 30, 1823, " Jackson Papers."

(2) St. Augustine,
29 Sept. 1823.

Sir :—

Governor Duval has requested me to act as one of the Commissioners provided for to run the boundary line as concluded on by the late Treaty with the Florida Indians —— I have said to him that I would so far comply with his wishes as to write a *private letter* to you explaining my views on the subject, and stating how far my services may be demanded if required by the Executive —— The situation of Commissioner adverted to, is not to be coveted, but I am willing to act in said capacity provided in so doing I can be instrumental to the immediate accomplishment of the objects to be effected by the treaty lately concluded with the Florida Indians, and render any service to the Territory of Florida —— The boundary line of the Country South allotted to the Indians can only be run at a certain season of the year, & if that season is permitted to escape a postponement to a subsequent one is inevitable —— This season is confined to the winter months or between the 1st of Jany & 1 of April * * * . The sooner the line of demarkation is defined, the sooner will the Indians concentrate, and any delay on the part of the U. States may produce an opinion among the Indians that the National Government is not determined on an object of vital importance to the prosperity of Florida —— It is not necessary to disguise the fact to you, that the treaty effected was in a degree a treaty of imposition —— The Indians would never have voluntarily assented to the terms had they not believed that we had both the power & disposition to compel obedience.

The Impression made therefore should not be lost ; a military Post should be immediately established at the Bay of Tampa, & the boundary line commenced & run as soon as the season will permit —— * * *

It is natural to wish to succeed in what we undertake—Success *would* be *doubtful* if the Commissioner was unsupported at least with the presence of a military force within striking distance of his operations, & failure inevitable if he attempts to contend against the elements.

From all the information I can gather relating to the country allotted the Indians, the hunting grounds in particular are inundated during the Spring & Summer rains. It is in winter only that they can be traversed, it is at that season only that they can be penetrated with Comfort & without sacrifice of health —— I am willing therefore to

tion,[a] the means used to effect the object. Gadsden's practices throughout were merciless. Anticipating that a small number only might attend the meeting on the 5th of September, he proposed holding the many responsible for what the few accomplished. Again and again he urged the immediate establishment of a strong military post at Tampa Bay; [b] so that, if he could succeed in inducing the Indians to

---

act as Commissioner, provided I can be immediately appointed & can receive the necessary orders for the immediate execution of the duties as such * * *

Should the above view of the subject correspond with your own: & my services be required: & the Executive feel disposed to associate any one with me, I take the liberty to name to you Lt. James Ripley of the Army, with the remark that his appointment would be gratifying in the extreme to me. Lt. Ripley commanded the Guard on the Treaty ground & rendered the Commissioners essential services during the complicated duties of their mission. He possesses the qualifications necessary in a pre-eminent degree —— The only objections to the propositions submitted anticipated by me, are the possible unwillingness of the Executive to act before the ratification of the Treaty —— But may not this obstacle be obviated on the plea of policy or necessity —— If the running of the line is postponed untill the Treaty is ratified it is very problematical whether it can then be run this season —— To delay concentrating the Indians another year would be seriously felt in the Territory of Florida —— It would be subjecting her fate to another embarrassment & she has already labored under many —— The expense I hope will prove no objection for I should be willing (if necessary) to make no demands on the Treasury untill advised of an appropriation: advancing the requisite amount myself. * * * A surveyor I would not require but would prefer the selecting a subaltern officer * * * Or if you would prefer it a Lt. of Engineers might be detailed as surveyor * * *

(Extracts from Letter from Gadsden to Calhoun, "Miscellaneous Files," Indian Office, MS. Records.)

[a](1) WAR DEPT.
31st July, 1823.

My dear Sir.

Such is my confidence in your judgement and character, that I am always happy to be put in possession of your views on any point connected with the publick interest,

Your knowledge of the Indian character enables you to speak with great certainty of the probable effect of any measure on them; & with this impression, the whole of your suggestions in relation to the pending treaty with the Indians in Florida would have been carried into effect, if there was sufficient time. As the treaty will be held in Sept[r] it will be impossible to move the troops from Baton Rouge to Tampa Bay, as you suggest. All of the other points will be attended to. I have great confidence in the Com[rs], particularly our friend, and I am very solicitous for their success. * * *

(Extract from letter of Calhoun to Jackson, " Jackson Papers.")

(2) Calhoun to Gladsden, Segui, and Duval, July 31, 1823, " Indian Office Letter Books," Series I, E, p. 473.

[b] Duval seems to have been in close accord with Gadsden. Note this letter to Calhoun announcing the sucessful negotiation of the treaty of Camp Moultrie. (" Treaty Files," 1802–1853, Indian. Office MS. Records :)

ST. AUGUSTINE
26 Sept. 1823.

Sir,

On the 21st instant you were advised by mail of our having concluded a Treaty with the Florida Tribes of Indians. The 2[d] Article of the Treaty, accompanying this will inform you of the Boundaries assigned them, which with the other articles agreed on will be found in our opinion to correspond with the spirit of our instructions, as well as the humane policy of our government. The want of a knowledge of the country South of Charlott's Harbor, and the impossibility of inducing any satisfactory information relative to that region, necessarily prohibits the Commissioners from confining the Indians to that quarter agreeably to the views of the Executive as first expressed in our instructions. A Northern Location, though desired by a Majority of the Indians, was violently opposed within the limits recommended by Gen[l] Jackson; to have extended beyond the limits would have been injurious to the best interests of Florida —— A Southern Location was objected to by the Indians on the ground that the Country South of Tampa did not contain a sufficient quantity of good land to furnish the subsistence of life—That force only could drive them into those limits, and that they were well convinced that the Americans possessed the power, and they not the ability to

move direct from the treaty ground to the spot assigned them, they would " find the seacoast occupied previously by a force capable of commanding obedience or chastising for dereliction."

The Florida tribes were diverse in origin and characteristics. It was therefore possible that some of them would prefer removal beyond the Mississippi to concentration with friend and foe in a bar-

resist—The Indians therefore threw themselves on the protection of the U. States ; and appealed feelingly to the humanity of the Commissioners not to locate them in a country in which they must inevitably starve.—We knew nothing of the Country but from vague, and contradictory representations : the appeal therefore was listened to so far as to embrace within the limits assigned the Indians a small tract of country about 30 miles North of Tampa Bay, containing within its boundaries many of the Settlements of the Southern Chiefs—Even this extension *North* was not considered as removing the objections urged : to satisfy therefore all parties and convince even the Indians of the humane disposition of the American government towards them, an article was incerted that if on examination by the Commissioners &c appointed to run the line it should appear that there was not a sufficient quantity of good land within the limits allotted them, then the North line should be extended so as to give satisfaction on this point.—

The reservations made in the Appalachicola district were in favor of six influential chiefs, whose assent to the Treaty could not have been obtained without this equitable provision for them & their connections—They are all represented to be men of industrious habits, and who have made some advances in civilisation. Blunt & Tuske-Hajo have been long friendly to the Americans, and rendered essential services to Genl Jackson during the operations in Florida, on the termination of which they were permitted to reside where they now do under the protection of the United States, with a promise that when the Indians in Florida were disposed of, the provisions now made for them should be taken into consideration —— We view these reservations as among the most favourable terms of the Treaty : The lands allotted each chief & their connections are so limited, as to force the occupants into the civil habits and pursuits ; while so large a subtraction is made from the Indian population to be concentrated, as to render that population more easily manageable.

The Treaty however was the best we could effect and we are inclined to the opinion that the boundaries to which the Indians have been limited will be found, on reflection, to be the most judicious in a National, as well as Territorial point of view — Justice has been done to the Indians by assigning to them a sufficient quantity of tillable land, with the addition of an extent of Territory alike favourable as hunting grounds, and for the grasing of cattle ; while the position is so central as to admit of being encircled by a white population capable of overawing and controlling their uncivilised propensities.

We deem it our duty before closing our mission to invite your attention to some important subjects as intimately connected with the accomplishment of the views which have dictated the policy pursued by the U. States towards the Indians —— It was a misfortune to Florida as a frontier Territory and with her maritime exposure to have any Tribes of Indians within her boundaries — It would have been a national benefit to have removed them to a more interior position : but as this seems to have been impracticable : the only course left was that which has been adopted —— The confining the Indians within certain limits, and in that part of the Territory least objectionable —— This being accomplished it is indispensable for the benefit of the Indians ; as well as the future security of Florida that all intercourse with foreign countries or Individuals exercising an influence over them be cut off, and that an exclusive control be obtained and maintained by the American Government—This is only to be effected by the immediate establishment of Military posts at the Bay of Tampa, Charlotts Harbor, and at some other point near Cape Florida on the Eastern Coast, with such other salutary laws regulating the Trade with ·them as your own sound judgement may dictate——It is scarcely necesary to state to you that a Majority of the Indians now inhabiting the Territory of Florida and included as parties to the treaty just effected, are wanderers, if not Refugees from the Southern Indians——Many of them are of the old Red Stick party whose feelings of hostility have only been suppressed not eradicated, and even the native Seminoles have ever been of a most erratic disposition——These Indians are now scattered over the whole face of Florida, but a small portion of their having any settled residence ; a majority wandering about for such a precarious subsistence as the esculent roots of the woods, or the misfortunes of our navigators on the Florida keys may afford.——

To bring together these discordant and fermenting materials ; to embody such a population within prescribed limits, and to conquer their erratic habits will require in

ren, unhealthy region, and Gadsden asked for instructions.[a] Calhoun replied, " I agree with you as to the importance to the Territory of Florida of removing the Indians West of the Mississippi; but there are no lands which the Government can assign them in lieu of those they may abandon, as all the public lands in that direction, that could be so disposed of, are occupied either by the Cherokees or Choctaws. The Government is, however, willing to encourage the removal of the Florida Indians as far as it can, and if all, or any part of them should be disposed to emigrate, and join the Cherokees or Choctaws, or any other tribe farther west that may be willing to receive them, you are authorized to include a stipulation in the proposed treaty on the subject, allowing them, in the event of their emigration, what may be deemed by the Commissioners a fair consideration for the lands relinquished by them in Florida, and agreeing on the part of the United States to pay the expenses attending their removal." [b]

The Indians preferred to stay in their own peninsula ; and, irrespective of the small individual reservations for the chiefs of the Appalachicola, were assigned a strip of territory, (at no point less than 15 miles from the coast)[c] running in a northwestwardly direction from Lake Okeechobee to the neighborhood of the Withlacoochee River, with the provision that the northern boundary should be extended until a sufficiency of " good tillable land " had been obtained.[d] In

some degree the exercise of authority, with the presence of a military establishment adequate to enforce it —— These Posts therefore, in our opinion, should be established before the boundary line is run and marked —— Such a military disposition of an adequate force would produce an impression upon the Indians most favourable to an immediate concentration within the limits allotted ——

The Military establishments recommended from the protection they would afford, will further induce an early settlement of the country now open to the enterprise of emigrants : the presence of which population will assist materially in forcing the Indians within the limits allotted them & obtaining that control so much desired.

As an act of justice to L. Ripley who commanded the detachment of Troops on the Treaty ground ; & of L. H. Brown the Asst. Commissary of Subsistence we most cheerfully testify to the zealous, active & faithful discharge of the various duties assigned them.

Col. Humphreys Indian Agent, & M[r]. Richards the Interpreter likewise rendered us essential services during the complicated difficulties we had to encounter—In assembling and marching the Western Indians through a wilderness of 250 miles in extent to the Treaty ground, they have been exposed to privations & expenses giving them strong claims on the Department of War for extra compensation ; the equitable adjustment of which is submitted to your consideration by

Your most obt. Servants,

WM. P. DUVAL.
JAMES GADSDEN.
BERNARD SEGUI.

The Honb.
J. C. CALHOUN, Sec. of War.

[a] Gadsden to Calhoun, June 11, 1823, " Miscellaneous Files," Indian Office MS. Records.

[b] Calhoun to Gadsden, June 30, 1823, " Indian Office Letter Books," Series I, E, p. 458 ; American State Papers, " Indian Affairs," II : 434–435.

[c] Gadsden to Calhoun, September 21, 1823, " Miscellaneous Files," Indian Office MS. Records ; William P. Duval to Calhoun, September 26, 1823, " Treaty Files," 1802–1853, Indian Office MS. Records.

[d] The account of the two successive extensions of this line belongs to the story of the Florida Indian sufferings and will come later.

November, Monroe commissioned Gadsden to run the lines, in December, the Senate ratified the treaty, and in May, following, Congress appropriated [a] various sums to carry it into effect.[b]

While the Florida Indians were being collected in readiness for transportation, the War Department reopened negotiations with the Creeks under the appropriation act of May 26, 1824; and as the treaty which our old friends, Duncan G. Campbell and James Meriwether, were now about to frame is the one that precipitated J. Q. Adams's famous controversy with Governor Troup, it behooves us to preface an account of it with a few remarks concerning the situation of the Creek community, not forgetting to bear in mind the way in which Indian affairs often became, to the detriment of the Indians, mixed up with local and even with national politics.[c]

At the time when their history becomes most interesting to us the Creek towns numbered fifty-six and were divided, not politically, but geographically, into the Upper of Georgia and the Lower of Alabama. As near as can be made out, Little Prince was their great chief, the king, so to speak, of the Creek Nation, with Big Warrior as a close second. William McIntosh, the leading actor in the coming drama, was not a head chief at all, but a chief fifth in rank, yet he seems to have been the recognized leader of the lower towns. He was a half-breed of Scotch extraction, a cousin of Governor Troup, and a clever, capable man, shrewd and unscrupulous. He had served with distinction under General Jackson in both the Creek and Seminole wars, and was generally known for his friendliness toward the whites. Big Warrior represented more nearly a Creek of the olden time. He

---

[a] 4 United States Statutes at Large, 37.

[b] Duval complained that the amount was not large enough, and it certainly was not; but the Government had had so much experience with him in the overcharging of his accounts as superintendent of Indian affairs in Florida that it might well hesitate to place too much reliance upon any estimate that he might furnish. As it was, his method of disbursing the money, after it had been appropriated, will scarcely bear investigation. His ration contract was a disgraceful affair, and there is some suspicion that he appropriated to himself the $500 which he pretended to have paid Enehe-Mathlá, and which was due to Enehe-Mathlá under the additional article of the treaty of Camp Moultrie.

[c] The appointment and subsequent removal of D. B. Mitchell is a case in point. When Colonel Hawkins died, the Government tendered the position of Creek agent to Gen. David Meriwether; but before he could accept it it was conferred upon D. B. Mitchell, who resigned the governorship of Georgia in order to assume the new duties. Just what influenced his action it is difficult to say. Jackson always claimed that it was the $85,000 Creek indemnity which was then being considered in Congress and of which W. H. Crawford, Secretary of the Treasury and Mitchell's friend, would have the disposal. In 1821, through the instrumentality of Jackson and his friends, the Creek agent was removed, it having been charged, and to the satisfaction of Monroe proved, that he had been engaged in smuggling Africans from across the Florida line, for which nefarious purpose he had made use of the Creek indemnity. His successor was Col. John Crowell, a former Congressional representative from Alabama and a man whose quarrel with the Methodist missionary, Rev. William Capers, (Harden's "Troup," pp. 249–251), and indiscreet affiliations with the Clarke, or anti-Troup faction, greatly complicated the Creek troubles. Another cause of dissatisfaction, on the part of the Georgians, with Crowell's administration as Creek agent was the tacit permission which he gave to his own relatives to trade unlawfully in the Creek country. This was supposed to influence his attitude toward the proposed diminution of Indian territory.

was the recognized chief of the Red Sticks and, in saying that, we have told all, for the Red Sticks were the "Hostiles," those who resented and had already tried to resist the encroachments of the civilized settlements. In character Big Warrior was supposed to be a wily and treacherous savage, but that was from an American point of view. Little Prince was a different man from either of the others, neither actively friendly nor actively hostile toward the United States. He did what he could, by peaceful and political measures, to prevent friction; then, failing, yielded to the inevitable.

Such were the men with whom Campbell and Meriwether had to deal when they started out in 1824 to negotiate a new Creek cession. Anticipating their coming, some of the Creek chiefs determined upon a bold step, encouraged thereto by the Cherokees. On the 25th of May they met at their capital town, Tuckaubatchee, and passed a resolution[a] (in effect a law of the nation, because done in general council and signed by Little Prince) that they would neither sell nor exchange another foot of land. Toward the end of September, Agent Crowell notified the Creeks[b] that the United States commissioners would expect to meet with them at Broken Arrow, the national council square, some time in the near future, preferably the 25th of November;[c] and, on the 29th of October,[d] the chiefs met at Pole Cat Spring to discuss the matter. The result was an announcement to the world of the decision reached at Tuckaubatchee five months before. Thus fortified they awaited the conference.

Since receiving their instructions in July, the commissioners had been making preparations for a large meeting, Crowell having informed them that they might expect some five thousand Indians to attend.[e] Campbell, at least, was sanguine of success; for, while conferring with the Cherokees, he had found out that the Creeks were

---

[a] " * * * on a deep and solemn reflection, we have, with one voice, [resolved] to follow the pattern of the Cherokees, and on no account whatever will we consent to sell one foot of our land, neither by exchange or otherwise." Signed by Little Prince, Big Warrior, Hohi Hajo, Abeco Tustenugga, Yahole Mico, Mad Wolf, Tustenugga Mallo, Tuskenaha, George Anson, Fooshache Fixeco, Powes Hajo, Mad Town, Young King, Jahaha Halo, (Article taken from "Montgomery Republican," and printed in Niles' "Register," December 4, 1824, XXVII: 223.

[b] Crowell to Campbell, September 27, 1824, "Journal of Proceedings at Broken Arrow," in "Indian Office MS. Records."

[c] The 25th of November was the date decided upon by Crowell and the commissioners; but the Indians preferred the 6th of December. That date interfered with Campbell's arrangements so it was changed finally to the 1st of December. (Crowell to Campbell, September 27, 1824, and Campbell to Crowell, October 13, 1824, in "Journal of Proceedings at Broken Arrow.")

[d] At this meeting the chiefs revoked any authority heretofore given to any individual to dispose of Creek land and decided that this notice should be published in some United States newspaper "so that it may be known to the world that the *Creek people are not disposed to sell one foot more of their lands.*" Signed by Little Prince, Big Warrior, Hohi Hajo, Tomma Tustenugga, What-a-Mico, Poeth-la-Halo, Tuskenaha Tustenugga Hajo, Mad Wolf, Foshatchee Fixico, Mico Pico, Tuskéga Tustenugga, Alec Hajo, Soakate Mala, Talase Tustenugga, Young King, Wm. McGilvery, Charles Cornells. (Niles' "Register," Vol. XXVII : pp. 223–224.)

[e] Crowell to Campbell, September 20, 1824, "Journal of Proceedings at Broken Arrow."

divided among themselves on the question of a cession. He had not yet heard of the action taken at Tuckaubatchee. With Crowell he was on the best of terms, the two having been political supporters of Matthew Talbot as against Troup in the last gubernatorial contest. So little were they at variance, indeed, that Campbell was able to report to Calhoun, the 8th of August, " The Agent is intelligent and communicative and I am certain will afford us all the facilities within his control." [a]

The same difficulty of having no lands to the westward available for exchange, as was felt in the case of the Florida Indians, now confronted the Administration in dealing with the Creeks.[b] Nevertheless, in their " talk," after the organization of the treaty council, the commissioners assured the Indians that the President had extensive tracts of country under his dominion beyond the Mississippi which he was willing to give them in exchange for the country they were then occupying, removal being with him a first consideration because of the Georgia compact.[c] In reply four chiefs, Little Prince, Poethleyoholo, William McIntosh, and Hossay Hadjo, signed their names to an address, in which they said:

" The agreement between our Father, the President of the United States, and our Brothers of Georgia we have never before this time been acquainted with; nor are we now convinced that any agreement between the United States and the state of Georgia will have the effect of alienating the affections of a just Parent from a part of his children, or aggrandising the one by the downfall and ruin of the other. That ruin is the almost inevitable consequence of a removal beyond the Mississippi, we are convinced. It is true, very true, that ' we are surrounded by white people,' that there are encroachments made—what assurances have we that similar ones will not be made on us, should we deem it proper to accept your offer, and remove beyond the Mississippi; and how do we know that we would not be encroaching on the people of other nations? " [d]

In spite of the reluctance to a cession manifested in this, the first recorded Indian " talk " of the conference, and of the positive refusal in the decision of Tuckaubatchee and of Pole Cat Spring, which had come to their notice prior to their arrival at Broken Arrow on the 30th of November, the commissioners continued to press their demands, drawing freely from other negotiations and inaccurately from history to strengthen the unwelcome arguments. Their final threat was, " Brothers, we plainly see and we know it

---

[a] "Journal of Proceedings at Broken Arrow."
[b] Calhoun to Campbell, September 13, 1824, " Indian Office Letter Books," Series II, No. 1, p. 195.
[c] Talk, December 7, 1824, " Journal of Proceedings."
[d] Talk, December 8, 1824, " Journal of Proceedings."

to be true from the talks of the President, the Secretary of War, the Governor of Georgia, the Georgia Delegation in Congress, and the Legislature of Georgia for years past, that one of two things must be done, you must come under the laws of the whites or you must remove." [a] Finding all their efforts useless, they employed men to interview the chiefs privately,[b] but all propositions were indignantly rejected except those offered to McIntosh, and even he dared not close with an offer on the treaty ground. The commissioners therefore made a night excursion up the river to Coweta Town and there conferred with lesser chiefs of the McIntosh following.[c] Ere long Little Prince and Big Warrior suspected that all was not right and deprived McIntosh of his office as speaker of the Creek Nation. The disgrace determined his action. At all events, because of that and of covert threats against his life, he left Broken Arrow secretly, and the next we hear of him it is as the betrayer of his country.

The earliest intimation of any distrust felt by the commissioners of hearty cooperation on the part of Federal officials was in connection with the sub-agent, Captain William Walker, recorded by the journal entry for December 13. There we learn that it had just come to the knowledge of the commissioners that Walker, who was, by the way, a son-in-law of Big Warrior, had acted as secretary at the Tuckaubatchee and Pole Cat meetings. About the same time the commissioners received an express from the governor of Georgia inquiring particularly as to the conduct of Colonel Crowell. Evidently Troup would have been glad, for political reasons, to find some cause for complaint against the man whose removal he had requested a twelvemonth before; but the commissioners had none to make—not even though the agent had, at the outset, informed them verbally that he would not risk losing the confidence of the Creeks and so imperilling future negotiations by trying to persuade them against their better judgment. He would leave the whole business to the commissioners and would do nothing against them.

On the 14th of December, the commissioners, seeing that they were making no progress at all, proposed in council that the balance of the negotiations should be conducted by a select number of chiefs, and that they should adjourn from the square to a comfortable and convenient room. They were met by a flat refusal.[d] Four more days passed away in profitless speech-making, with Crowell neutral, the example of the Cherokees influential, the upper Creeks obstinate, and the commissioners exasperated. Clearly it was a waste of time and money to continue the negotiations. They were there-

---

[a] "Journal of Proceedings."

[b] "Crowell's Defense," Indian Office MS. Records.

[c] Commissioners to Troup, December 14, 1824, "Crowell's Defense," Indian Office MS. Records.

[d] "Journal of Proceedings."

fore suspended, subject to further instructions from Washington, whither Campbell straightway repaired, a letter from Troup in his wake notifying the President that " a treaty can be immediately signed upon the conditions which will be disclosed by the commissioners." [a]

On the 8th of January, Campbell submitted to the War Department his complaint and his suggestion.[b] After giving various prudential reasons why the commissioners had not seen fit to conclude a contract with the McIntosh party alone, he requested " the authority of the Executive * * * to convene the chiefs within the limits of Georgia; to negotiate with them exclusively, if we think proper, or inclusive of a deputation of chiefs from the upper towns, if such deputation should present themselves and evince a disposition to negotiate to further extent * * * ." The request was refused. On the 11th Campbell wrote again to inquire whether negotiations for a cession and removal might be resumed with the entire tribe; and, only in the event of a second failure, continued and concluded with the Georgia chiefs, subject to the assent of the others that the land vacated by the emigrants should be placed immediately at the disposal of the Government.[c] Again he was told that the President could authorize no treaty with the Creeks unless it were made " in the usual form, and upon the ordinary principles with which Treaties, are held with Indian tribes * * * ."[d]

Though so uncompromising in this particular, in other respects the Administration showed itself very ready to comply with the wishes of Campbell. Regardless of the intercession of General Jackson,[e] Walker was summarily dismissed on the plea that he had used his influence to defeat " the successful termination of the treaty," [f] the specific charge being " that he penned the publication of the Creek chiefs at Tokaubatche and the Pole-cat Springs; and that their meeting at the latter was at his house, and with his sanction and countenance * * * ." [g] Crowell was reprimanded for neglect of duty and ordered to cooperate in the future, whether he would or no, with the United States commissioners.[h] This was not all. Calhoun so far played into the hands of Campbell that he conferred upon him discretionary power to change the location of the treaty ground, and it was changed, most significantly, from Broken Arrow, in Alabama, to Indian Springs, in Georgia.

---

[a] December 23, 1824, " Miscellaneous Files," Indian Office MS. Records.

[b] American State Papers, "Indian Affairs," II : 574.

[c] American State Papers, "Indian Affairs," II : 575.

[d] Calhoun to Campbell, January 18, 1825, " Indian Office Letter Books," Series II, No. 1, pp. 309–310.

[e] " Indian Office Letter Books," Series II, No. 1, p. 375.

[f] Ibid., p. 298.

[g] Ibid., p. 300.

[h] Ibid., p. 310.

The Creeks were summoned to appear at the new treaty ground on the 7th of February.[a] Little Prince and Big Warrior refused to come themselves, but sent Poethleyoholo of Tuckaubatchee to act as their representative. Apparently his duty was to declare the present meeting unlawful, inasmuch as the McIntosh party, there predominating, had absolutely no authority to negotiate a cession, and to invite the commissioners to return three months hence to the National Council Square at Broken Arrow.[b] · Campbell, however, was determined to complete the business then and there and warned Poethleyoholo that if he and his people departed the treaty ground, as they had threatened, he should consider himself fully authorized to conclude a cession with those that remained.

Resort was had during the progress of the negotiations to the same underhand practices as had distinguished the proceedings at Broken Arrow. Campbell's brother-in-law, Colonel Williamson, seems to have been an advance agent employed to accomplish by bribery what the commissioners might possibly fail to do by treaty. On one occasion, in an endeavor to win over Interpreter Hambly (the individual who had figured so disreputably in the Seminole troubles, first as a friend of the British, then as an American spy), he boasted that he had been promised the disbursement of the Creek removal funds and would share the profits with Hambly if he would lend the commissioners his support.[c]

Under such circumstances we should scarcely expect to find that the treaty, finally negotiated, was the result of fair and square dealing. In an incomplete form,[d] it was interpreted to the council on the 12th of February and signed by the McIntosh party, certainly not by the dissenters; for very few of them were then in Indian Springs, the Cussetas and Soowagaloos having left secretly the night before. Poethleyoholo was still there, however, and is reported to have said to McIntosh, as he was in the act of affixing his name, "My Friend, you are now about to sell your country; I now warn you of the danger." When all was done, Crowell, true to his promise of cooperation,[e] signed as a witness and then prepared a formal protest

---

[a] Campbell to Crowell, January 12, 1825, American State Papers, "Indian Affairs" II: 576.

[b] "Journal of Proceedings," February 11, 1825, American State Papers, "Indian Affairs," II : 582.

[c] "Crowell's Defense," Indian Office MS. Records.

[d] Later investigations divulged that the fifth article was surreptitious. It provided for the distribution, "by the commissioners," of $200,000 of the purchase money, reputed to have been an arrangement "at the particular request" of the Indians, yet was never read or interpreted to them in council." (Crowell's Defense.) The "additional article" was not presented to the assembly until the 14th of February, and was then signed "by all the principal chiefs present." As the commissioners recorded in their journal, it affected McIntosh only. It was probably the price of his treachery since, of the two reservations for which it provided he should be compensated, one did not belong to him and the other was not worth one-fifth of the amount stipulated.

[e] Crowell to the Commissioners, February 7, 1825, "Journal of Proceedings."

to the War Department,[a] alleging that the whole proceeding of the commissioners had been contrary to the letter and to the spirit of their instructions. Although knowing this and knowing too that he had grossly misrepresented facts all along, Campbell was able to write with a clear conscience that a treaty had been concluded " with the Creek Nation Indians," [b] and again that " the attendance of chiefs was a full one, much more so than is usual when chiefs only are invited." His report to Governor Troup, February 13, 1825, was more in harmony with the facts in the case; for the assembly at Indian Springs might be what he " considered " the Creek Nation, but that certainly did not make it so. As a matter of fact, very few of the men present were chiefs, none of them were chiefs of first rank, while the representative of Little Prince and Big Warrior was a dissenter. Of the signers, McIntosh and possibly two others were the only chiefs in good standing, the rest were " underling chiefs, broken chiefs, and boys." [c]

The intense interest in Indian removal, which had revealed itself during the last few years, coupled with the consciousness that individual applications of the policy were an excitement to sectional jealousy and a ruinous expense, led Monroe to hesitate no longer in urging officially a general colonization west of the Mississippi. In his eighth annual message, therefore, he advised the adoption " of some well-digested plan " which would, while relieving the States and Territories, not be prejudicial to Indian interests.[d] Reprobating the idea of coercion, he proposed that, after the Government had extinguished the indigenous title, the eastern tribes should be invited to occupy by districts the country lying east of the Rocky Mountains. There they were not to be abandoned to their own devices, but each district was to be provided with schools and with a regular civil administration.

A week later, in the Senate, the Committee on Indian Affairs called for information respecting the number of possible emigrants and an estimate of the expense.[e] In the House, while the same proposal was being considered in committee, a resolution offered by Conway, the Delegate from Arkansas, was adopted, providing, " That the Com-

---

[a] Crowell to Calhoun, February 13, 1825, "Miscellaneous Files," Indian Office MS. Records.

[b] Campbell to Calhoun, February 16, 1825, "Miscellaneous Files," Indian Office MS. Records.

[c] In partial verification of this, note McKenney's report to President Adams, June 23, 1825, of which the following is an extract: " * * * It appears * * * that all those [presumably chiefs and headmen] who receipted for the annuity of 1824 are subscribers to one ' or other of the Treaties of 1814, 1818, and 1821, except one Pothleolo) ; and only one (McIntosh ') subscribed the late Treaty of the Indian Springs. * * *" " Indian Office Letter Books," Series II, No. 2, pp. 59–60.

[d] Richardson, II : 261.

[e] Benton to Calhoun, December 15, 1824, "Miscellaneous Files," Indian Office MS. Records.

mittee on Indian affairs be instructed to inquire into the expediency of organizing all the territories of the United States lying west of the State of Missouri and territories of Arkansas and Michigan" into an Indian Territory and of authorizing the President to adopt, at discretion, measures for colonizing all the tribes there.[a] An unexpected criticism of any such plan came from Smyth, of Virginia. In order to prevent a constant drain upon "the flower" of the eastern population, he was quite willing to limit the number of States west of the Mississippi to two tiers and to give "the Indians an unchangeable boundary beyond;" but remarked that, though the Government formed there might continue under the protection of the United States," it could not be admitted "as a part of the Confederacy." [b]

When sending in a special message on the 27th of January for a new appropriation to extinguish Indian titles, Monroe, encouraged by the friendly attitude of Congress toward his earlier proposal, took occasion to outline more fully a plan for general removal, not, however, disguising the truth that rising troubles over the Georgia compact had spurred, if not necessitated, his action.[c] In the Senate the plan was adopted by the Indian Committee "unanimously" and application made to Calhoun to draft a bill in conformity with it.[d] He did [e] so, but on the supposition that the committee had equally approved of his report which had accompanied the President's message and had provided for a rather peculiar distribution of the emigrant tribes.[f]

Calhoun's report of January 24, 1825, raises a question as to his own motive for advocating Indian removal. It will be noted that it was in contemplation to give the Indians a guaranty of perpetual possession in the new land, a thing which might mean much or little. Some of the tribes had had guaranties before, and they had meant nothing. The problem of the future would be whether one Congress, having no authority to bind its successors, could give a better pledge of security than the treaty-making power, acting under a questionable prerogative. Supposing, however, that that difficulty did not present itself to Calhoun, or, if it did, was dismissed with the reflection that an Indian guaranty might be at least as binding as the Missouri Compromise, the question remains, What was his motive? Did he, as the abolitionists claimed, plan to give the Indians a perpetual prop-

[a] " Niles' Register," XXVII: 271.

[b] Benton's "Abridgment of Debates in Congress," VIII: 211.

[c] Richardson, II: 280–283; American State Papers, "Indian Affairs," II: 541–542.

[d] Benton to Calhoun, January 28, 1825, "Miscellaneous Files," Indian Office MS. Records.

[e] Calhoun to Benton, January 31, 1825, "Indian Office Letter Books," Series II, No. 1, p. 334.

[f] "Gales and Seaton's Register," I, Appendix, pp. 57–59; American State Papers, "Indian Affairs," II : 542–544.

erty right west of Missouri and west of Lake Michigan, in order to block free-State expansion north of the interdicted line of 1820? The evidence points strongly to an opposite conclusion, or at least to an incrimination of others besides Calhoun; for, as we have seen, since 1815 there had been vague projects for converting the present State of Wisconsin into an Indian Territory. Doctor Morse specifically recommended it in 1820, and some of the New York Indians had already emigrated there. It was, therefore, not strange that the country west of Lake Michigan should have been included in Calhoun's plan. Indeed, the resolution of Conway had specifically embraced it. Moreover, years afterwards, on an occasion when there was really no object in misrepresentation, Calhoun referred [a] to the subject as though to ascribe the honor of it exclusively to Monroe. A good explanation for the introducing of the phrase, " west of the State of Missouri and Territory of Arkansas," is found in the vigorous protests made of late years by western people against a policy of relieving the older communities at the expense of the newer. It is hardly likely that it came from any conscious reference to the Missouri Compromise, especially as the slave belt west of Arkansas was to be a part of the Indian Territory.

On Washington's birthday Calhoun's bill, " for the preservation and civilization of the Indian tribes," was debated by the Senate in Committee of the Whole and ordered engrossed for a third reading.[b] It was passed on the 23d and sent to the House, but there pressure of business, as once before, must have prevented consideration. Independent action by the House on Monroe's proposal was effectually blocked by Forsyth's determination not to let the great plan of removing all the Indians retard the performance of obligations due to Georgia alone.

---

[a] Speech on the Oregon bill, Senate, January 24, 1843. Crallé, IV : 246.
[b] Gales and Seaton's Register, I : 639–645.

CHAPTER VII.

J. Q. ADAMS AND INDIAN REMOVAL.

The election of J. Q. Adams was inauspicious for Indian removal, but not because his Administration introduced any radical change in policy; quite the contrary, inasmuch as the continuity of attitude was preserved throughout. The trouble was, local prejudices of one kind or another were, for four long years, enlisted on the side of the Opposition to defeat by procrastination any measure that the President might ardently desire. Some commentators have it, that he desired Indian removal only as a bid for popular support, and that, in the very nature of things, it was impossible for a New England er to advocate it for its own sake—but that is immaterial to us. We are for the moment not so much concerned with motives as with facts, and it suffices us to know that Adams took up the work where Monroe laid it down and carried it on unflinchingly along the lines of no coercion.

Many of the disastrous events of the Tenth Presidential Administration, for instance, the Creek controversy, were precipitated at its birth and might have happened even if a more tactful man than J. Q. Adams had become the Chief Magistrate. The reception of the Indian Springs treaty in the Senate was not marked by any indication of the frauds that had attended its negotiation, although it was generally known that the Alabama Creeks had not consented to it.[a] For weeks past all Forsyth's remarks in the House had been directed toward the drawing out of an opinion approbative of treaty making with a part of a tribe, and a close observer would have concluded that his object was to forestall any criticism that might come up against Campbell and Meriwether; possibly also to prepare the War Department for a similar negotiation with the Cherokees. Moreover, Crowell's protest was on file in the Indian Office, and Crowell himself was in Washington informing Monroe and Calhoun of all that had passed. The Georgians were anxious to get the treaty in and ratified before the Eighteenth Congress adjourned,[b] but they were not quite able to manage it. It was transmitted to the Senate on the 3d of March and hastily advised and consented to.[c] President Adams pro-

---

[a] J. Q. Adams's Diary, May 20, 1825.

[b] Major Andrews's Report, August 1, 1825, Indian Office MS. Records.

[c] The Senate vote on ratification stood 38 in favor and 4 (Barton of Missouri, Branch of North Carolina, Chandler of Maine, and De Wolf of Rhode Island) against. (Harden's "Troup," p. 263, note). It is interesting to observe Barbour's name among those consenting.

claimed it on the 7th, without inquiring, perhaps out of courtesy to his predecessor, too closely into its history. The inaction was a compromise with fate, but was not long to last. Events were already happening in the South destined to force an investigation, and it came.

Included among the documents that accompanied Campbell's draft of the treaty to Washington was one bearing date January 25, 1825,[a] which ought to have convinced the Administration that all was not well in the Creek country. It was the appeal of the McIntosh party for protection. Notwithstanding, the negotiations proceeded to a finish. Then came the news of ratification and with it "sorrow and consternation" to the Upper Creeks. All along they had hoped that the President would interpose in their behalf to defeat the ends of McIntosh and Georgia. Thrown back now upon their own resources, there was nothing for them to do but to resort to desperate measures; so, after announcing that as they had sold no land, they would accept none of the money, they prepared to execute a law of their nation, prescribing capital punishment for anyone who should propose a cession in defiance of the national will.[b] So critical was the situation that before the end of March the newspapers of the country declared a Creek civil war in prospect.[c]

About this time, when it was so necessary to advance cautiously, Governor Troup developed an interest in State surveys. It first manifested itself in a request for the Federal Government to cooperate in the running of the Alabama line,[d] a thing impossible to do without disturbing the Creeks; but the President was discreet enough not to offer that as an excuse for refusal. He preferred rather to remark, as Monroe did the year before, that the running of an interstate line was not a Federal, but an interstate affair.[e] Shortly afterwards Troup made a similar request with regard to the Florida line[f] and was told that, while the same objections did not hold as in the case of Alabama, it could not be granted because there was no appropriation for it. These incidents were not calculated to increase the growth of friendly feeling between the United States and Georgia, rather the reverse.

In the meantime the governor, his interest in surveys undiminished, revolved in his own mind a plan for shortening the process of bring-

---

[a] American State Papers, "Indian Affairs," II : 579.

[b] The law was passed in a Creek council at Broken Arrow, July, 1824. Little Prince spoke of it as the law of the nation, and at ball play in August, 1824, General McIntosh proclaimed it before the assemblage. (Niles's Register, XXVIII : 333.)

[c] Niles's Register, XXVIII : 49.

[d] Letter, March 31, 1825.

[e] Barbour to Troup, April 26, 1825, "Indian Office Letter Books," Series II, No. 1, p. 467.

[f] Letter, April 13, 1825, transmitting a resolution of the Georgia legislature to the same effect.

ing the Creek ceded lands into the market. Election day was approaching and no better plan could be devised for winning votes than a display of interest in the concerns of settlers. The eighth article of the treaty of Indian Springs was as follows:[a] " Whereas the said emigrating party cannot prepare for immediate removal, the United States stipulate, for their protection against the incroachments, hostilities, and impositions of the whites, and of all others; but the period of removal shall not extend beyond the first day of September, in the year eighteen hundred and twenty-six." In consequence of this provision, Georgia was debarred from immediate entry, and so Troup had admitted in his proclamation of March 21, 1825.[b] It was not long, however, before it occurred to him that a survey did not come within the implied prohibition, particularly if the Indians were a consenting party to it; and to obtain that consent he opened up a correspondence with McIntosh. The general was a little afraid at first, and said he would be willing if the agent were.[c] Finally, on the 25th of April, he gave his unconditional consent.[d] It was the signal for his own destruction. On the 30th the enraged warriors of the opposing party surrounded his house at break of day and, as an act of penal justice, shot him down in cold blood.[e] A similar vengeance overtook Samuel Hawkins and Tustunnuggee Tomme.[f]

Here was the opportunity for which Governor Troup had so long waited. Insinuations against Agent Crowell—working, from a fear

---

[a] 7 United States Statutes at Large, p. 238.

[b] " Miscellaneous Files," Indian Office MS. Records.

[c] McIntosh to Troup, April 12, 1825, Harden's " Troup," p. 273.

[d] McIntosh to Troup, April 25, 1825, Harden's " Troup," p. 276.

[e] Niles's Register, XXVIII : 212; Letter of Col. A. J. Pickett of Alabama, descriptive of the murders; White's "Historical Collections of Georgia," pp. 170–173.

[f] Perhaps retribution would be a more fitting word to use. These men were all cognizant of the law against a further cession, cognizant also of the punishment that was to be meted out to violators of it. Crowell, in his defense to the War Department, submits the testimony of a man named Joel Bailey, who was authorized to offer $40,000 to McIntosh for his signature to the fraudulent treaty, $25,000 of it to figure as the price of the two reservations and $15,000 to be bona fide hush money, the price of his trouble. McIntosh accepted the proposition, but only on condition that he be permitted to affix his signature in his own house and not in the national square, because " he would be put to death on account of the law." The commissioners refused to agree to the change. Other affidavits testified to McIntosh's full realization of the enormity of his offense and of the inevitable consequences. His motive may have been even lower than is usually supposed, for in a burst of anger he told Nimrod Doyle that he intended to sell his country out of revenge for having been " broken as Speaker." (Crowell's Defense, Indian Office Manuscript Records.) Scarcely was the deed done before fear must have made him repent it. On the 17th of February and again on the 19th some of his fellow-conspirators conferred with Troup and begged assurance of protection should an outbreak occur. On the 20th they informed the governor of the extreme danger surrounding his cousin, and forthwith Col. Henry G. Lamar was dispatched to the Creek country with a message, threatening retaliation should any harm be done the fugitive. (Harden's " Troup " pp. 264–269.) The " hostile " Creeks seemed generally suspicious of the Georgians (Lamar's Report, March 10, 1825, Harden's " Troup " pp. 268–269), but certainly they were not to be intimidated. The danger continued as great as ever, and Chilly McIntosh personally pleaded, March 3, 1825, with his father's cousin for that father's safety. Troup promised aid, and yet, before the month was out, entered upon another project (the gaining of General McIntosh's consent to a survey of the ceded lands) which was to precipitate his relative's death, the long-deferred execution of a sentence of legal justice.

that he would retard [a] the emigration of the Creeks, for his removal—could now be resolved into implications of connivance at and instigation to murder; and the duty of setting them forth as charges before the War Department was intrusted to Chilly McIntosh, who was about to go to Washington to describe the circumstances of his father's death. Impressed by the report, Barbour ordered the suspension of the agent,[b] but held back the letter upon the receipt of news from the accused man that the real cause of trouble was Troup's determination to survey the ceded lands before the time permitted by the treaty.[c] Justice demanded an investigation, and a special officer, Maj. Timothy Andrews, was appointed to make it. His orders were explicit. With discretionary power to suspend the agent should the facts warrant it, he was to repair to the Creek Agency and, " after inquiring into the charges and applying to Governor Troup for specifications and evidence, hear and report upon Crowell's defence." [d] At the same time General Gaines was detailed for guard duty in Georgia, since, despite the assurance from the Creeks that the white people had nothing to fear,[e] Troup was ordering out the State militia for the protection of the frontier.[f]

In the interval, for reasons cited in the executive message of May 23, 1825,[g] the Georgia legislature was convened in extra session, and a joint committee of its members, with Lumpkin at their head,[h] ap-

---

[a] Troup to the Georgia Congressmen, February 15 and 17, 1825, " Crowell's Defence."

[b] Barbour to Crowell, May 17, 1825, " Indian Office Letter Books," Series II, No. 2, p. 13.

[c] Barbour to Troup, May 18, 1825, " Indian Office Letter Books," Series II, No. 2, p. 15.

[d] Barbour to Andrews, May 19, 1825, " Indian Office Letter Books," Series II, No. 2, p. 18.

[e] Niles's Register, XXVIII : 196.

[f] Troup chose to regard the slaying of McIntosh and of his two followers, really the enforcement of an article of Creek internal police, as an act of hostility against the United States and requested (letter, May 3, 1825) President Adams to order troops to the spot for the chastisement of the non-treaty party. His ungovernable temper displayed itself in all his correspondence of the time. On the 3d of May, 1825, he wrote to Joseph Marshall, " My revenge I will have. It will be such as we have reason to believe the Great Spirit will require ! Such as our Christ would not think too much ! ! " (" Examination of the Controversy between Georgia and the Creeks "), and on the 7th of June, 1825, to General Ware, " I sincerely trust, if these infuriated monsters shall have the temerity to set foot within our settled limits, you may have the opportunity to give them the bayonet freely, the instrument which they most dread and which is most appropriate to the occasion * * * " (" Georgia Journal," June 7, 1825). Meanwhile, the Creeks showed little concern for all this bluster. They were " confiding in the benevolence and justice " of the United States Government. (Letter from Mr. Compere, resident missionary in the Creek Nation, to the editors of the " Southern Intelligencer," May 10, 1825.)

[g] " Niles's Register," XXVIII : 238–40.

[h] Wilson Lumpkin was also chairman of the select committee appointed by the House to inquire, with special reference to the grievance of colonizing blacks, into the disposition, evinced of late by the Federal Government " to interfere improperly " in Georgian affairs. The report (" Niles's Register," XXVIII : 271) of the committee, indorsing the spirit of Troup's message, was decidedly rebellious in tone and excited, as did the attitude of Georgia and her governor generally, much comment abroad. (" Niles's Register," XXIX : 18, 53, 97.) The neglect of the Georgia house to call up Lumpkin's report may rightfully be regarded, as it was in Great Britain, as " a significant reproof " of Troup's conduct. (" Liverpool Advertiser," August 9, 1825.)

pointed to substantiate the suspicions against Crowell. Their procedure was altogether ex parte. Nevertheless, the governor seems to have held [a] their findings as equivalent [b] to the presentment of a true bill by a grand jury,[c] and, when Andrews arrived, demanded the immediate execution of the sentence of suspension.[d] Out of courtesy to the Georgian authorities, Andrews complied, but reluctantly, and when, in an open letter,[e] he notified the agent of what he had done, intimated that he was satisfied in his own mind that Crowell was the victim of gross calumny. Naturally enough, this letter and its manner of publication aroused the ire of Governor Troup, who, without more ado, ordered Andrews to consider his relations with the State of Georgia at an end.[f] On the 4th of July, Andrews retorted, vindicating his own conduct by denouncing that of the State.[g] A quarrel so undignified could scarcely redound to the credit of either party, and its bitterness was soon to be intensified by the disclosures of General Gaines.

The frauds connected with the treaty of Indian Springs were not to end with its negotiation. With a view to obstructing whatever designs Colonel Campbell may have had for the disposition of the $200,000 of purchase money, Crowell wrote to the War Department on the 12th of March and was told that the President, with all due regard to the stipulations of the treaty, could see no reason why the funds should not be distributed as the annuities were; that is, through the medium of the chiefs.[h] The point at issue was adroitly dodged, for Crowell and Campbell differed materially in the connotation of the word "chief," and the Department ignored the fact. It went farther and ordered, in favor of Campbell and Meriwether, an immediate requisition upon the Treasury, instructing them simultaneously to apportion the money among the chiefs according to the annuity schedule which would be furnished by Colonel Crowell. The money, being intended for the whole Creek Nation as a recompense for a cession of land belonging to the nation, was not to be devoted exclusively to the McIntosh party, but doled out, irrespective of faction, whenever a chief should manifest his willingness to emigrate.[i]

---

[a] Report, June 10, 1825.

[b] Troup to Andrews, June 20, 1825, "American State Papers," "Indian Affairs," II: 804.

[c] In the United States circuit court for Milledgeville, the grand jury, at the May term, did bring in a presentment lodging suspicion against white men, names unmentioned, as the seducers of the Indians. ("Niles's Register," XXVIII: 196.)

[d] Troup to Andrews, June 14, 1825, American State Papers, "Indion Affairs," II: 803.

[e] Andrews to Crowell, June 21, 1825, American State Papers, "Indian Affairs," II: 852.

[f] Troup to Andrews, June 28, 1825, American State Papers, "Indian Affairs," II: 807.

[g] American State Papers," "Indian Affairs," II: 807.

[h] McKenney to Crowell, March 19, 1825, "Indian Office Letter Books," Series II, No. I, p. 420.

[i] Barbour to Campbell and Meriwether, March 22, 1825, "Indian Office Letter Books," Series II, No. I, pp. 420–421.

When Gaines took up his station on the Georgia frontier, pursuant to the order of the 18th of May, he was instructed to apply to Campbell and Meriwether for the unexpended portion of this first installment.[a] He did so, but the money was not forthcoming. The reason for its detention came within the range of Major Andrews's investigations and appears to have been a prior investment in cotton and negro slaves.[b]

But to return to General Gaines, who, being sent into the Indian country " in a civil and military capacity, to investigate the causes of the disturbance—to remove the causes of discontent and to reconcile the contending parties "—came into direct contact with certain commissioners whom Governor Troup had appointed, under authority of the legislature, to collect evidence against the agent in Alabama and the Creek Nation.[c] These men were reputed to have been chosen with an eye single " to the qualifications of uprightness, integrity, and intelligence; "[d] but their actions greatly belied their character. On learning of their appointment, Colonel Crowell communicated with them, hoping to secure, by an exchange of favors, the privilege of cross-examining those witnesses testifying against him; but soon found out, to his dismay, that that was not their intention. Rumors indeed were rife that they had brought money with them with which to bribe witnesses.[e] Were that the case there was, of course, an explanation for reticence. General Gaines was intolerant of subterfuges and, when these same commissioners attempted to work upon the weaknesses of Indians with whom he had to deal, he bade them begone.[f] In this manner did he prepare to enter the same category with Andrews.

General Gaines's quarrel with Governor Troup dates, however, from his letter of the 10th of July[g] in which he inclosed a certificate, signed by William Marshall of the lower Creeks, testifying that the consent to a survey which Troup claimed to have received from General McIntosh was never agreed to in council. It is unnecessary for us to enter into the details of this dispute. It was both personal and political. Of greater moment was the effect produced by Gaines's information upon the War Department. Since the middle of May, President Adams had held several Cabinet conferences on the subject of the Creek controversy and had uniformly inclined to a just yet conciliatory policy.[h] Up to date, his aim has been to shift the

[a] Barbour to Campbell and Meriwether, May 18, 1825, " Indian Letter Books," Series II, No. 2, p. 17.

[b] " Major Andrews's Report," August 1, 1825, Indian Office MS. Records.

[c] Resolution, June 11, 1825.

[d] Message of Troup, November 26, 1825, " Niles's Register," XXIX : 203.

[e] " Major Andrews's Report," Indian Office MS. Records.

[f] " General Gaines's Report," " Miscellaneous Files," Indian Office MS. Records.

[g] American State Papers, " Indian Affairs," II : 800.

[h] " Diary," May 15, 17, 19, 20, 31 ; June 15.

responsibility for a survey from the Federal Government to Georgia and by that means to deter Troup from making it. He now ordered it to be postponed, but was met with the rejoinder that, since the legislature had authorized it,[a] it should proceed. Soon came further disclosures from General Gaines, the burden of which was that forty-nine fiftieths of the Creek Nation were opposed to the treaty of Indian Springs. Thereupon the President forbade the survey and declared his intention of referring the whole matter to Congress.[b] Troup, in turn, waited for the legislature.[c]

The several disputes with Andrews, Gaines, Barbour, and Adams had been extensively used in Georgia as campaign material, consequently the reelection of the governor in October was interpreted by himself as a complete vindication of the course which he had pursued, and his message to the legislature was a triumphant expression of past and future policy, in which the doctrine of States Rights was the dominant note. Knowing that the President intended to impeach the treaty of Indian Springs, he courted a confession of faith in its validity, and received one.[d] He was then ready for any emergency that might arise.

Toward the end of November a delegation from the upper Creeks, four of whom lived within the limits of the ceded land, arrived in Washington and paid their respects to the President.[e] They had come, they said, at the suggestion of General Gaines, "to make complaint, to tell our sorrows, to utter our grievances to our Great Father, to show that the Treaty was made by fraud, by thieves, by walkers in the night."[f] Barbour then produced an agreement which the dissenting Creeks had made with General Gaines in council at Broken Arrow, that they would make a cession of all their lands in Georgia for an equal acreage West, plus a bonus of $300,000. Poethleyoholo acknowledged the agreement, but wanted time to reflect. A later council at Tuckaubatchee, which had intrusted this mission to him and his colleagues, expected the new treaty to be made "under a clear sky." Besides, Gaines had made a mistake in saying how much land they would cede. Their people had never promised, nor were they, the delegates, instructed to take anything but the natural boundary of the Chattahoochee as the line of division between the Creek country and Georgia. Adams demurred, knowing that "that would still leave a bone of contention," and suggested

---

[a] Act of June 9, 1825, American State Papers, "Indian Affairs," II : 741.

[b] Barbour to Troup, July 21, 1825, American State Papers, "Indian Affairs," II : 809.

[c] Troup's excuse for thus waiting is given in his message of November 26, 1825. He claimed he had not weakened in his contention that Georgia had an absolute title to her own soil and jurisdiction, but he felt that it was meet that, in a strife "between states equally independent," corresponding departments should be listed against each other.

[d] Resolutions, December 23, 1825, American State Papers, "Indian Affairs," II : 741.

[e] "Diary," November 26, 1825.

[f] Talk of Poethleyoholo, November 30, 1825, "Indian Office Letter Books," Series II, No. 2, p. 272.

"laying the whole matter before Congress instead of going ahead and trying to negotiate a new treaty." [a]

On the 6th of December, the President transmitted his first annual message to Congress,[b] and promised to make the treaty of Indian Springs and later transactions in connection with it the subject of a special communication. His failure to do so, made much of by the Opposition,[c] may possibly be attributed to Clay's report in Cabinet meeting that Webster was opposed to such a proceeding on the ground that it would end in nothing.[d] Furthermore, Forsyth remarked to Barbour that he would prefer a treaty on the basis of the Chattahoochee to a recommendation to Congress to annul the treaty as fraudulent, and Meriwether admitted that there was a great convenience in having a river for a boundary.[e]

Under these circumstances, and in consideration of the fact that Gaines's aid-de-camp had corroborated Poethleyoholo's account of the promise made at Broken Arrow, negotiations were about to be resumed with the Creek delegation when Senator Cobb threatened Barbour that, if the Administration yielded the point to the Indians, Georgia would be compelled to support General Jackson.[f] Such threats were lost upon President Adams, and the negotiation went on,[g] notwithstanding the fact that the Georgia delegation, when applied to as a body, declined to make any choice between sending the treaty to Congress and negotiating for the Chattahoochee line.[h] In their opinion there was no real occasion for either course, since no good cause had yet been shown for invalidating the treaty of Indian Springs.

The story of the treaty of Washington can best be told in the light of events attending its ratification and execution.[i] Two distinct Creek delegations were in the city, but only one, Poethleyoholo's party, can be said to have had a hand in its making. The other Creeks were of the McIntosh following, and had come to assert their rights under the earlier contract. Poethleyoholo refused to let them sign the new one, as they had not been delegated to negotiate it. None the less, they consented to its terms, especially when certain provisions had, at Adams's suggestion,[j] been inserted in their favor. Their consent took the form of a written declaration,[k] independent of the treaty

[a] " Diary," December 1, 1825.

[b] Richardson, II : 306.

[c] " Gales and Seaton's Register," III : 1536.

[d] " Diary," December 7, 1825.

[e] Ibid., December 22, 1825.

[f] Ibid., December 23, 1825.

[g] Ibid., January 9, 1826.

[h] Georgia Delegation to Barbour, January 7, 1826, American State Papers, " Indian Affairs," II : 747.

[i] 7 United States Statutes at Large, 286.

[j] " Diary," January 18, 1826.

[k] " Indian Office Letter Books," Series II, No. 2, p. 388.

proper. After some slight disagreement in the Cabinet as to the
advisability of sending in to the Senate all the papers relating to
the Georgian controversy, the President deferred to the wish of
Barbour[a] and transmitted only the simple treaty, the Secretary's
report of its negotiation, and his own special message.[b] They were
at once referred to the Committee on Indian Affairs, who reported
March 17, 1826, recommending that the Senate " do not advise and
consent." On the 31st of March, Adams submitted the supplementary article which, providing (as everyone seems at the time to have
believed) for a cession of the remaining Creek lands between the
Chattahoochee and the western line of Georgia, removed the great
objection, and the same committee reported it on the 4th of April
without amendments. It was then considered in Committee of the
Whole. " Berrien wanted the first article changed so as to abrogate the Indian Springs treaty without reflecting upon its negotiation," inasmuch as the Georgia legislature had resolved upon a
vote of confidence in Campbell and Meriwether,[c] and without undoing what was already done; but his amendment to that effect was
lost. On the final question of advising and consenting to ratification, the entire Senate, with the exception of Berrien and Cobb, of
Georgia; King, of Alabama; Macon, of North Carolina; White, of
Tennessee, and Williams, of Mississippi, voted in the affirmative.[d]
Their objection was supposed to be purely constitutional,[e] the idea
being that the President and Senate were not competent to abrogate
a treaty under which vested rights had accrued; but Berrien afterwards confessed to Governor Troup that he and Cobb had voted
against the treaty because it did not contain " sufficient inducements "
for the McIntosh party to emigrate.[f]

There was yet much to be done before the treaty of Washington
could pass muster. Between the time of ratification and the Senate
consideration of the House bill appropriating money to execute the
contract, Barbour informed the chairman of the Indian Committee
in the lower branch that Poethleyoholo's delegation and their Cherokee secretaries were planning, under the peculiar wording of the
third article, to keep back for their own use a large part of the purchase money.[g] This news, being communicated to the Senate, led to
an investigation which revealed the fact that the Secretary of War
had known of their intention before the treaty was fully negotiated,
but had let the matter pass with the remark that it was their own

a " Diary," January 30, 1826.
b Richardson, II : 324–326.
c Resolutions, November 18, 1825, " Niles's Register," XXIX : 227–228.
d " Niles's Register," XXX : 256.
e " Niles's Register," XXX : 297–298.
f Berrien to Troup, April 22, 1826, American State Papers, " Indian Affairs " II :
748–749.
g Schedule, American State Papers, " Indian Affairs," II : 667.

affair and, so long as it was not made a part of the document which he was framing, he would not interfere. The southern members saw in this transaction a chance to turn the tables upon the Administration and even to excite a laugh at its expense by repeating a story which Benton told of how Barbour had rejected with scorn a proposition of his to distribute the usual presents to the Indian negotiators.[a] Barbour, however, was proof against every attack. The Senate then turned to more serious business, and offered an amendment to the appropriation bill designed to outwit the chiefs; but the House refused to concur. Eventually a committee of conference was appointed and its report, which planned to distribute the money to the " chiefs " in " full council," with slight modification, adopted.

From fear that the treaty of Washington would not accomplish so much for Creek removal as its predecessor would have done, Berrien immediately moved a resolution in the Senate to make good the deficiency.[b] The McIntosh party had persuaded him that " if sufficient inducements " were offered they would get most of their tribe to emigrate; and some of the Senators had promised that if Georgia would be satisfied not to burden the new treaty with any such provision they would give their votes for legislation to effect the same object. Such was the history of the enactment of May 20, 1826, by which $60,000 were appropriated to aid the emigrating Creeks.[c]

From first to last Governor Troup denied the power of the United States to annul the treaty of Indian Springs, and informed the President that since Georgia " in declaring its inviolability " had " already proclaimed the invalidity " of any later contract, designed to supercede it, he should proceed " to occupy the Creek lands, September 2, 1826." [d] The treaty of Washington had guaranteed possession to the Creeks until January 1, 1827; consequently, when they, through Agent Crowell, protested against the advance of the surveyors, who were running the Georgia-Alabama line through their country, Barbour sustained the objection and wrote to Troup, " It is expected that Georgia will desist from any further prosecution of the survey until it is authorized by the treaty." [e] The letter was delayed in its journey, and Troup did not answer it for nearly three weeks. He was then able to say that the alarm had come from " officious intermeddlers," since the surveyors had almost completed their work and as yet there had been no interruption whatsoever.[f]

[a] " Thirty Years' View," I : 60 ; " National Intelligencer," June 1, 1826.
[b] " Gales and Seaton's Register," II : 620.
[c] 4 United States Statutes at Large, 187.
[d] Troup to Adams, February 11, 1826, American State Papers, " Indian Affairs," II : 737.
[e] Barbour to Troup, September 16, 1826, American State Papers, " Indian Affairs," II : 744.
[f] Troup to Barbour, October 6, 1826, American State Papers, " Indian Affairs," II : 744.

One difficulty passed, another arose. When the Georgia legislature convened for its winter session, the governor announced that the treaty of Washington, though intending as much, had not secured for Georgia quite all of the Creek lands within her conventional limits; but, as the mistake had been made by the Federal authorities, he should be governed by the original intention.[a] The legislature approved his spirit, even declaring in resolutions of the 22d instant that, " in so far as the treaty of Washington had divested Georgia of any rights acquired in 1825, it was illegal and unconstitutional." [b] Thus morally supported the governor allowed the surveyors to proceed with the Alabama line beyond the western limit of the late Creek cession. It was not customary to run State boundaries through country where the native title had not been extinguished. Inferentially, then, this act of Troup's implied a surrender of the whole Creek territory lying within the limits of Georgia, which was contrary to the terms of the treaty of Washington.

The differences between the State and Federal authorities had now been brought to a square issue. The Creeks complained to Crowell and Crowell communicated with Barbour,[c] but nothing was done until news reached Washington that the Indians had arrested the progress of the surveyors and were themselves menaced by a Georgia " troop of horse." Adams at once called his Cabinet together and conferred with them on the course to pursue. Let us give the story in his own words:

Act of Congress of 30th March, 1802, consulted. Section 5 forbids surveying. Section 16 authorizes the military force of the U. S. to apprehend any person trespassing upon the Indian lands and convey him to the civil authority in one of the three next adjoining districts. Section 17 authorizes the seizure and trial of trespassers found within any judicial district of the U. S. It was proposed to order troops to the spot to apprehend the surveyors and bring them in for trial by authority of Section 16. I have no doubt of the right, but much of the expediency, of so doing.

Mr. Clay urged the necessity of protecting the rights of the Indians by force. Their rights must be protected, but I think the civil process will be adequate to the purpose. The Georgia surveyors act by authority and order of the State. To send troops against them *must* end in acts of violence. The Act of 1802 was not made for the case, and before coming to a conflict of arms, I should choose to refer the whole subject to Congress. Governor Barbour proposed sending a confidential agent to warn the Georgians against proceeding.[d]

Adams's preference for a civil redress having prevailed, Barbour instructed the United States district attorney, R. W. Habersham,[e] to

[a] Message, December 9, 1826, American State Papers, " Indian Affairs," II : 749.

[b] American State Papers, " Indian Affairs," II : 734.

[c] American State Papers, " Indian Affairs," II : 864.

[d] "Diary," January 27, 1827.

[e] Barbour to Habersham, January 30, 1827, American State Papers, " Indian Affairs," II : 864.

get without delay the proper process for arresting the surveyors and deliver it to Marshal Morel, who was to lose no time in executing it.[a] At about the same time three other letters issued from the War Department—one to Crowell,[a] cautioning the Creeks against the use of violence and promising that their rights should be respected; a second to Troup,[a] warning him that the President would employ all necessary means to perform his constitutional duty of executing a "supreme law of the land;" and a third to Lieutenant Vinton,[b] intrusting him with the special mission of endeavoring to prevent a resort to force either by the Georgians or the Indians. The reception of these letters in Georgia reacted powerfully against the Administration.[c] Habersham, considering loyalty to his State preeminent, resigned his position rather than proceed against the surveyors, and public opinion applauded.[d] The action of Troup was characteristic of the man. On the 17th of February he defied the Federal Government to do its worst.[e]

A little uncertain of his own ground, the President had in the interval decided to seek the support of Congress, and his message of the 5th of February,[f] which he himself records to have been "the most momentous" he had ever sent,[g] was referred, with accompanying documents, by both Houses to a select committee. At the head of one was Benton, of the other, Everett, and their reports of the 1st and 3d of March, respectively, were just what might have been expected. The one, without criticising the President, supported the claims of Georgia; the other unequivocally, yet in the calm, judicious spirit of Adams, with whom Everett had consulted,[h] upheld the treaty of Washington. Both advised the expediency of purchasing the remaining Indian land in Georgia.[i]

As a matter of fact, that is what the President was already attempting to do. Colonel Crowell was even then, under instructions of the 31st of January,[j] endeavoring to persuade the Creeks to make a cession. Additional orders[k] issued in April after it had been discovered that the difference between the cessions of 1825 and 1826 was only a matter "of about 192,000 acres *of pine barrens*." Crowell,

---

[a] Barbour to Morel, January 29, 1827. American State Papers, "Indian Affairs," II : 864.

[b] Ibid., p. 865.

[c] Public opinion in Georgia had already expressed itself against the treaty of Washington. (Extracts from "Georgia Journal" and "Milledgeville Recorder," reprinted in "National Intelligencer" May 27, 1826.

[d] Phillips, p. 62.

[e] Niles's Register, XXXII : 16.

[f] Richardson, II : 370–373.

[g] Diary, February 4, 1827.

[h] Diary, February 15, 1827.

[i] Gales and Seaton's Register, III : 498, 1534.

[j] "State Papers," Twentieth Congress, first session, Vol. VI, No. 238, p. 7.

[k] "Indian Office Letter Books," Series II, No. 4, p. 31.

however, could make no impression upon the Creeks, and in June came in person to Washington to report his failure.[a] Thomas Mc-Kenney was then sent on a special mission among the Southern Indians to advocate removal. In the course of time he came to the Creek agency and, after experiencing considerable opposition from Poethleyholo and his Cherokee friends,[b] secured the greater part of " the bone of contention."[c] The rest was surrendered at the beginning of the next year.[d]

The treaty of Indian Springs, although professedly made by Georgian Creeks, provided for a cession of Alabama land which went back to its Indian owners under the treaty of Washington. Alabama, therefore, advanced a claim of vested rights;[e] and, when that claim was ignored passed two acts which were a sort of anticipation of future troubles. One extended " the civil and criminal jurisdiction of the State over so much of the Creek land ceded in 1825 as lies in Alabama." The other prohibited " the Creek Indians from hunting, trapping, and fishing within the settled limits of the State." The Administration was immediately apprised of the proceeding,[f] but took no action until Senator Cobb complained of the distinction made between this and the very similar purposes of adjoining States,[g] At a loss how to answer him, Barbour consulted the President and was told to say, " The bearing of the lawful power of the Union is upon the acts of individuals, and not upon the legislation of the States." [h] Nevertheless, Barbour mildly admonished Governor Murphy that the President hoped the acts aforesaid would not be allowed to conflict with laws of the United States regulating Indian affairs,[i] and a controversy was averted by the respect shown for a decision rendered in the United States district court for Alabama that such legislation was unconstitutional and therefore null and void.

After the treaty of 1826, the Creeks were in a fair way to emigrate. Georgia had virtually won her point in the conflict with Adams, and yet she had done the cause of Indian removal, considered as a humane and judicious measure, an irreparable injury. Those in the North who before had been disposed to advocate it out of an honest regard for the general welfare of both races were now opposed, the more so because, as time went on, it became evident that Georgia was deter-

[a] Diary, June 20, 1827.

[b] McKenney to Folsom and Leflore, December 13, 1827, " Indian Office Letter Books," Series II, No. 4, pp. 177–178.

[c] 7 United State Statutes at Large, p. 307.

[d] Phillips, p. 65.

[e] Resolutions of Alabama Legislature, January 14, 1826 ; Letter of Governor Murphy, American State Papers, " Indian Affairs," II : 644.

[f] Diary, February 8, 1827.

[g] February 23, 1827, " Miscellaneous Files," Indian Office MS. Records.

[h] Diary, February 26, 1827.

[i] Barbour to Murphy, March 2, 1827, " Indian Office Letter Books," Series II, No. 3, p. 415.

mined not to give the policy a general application until her own territory had been disencumbered; that is to say, she persistently sacrificed the great and benevolent plan of colonizing all the Indians to the inordinately selfish desire of immediate personal relief. She diverted every suggestion for general removal into the narrow channel of Creeks and Cherokees. Never once, until the great debate of 1830, did she permit a full discussion of the question at issue. She clogged nearly every resolution that called for an inquiry into the expediency of Indian emigration with a manifestly irrelevant reference to the compact of 1802; and, all the while, she antagonized the North by her indiscretions, of which threats of coercion were the most prominent. From one view point, however, she really advanced the cause of removal, such as it was, inasmuch as she so continually agitated the question that the nation could not forget it, and sister States, not to be behindhand where benefits were to be secured, united their complaints with hers, thus making it appear to be a more or less universal demand.

The controversy with the Creeks was not the only event during these years that established a line of connection with Indian removal. Nothing but disaster had resulted from the concentration of the Florida tribes. Indeed, it can hardly be said that they ever were concentrated, at least, not until after the northern line of their original reserve had been twice extended,[a] in order to give them a "reasonable" amount of tillable land. Their period of sufferings began, however, with the attempted concentration which the Government expected to accomplish in short order by assembling them in one or two large bodies and marching them with a military escort down to the desolate country assigned them north of Charlotte Harbor. The Indians came in large numbers, drawn thither by the hope of receiving plenty of free rations, as promised by the treaty. They were disappointed; for Gadsden, aiming to please an economical Administration and to ward off the criticism of a still more economical Congress, had sent in an estimate of the amount of rations that would be needed that was altogether too small. Moreover, through some irregular practices of Governor Duval, the deficiency was exaggerated[b] and the Indians roamed about and waited—hungry.

An opening experience such as this was not likely to increase the confidence of the Seminoles in the justice of the General Government. Some of them would go no farther; some went on, saw the country, and turned back; others went on likewise and stayed—to suffer. They had positively nothing to live upon, for the "sustenance" which the United States had promised them for one year, was all exhausted before they went down. It was of no use for them to wander back to

---

[a] "Indian Land Cessions in the United States" p. 705.
[b] American State Papers, "Indian Affairs," II: 614–644.

their old haunts, the title had passed to the white people, and they were homeless, except for that barren tract north of Charlotte Harbor. None the less, it was very certain that, if the Florida politicians had thought to dispose of them forever by shutting them up in the swamps, they were much mistaken. Famishing at last, many of them skulked around the settlements, stealing when they could and, when provoked, murdering; yet as a body they were not hostile. Such depredations as were committed were the acts not of tribes, but of individuals reduced to desperate straits, vagabonds by necessity.[a]

Both Florida and Georgia had a grudge against the Seminoles, mainly because now, as formerly, they were supposed to harbor fugitive slaves, and Governors Duval and Troup were only too ready to order out the militia against them in the winter of 1827. At about the same time the Florida legislative council memorialized Congress for their removal.[b] A year previous the subject of their destitution and its causes had been thoroughly investigated in Congress, with the result that $20,000 had been appropriated for their relief.[c] It was not enough. Besides, so unproductive was their country that the prospects were, they would be " charity patients " of the Government until 'they disappeared. The suggestion to remove was made to them as soon as the President had assured himself that their condition was " truly lamentable," and that they had a positive " horror " of the country allotted them in the peninsula. He did it in all kindness, especially as the Department of War had good reason to suspect that they had been actually terrified into a compliance with the treaty of Camp Moultrie.[d] At first it was contemplated to get them to accompany the Creeks,[e] an idea that had to be abandoned when Campbell's success seemed so uncertain.

In lieu of immediate removal the Seminoles were accommodated with the Big Hammock,[f] but, failing even there to find subsistence,

---

[a] McKenney to Walton, June 20, 1825, " Indian Office Letter Books," Series II, No. 2, pp. 53–54. " Niles's Register," XXXI : 369.

[b] " Niles's Register," XXXI : 365.

[c] Act of March 22, 1826, 4 United States Statutes at Large, p. 194.

[d] McKenney to Duval, Gadsden, and Segui, December 15, 1825, " Indian Office Letter Books," Series II, No. 2, p. 313.

[e] McKenney to Barbour, November 28, 1825, ibid., p. 258.

[f] In the spring of 1826 " Niles's Register," XXX : 259–260) a Seminole delegation came to Washington. In answer to their request for " good " land, President Adams offered to let them have the Big Hammock as a loan; but they were too sharp to accept readily. They wanted a piece of land from which they would never have to move again. They were told that that could only be west of the Mississippi. They did not want to go there. It was a strange place. They denied hiding the runaway slaves, and instead accused the white people of stealing theirs. They did not care to compete in the matter of education, for they were too far behind the Europeans to begin with. All they asked was to be left alone. They gave a very ancient origin to the white man's duplicity, and, at the same time, explained the source of his superior knowledge. Long ago an old blind man promised a book to the representative of the race that should first kill a deer. The white man killed a sheep, and the blind man, not detecting the difference, gave him the book and taught him to read. Later on the red man came in with a deer, but he was too late.

continued to overrun the country, and notice was taken of the fact by the grand jury of the superior court of East Florida. That and other things like it ushered the matter into Congress, and the President was asked to furnish information.[a] Barbour reported that one of two things must be done—the Indians removed to a more productive country or supplied regularly with provisions.[b] The President preferred removal, and Joseph White, the Delegate from Florida, was permitted unofficially to offer a district north of Arkansas and west of Missouri.[c] Before Colonel White could leave Washington, the Florida legislature passed an act providing for the chastisement of such Indians as refused to stay on their own territory. The Secretary deprecated the deed, knowing the proud Seminoles would never submit to an indignity of the kind " without seeking revenge," and expressed a hope that " their present miserable and perishing condition may induce in the citizens of Florida dispositions of forbearance and kindness, and especially as there is reason for believing they will soon be relieved from them altogether." White interviewed the Indians May 24, 1827, but nothing resulted. They refused even to send out an exploring party,[d] but he did not despair, not though Agent Humphreys was suspected of counteracting his influence. On the contrary, he communicated from time to time with the War Department, urging a renewal of the offer. Finally the new Secretary, Peter B. Porter, had to admit that lack of funds was the insuperable obstacle.[e] When Congress met, therefore, Colonel White moved an inquiry into the expediency of a special appropriation, but Congress was waiting for Andrew Jackson.

Having bestirred himself to make things uncomfortable for the Creeks and Seminoles, it would have been strange if Governor Troup had left the Cherokees in peace. Soon after the consummation of the treaty of Indian Springs, John Forsyth, at his request, asked for a similar negotiation with Path Killer's faction, who had some time since applied through General Jackson for an exchange.[f] Ross, Lowry, and Hicks, being then in Washington, were asked what they thought about it and expressed their disapproval[g] so strongly that the President, mindful of the instructions to Campbell against contracting with a part of a tribe only, was obliged to reject Forsyth's proposal;[h] but he did it tactfully by assuring the Georgians that he

[a] House resolution, January 5, 1826.

[b] Barbour to the chairman of the Committee on Indian Affairs, House of Representatives, January 30, 1827.—" Indian Office Letter Books," Series II, No. 3, 346.

[c] Barbour to White, February 26, 1827, ibid., p. 409.

[d] Niles's Register, XXXII : 291.

[e] Porter to White, July 11, 1828 ; McKenney to Gadsden, August 1, 1828, " Indian Office Letter Books," Series II, No. 5.

[f] Forsyth to Barbour, March 9, 1825, " Cherokee Files," Indian Office MS Records.

[g] Barber to Forsyth, March 23, 1825, " Indian Office Letter Books," Series II, No. 1, p. 423.

[h] McKenney to Barbour, March 11, 1825, ibid., pp. 397–398.

was desirous of executing the compact of 1802 and in full accord "with the policy recommended by Mr. Monroe to Congress at their last session on the subject of a general removal of the Indians to the West of the Mississippi."[a] Troup was vexed, but he bided his time.

Just in proportion as the Georgian demands took on a more decided form the Cherokees became politically more capable of resistance, and yet, in the end, the very thing that they fancied would render them invulnerable proved their weak point of attack. In the summer of 1826, they had a serious dispute with Troup over his pretended right to prospect for a canal through their territory; and, although the Federal Government supported their view of the case, they deemed it prudent to prepare for future aggressions. Wise in their day and generation they saw that the strongest argument for removal was their own adherence to primitive customs, which made it appear that they were unprogressive, or, if you will, uncivilized, and they resolved to disabuse the world of that idea. It was not enough to have their own alphabet, their own printing press, their own churches and schools, their own laws, regulating public and private relations, they must have a republican form of government. But how to get it was the question. An opportunity soon came in the death of Path Killer, the leader of the nomads, whose place the other chiefs resolved not to fill, but to vacate their own and call a constitutional convention.

In 1820 the Cherokee country had been laid off into districts, so that the materials were all ready for the election of delegates, authorized in June, 1827, by a resolution of the national council. The election of July 1, 1827, was "warm and closely contested in some districts,"[b] but on the 4th—most revered of dates to an American—the delegates met in constituent assembly at New Echota and effected the change which, intended for their salvation, was, by a strange perversity of fate, to prove their ruin. The constitution, there drafted and so closely modeled upon that of the United States as to be, as far as it went, a reproduction, was ratified by the nation before the end of the month, and a new era of Cherokee history then began.[c] The movement was revolutionary, yet when John Ross, his Scotch blood all aglow with the enthusiasm of a righteous cause, exchanged his chieftainship for a presidency, little did he think that, in this supreme imitation of a modern ideal, Georgia was to find her great support; but so it was. Here, by a very free construction of the constitution of 1787, was an open violation of its fourth article.[d]

---

[a] Barbour to Forsyth, March 23, 1825, ibid., p. 423.

[b] "Niles's Register," XXXII : 255.

[c] "Niles's Register," XXXIII : 214.

[d] Art IV, sec. 3, c. i.: "New States may be admitted by the Congress into this Union, but no new State shall be formed or erected within the Jurisdiction of any other State * * * without the Consent of the Legislatures of the States concerned as well as of the Congress."

Georgia saw in this formulation of a fundamental law an intent of the Cherokees to perpetuate their existence as a distinct community within, saving the past cessions, what were approximately their ancient and her chartered limits. It was not to be tolerated. She looked for sympathy to the Federal Government and gained from one of its officers a suggestion of what her own policy should be.[a] By a law, assented to December 26, 1827, she enacted [b] that a certain portion of the Cherokee land should, for purposes of criminal jurisdiction,[c] be annexed to the counties of Carroll and De Kalb. The day following, resolutions [d] were adopted indicative of her indignation at what she chose to call the unfaithfulness of the Federal Government in not adhering to the compact of 1802. These were duly communicated to the Senate,[e] but not before the House had instructed its Judiciary Committee,[f] and later on its Indian Committee,[g] to inquire into the circumstances of the new Cherokee republic and to report upon the expediency of arresting its design. Late in February and early in March, the House considered [h] the advisability of calling upon the President for illustrative material, and there the matter ended, except that the Indian appropriation bill for that year contained a specific grant of $50,000 for carrying into effect the compact of 1802.[i]

The Department of War, under conditions to be described hereafter, had just concluded a treaty of exchange and perpetual limits with the Arkansas Cherokees,[j] whereby inducements were held out to the Eastern to emigrate, among whom, as negotiations in the usual mode were presumed to be no longer possible,[k] and, indeed, not desired by Senator Cobb,[l] a confidential agent, Capt. James Rogers, was sent to " explain to them the kind of soil, climate, and the prospects that await them in the West, and to use, in his discretion, the best methods to induce the Indians residing within the Chartered limits of Georgia to emigrate * * *."[m] The choice

---

[a] McKenney in reporting to Barbour the first information of the Cherokee purpose, February 20, 1827, said, " I think it much to be regretted that the idea of *Sovereignty* should have taken such deep hold of these people. It is not possible for them to erect themselves into a state of such independence and a separate and distinct Government, and the sooner they are enlightened on the subject I think the better. The most they can ever hope for if they retain their possessions within the States, is to hold them under the laws of the States as Citizens * * *." (" Indian Office Letter Books," Series II, No. 3, p. 390.)

[b] Niles's Register," XXXV : 41–42.

[c] A law of the previous year had debarred persons of Indian blood from appearing as witnesses in Georgia courts of justice. Ibid.

[d] "Acts' of Georgia Assembly," 1827, p. 249.

[e] Niles's Register," XXXIII : 406.

[f] Gales and Seaton's Register, IV, Part 1, p. 914.

[g] Ibid., p. 925.

[h] " Niles's Register," XXXIV : p. 45.

[i] Act of May 9, 1828, 4.United States Statutes at Large, 300.

[j] May 6, 1828, 7 United States Statutes at Large, 311.

[k] McKenney to Porter, July 9, 1828, " Indian Office Letter Books," Series II, No. 5, p. 33.

[l] McKenney to Montgomery, July 22, 1828, ibid., p. 47.

[m] Same to same, May 27, 1828, ibid., No. 4, p. 466.

of Rogers was unfortunate.   He was himself a half-breed Cherokee
and carried with him, into Georgia, " scrip " which " was designed
merely as the sanction of the Department to such steps as he might
esteem it best to take in impressing his Countrymen with the advantages that awaited them in the exchange of homes."[a]   As for
himself, he was to be paid according to the worth of his services,
$500 down and $500 more if he succeeded.   Thus liberally supplied
in fact and in prospect, he indulged his appetite for drink, became
intoxicated, and the chances were he would remain so.[b]   Another
half-breed was soon associated with him, but together they made
little progress.   Mitchell, of Tennessee, who was interested in the
project because his own State would profit by it incidentally, complained that there was not a free enough use of money, but McKenney thought the strong box had best be guarded.[c]   Soon came a report
that the Indians in the outlying districts were starving, and the
Government added that fact to its list of inducements.[d]   Little by
little the common men of the tribe professed a willingness to go, but
were held back by their chiefs, who in general council at New
Echota, October 13, 1828, ably disposed of the Georgia claim;[e]
seemingly all to no purpose; for McKenney, not long after, advised
Porter to have a military force in readiness to protect the emigrants
against their own kin.[f]   Georgia, meanwhile, was getting impatient,
and decided, upon Governor Forsyth's advice,[g] to pass a law enacting that on and after June 1, 1830,[h] the Cherokee country was in all
respects to be subject to her exclusive jurisdiction.

During the last year of Monroe's Presidency, conditions in the
West enabled the Department of War to take initiatory steps toward
removing one very serious difficulty in the way of Indian colonization.   More than once, as already noted, removal had had a set-
back through the inability of the Government to offer any unen-
cumbered western lands for exchange.   The Quapaw and Osage
cessions of 1818 had proved wholly inadequate, the supply of grants
was soon exhausted, and to get more it would be necessary to treat
with the two Dacotah tribes—the indolent Kaws and the fierce
Osages.   The man for the work was Gen. William Clark.

Ever since 1818, Indian emigrants from the North had been forcing
their way into southwestern Missouri, attracted there, just as the
southern wanderers were to Arkansas, by the desire to be near their
old neighbors.   Some of them had come under treaty stipulations,

---

[a] McKenney to Hon. J. C. Mitchell, July 10, 1828, ibid., No. 5, p. 34.
[b] McKenney to Porter, July 26, 1828, ibid., p. 54.
[c] McKenney to Mitchell, August 23, 1828, ibid., p. 95.
[d] McKenney to Montgomery, August 26, 1828, ibid., p. 101.
[e] " Niles's Register," XXXV : 198–199.
[f] December 1, 1828, " Indian Office Letter Books," Series II, No. 5, p. 214.
[g] Message, November 4, 1828, " Niles's Register," XXXV : 221–224.
[h] Act of December 20, 1828, Dawson's " Compilation of Georgia Laws," p. 198.

many voluntarily. In 1824 they were said to number about eight thousand souls and more were coming.[a] Naturally the young State was not at all pleased, and lost no time in representing to the Government how shortsighted was the policy that expected to find a " permanent home " for the Indians within her limits. Why should she be any more content to have the tribes as " fixtures " than Illinois or Georgia? A possible way of gaining relief had seemed to open up within a few months of her admittance to statehood but nothing had been done. The facts were these:

Around Cape Girardeau were certain valuable lands, claimed under Spanish grant by the Shawnees and Delawares, which Governor Clark proposed to purchase by the method of exchange,[b] supposing the Osages and Kaws could be induced to relinquish, for the purpose, a portion of their extensive hunting grounds in the trans-Missouri region,[c] where it might also be possible to place all the northwestern emigrants.[d] Even if Missouri were willing, the southwestern section of the State, out of which Clark had carved the Kickapoo and Delaware reservations, could not be expected to accommodate very many tribes. It was not even enough to recompense the Shawnees, especially as they hoped to reunite all their scattered bands and collect once more on a single tract. An equivalent for Ohio and Cape Girardeau lands combined would have to be found somewhere else. Lack of funds prevented in 1820 an immediate negotiation with the Dacotahs, but the idea was not forgotten. David Barton and Duff Green independently revived it late in 1822,[e] and again Calhoun pleaded poverty.

All through these years, Missourians in Congress never lost an opportunity to protest against saddling their State with emigrant Indians, and, in the Senate, from his position as chairman of the Committee on Indian Affairs, Thomas Benton was able to connect in the minds of his colleagues the two schemes of relieving Missouri and negotiating for a cession with the Kaws and Osages,[f] the one being a concomitant of the other. Such a connection is what actually did happen eventually, but it came about independently of legislative action.

In February, 1825, John Lewis (Quoit-awy-pied), an Ohio Shawnee,[g] represented to the Government that all the northwestern tribes were anxious for removal and wished to discuss the matter with a

---

[a] " State Papers," Eighteenth Congress, first session, Vol. IV, No. 56.

[b] Calhoun to Clark, April 24, 1820, " Indian Office Letter Books," Series I, D, p. 410.

[c] Same to Same, July 28, 1820, ibid, p. 475.

[d] Duff Green to Calhoun, December 9, 1821, " Miscellaneous Files," Indian Office MS. Records.

[e] " Indian Office Letter Books," Series I, E, p. 329 ; Duff Green to Calhoun, December 4, 1822, " Miscellaneous Files," Indian Office MS. Records.

[f] Committee Report, May 14, 1824, American State Papers, " Indian Affairs," II : 512.

[g] " Miscellaneous Files," Indian Office MS. Records.

Government agent at a great meeting which was to be held at Wapaghkonetta, Ohio, the following month. General Cass was sent to confer with them and, at the same time, informed that the Shawnees of Missouri were willing to have their Ohio brethren unite with them wherever they (the former) might be located.[a] Simultaneously General Clark was instructed that if, in order to accommodate the Shawnees, it were expedient to procure a cession from the Osages, he would be duly empowered to negotiate.[b] Accordingly, on the 15th of March he was commissioned,[c] under a charge of strictest economy, since there was no special appropriation for it, "to treat, should you find it necessary, with the Osage and Kansas Indians, with the view of procuring an extinguishment of their titles to land upon which to locate the Shawnees and any other tribes who may be disposed to join them from the East of the Mississippi.[d]

The Wapaghkonetta meeting, from which so much had been expected,[e] was a failure.[f] It turned out that John Lewis was an Indian absolutely without credit in his own nation,[g] and the assembly would have nothing to say on the subject of removal. Clark's double mission in the West was more successful. He wisely began with the Kaws and Osages and brought matters to a conclusion on the 10th of August. Separate treaties were negotiated; but, for the purpose in hand, the Osage was the more important of the two.[h] The cession for which it provided was immense, covering all the Osage claim between the Canadian and Kansas rivers except a comparatively small reservation extending across the southern part of the present State of Kansas from a point 25 miles west of the Missouri boundary, presumably, to the old United States line. The Kaw cession was smaller,[i] but came in very conveniently later on, when the trans-Missouri region was definitely set apart as an Indian Territory.

Now that the crowning obstacle in the way of Indian colonization had been removed, it became an interesting question whether the Administration would avail itself of the opportunity. As far as Adams personally was concerned, the controversy in Georgia was probably doing more harm than good. Removal, after all that had occurred and was occurring, would look too much like an abject surrender to

---

[a] McKenney to Cass, March 9, 1825, "Indian Office Letter Books," Series II, No. 1, p. 395.

[b] McKenney to Clark, March 9, 1825, ibid, pp. 394–395.

[c] Benton, in his "Thirty Years' View," I: 28–29, ascribes to himself the honor of instructing General Clark to negotiate with the Kaws and Osages.

[d] Barbour to Clark, March 15, 1825, "Indian Office Letter Books," Series II, No. 1, p. 405.

[e] "Niles's Register," XXVIII: 49.

[f] Ibid., p. 260.

[g] John Johnston to McKenney, April 11, 1825, "Miscellaneous Files," Indian Office MS. Records; McKenney to Cass, June 1, 1825, "Indian Office Letter Books," Series II, No. 2, p. 44.

[h] 7 United States Statutes at Large, 268–270.

[i] Ibid., 270–272.

State tyranny for it to be generally advocated in the earnest spirit of Monroe. The President's discussions with his Cabinet show, however, that he was willing to enlist himself on the side of any project that would best subserve the true interests of both races.

The successive changes in Barbour's ideas are very instructive. In the early part of his career as Secretary of War he seems to have vacillated between indorsing Monroe's plan of removal by tribes and Crawford's plan of incorporation. The question of choice perplexed him and so, October 3, 1825, he requested McKenney to report on the probable and ultimate consequences of the two projects.[a] Evidently he had not yet realized how intense and universal was the desire to get rid of the Indians. McKenney reported November 30;[b] but Barbour had already made up his mind and had submitted a plan of incorporation to the President.[c] Weeks passed and he was inflexible, though Adams and Clay both tried to convince him of its impracticability.[d] It was soon to be brought to a square issue; for, early in the new year, the House Committee on Indian Affairs sought his advice.

The bill for the preservation and civilization of the Indians, passed by the Senate the previous session, had not been entirely lost; but, as heretofore remarked, had been pushed aside in the House by other business after having been referred to the standing committee and by them amended. It was now to be revived and sent for suggestive comments to the Secretary of War.[e] Barbour considered the matter carefully and then submitted an elaborate report,[f] accompanied by the outline of a new bill, the most prominent feature of which was removal, not by tribes as formerly, but by individuals.[g]

Taken as a whole, the report shows how far above the majority of his contemporaries Barbour was in his conception of justice. He read the times aright, did not mince matters or cater to local preju-

---

[a] "Miscellaneous Files," Indian Office MS. Records.

[b] American State Papers, "Indian Affairs," II : 585.

[c] J. Q. Adams's Diary, November 21, 1825.

[d] Ibid., December 22, 1825.

[e] John Cocke to Barbour, January 11, 1826, "Miscellaneous Files," Indian Office MS. Records.

[f] Gales and Seaton's Register, Vol. II, Part 2, Appendix, pp. 40–42.

[g] Among the "Miscellaneous Files," of this year I found a bill in manuscript, but have not been able certainly to determine whether it was the one Barbour sent or the one he received. I rather incline to the latter opinion for two reasons: First, its presence in the "Miscellaneous Files," where letters that came in were preserved, and its absence from the letter books where all outgoing letters and reports were recorded; secondly, Barbour says he sent the "project" of a bill. This is a bill complete. If it be the one Barbour received, then the credit of originating the plan of removal by *individuals* as distinct from removal by *tribes* belongs probably to some unknown member of the Eighteenth Congress. "Section 4. And be it further enacted, That in all cases, where the proper authority of any tribe may decline entering into stipulations respecting the removal of such tribe, it shall be the duty of the Commissioner or Commissioners to enter into such arrangements with any individual of the tribe, and under the directions of the President to make the necessary provision for the removal of such individuals. But the arrangements with such Individual shall in no case affect the rights of the tribe."

dices, but frankly criticized the Government for its existing policy toward the Indians. " Missionaries," said he, " are sent among them to enlighten their minds, by imbuing them with religious impressions. Schools have been established by the aid of private, as well as public donations, for the instruction of their youths. They have been persuaded to abandon the chase—to locate themselves, and become cultivators of the soil—implements of husbandry and domestic animals have been presented them, and all these things have been done, accompanied with professions of a disinterested solicitude for their happiness. Yielding to these temptations, some of them have reclaimed the forest, planted their orchards, and erected houses, not only for their abode, but for the administration of justice, and for religious worship. And when they have so done, *you* send *your* Agent to tell them they must surrender their country to the white man, and re-commit themselves to some new desert, and substitute as the means of their subsistence the precarious chase for the certainty of cultivation. The love of our native land is implanted in every human bosom, whether he roams the wilderness, or is found in the highest stage of civilization. * * * We have imparted this feeling to many of the tribes by our own measures. Can it be matter of surprise, that they hear, with unmixed indignation of what seems to them our ruthless purpose of expelling them from their country, thus endeared? They see that our professions are insincere—that our promises have been broken; that the happiness of the Indian is a cheap sacrifice to the acquisition of new lands; and when attempted to be soothed by an assurance that the country to which we propose to send them is desirable, they emphatically ask us, what new pledges can you give us that we shall not again be exiled when it is your wish to possess these lands? It is easier to state, than to answer this question. A regard to consistency, apart from every other consideration, requires a change of measures. Either let him retain and enjoy his home, or, if he is to be driven from it, abstain from cherishing illusions we mean to disappoint, and thereby make him feel more sensibly the extent of his loss. * * * "

The points in Barbour's project were five and may as well be given in his own words:

First, The country West of the Mississippi, and beyond the States and Territories, and so much on the East of the Mississippi as lies West of Lakes Huron and Michigan is to be set apart for their exclusive abode.

Secondly, Their removal as individuals, in contradistinction to tribes.

Thirdly, A Territorial Government to be maintained by the United States.

Fourthly, If circumstances shall eventually justify it, the extinction of tribes, and their amalgamation into one mass, and a distribution of property among the individuals.

Fifthly. It leaves the condition of those that remain unaltered.

The logical outcome of Barbour's plan would have been the collocation of all the tribes in a compact mass with tribal lines obliterated; and, by and by, the erection of a great Indian State in the Union.[a] Was it feasible? Congress evidently thought not, although the House considered it to the extent of inquiring the probable cost of the venture as compared with that of the then present system.[b] We shall hear of it again in connection with Isaac McCoy.

In the second session of the Nineteenth Congress the subject of removal came up very early,[c] and resulted in a discussion as to the remaining obstacles to removal. There was one that was very serious. It had not taken the emigrant Indians long to find out that there was no certainty of tenure in their new lands. Both Choctaws and Cherokees had experienced it in a forcible manner and were deterred from general emigration in consequence. The fault lay with the Government. Without noticing the breakers ahead, it had designed to place these two southern tribes wholly or in part within the limits of Arkansas, upon land where white people had already " squatted.". This was flying in the very face of a dangerous experience. A more unstatesmanlike policy could not have been conceived. However, in the case of the grant to the Choctaws, the Government promised, through its commissioner, Andrew Jackson, that it would remove the settler, who had really no right there anyway. Local influence proved too strong, the Indian too weak, and it did not do so. As a result, the Choctaws were practically compelled, in 1825, to retire west of the Arkansas line.[d] It was the same way with the Cherokees, although they managed to cling to their treaty rights a little longer.

Under article 5 of the treaty of 1817, the Cherokees were assigned a tract of country, the eastern line of which began at Point Remove on the upper bank of the Arkansas River and ran northeastward to White River; the western was not defined and could not be until the exact acreage of the cessions upon which it depended had been determined; but, not liking to be kept in ignorance of their exact claim,

---

[a] As narrated in an earlier chapter, the idea was by no means a new one. The Revolutionary fathers may possibly have speculated about something of the kind when they negotiated and confirmed the treaties of Fort Pitt and Hopewell, 1778 and 1785, respectively. By the sixth article of the former. (7 United States Statutes at Large, 14), the contracting parties agreed that, if mutual interests demanded and Congress approved, Indian tribes friendly to the United States should be invited to form a State, of which the Delawares should be the recognized head, and join the contemplated confederacy of the old Thirteen. By the twelfth article of the latter (ibid., p. 20) the Cherokees were given the right to send a deputy to the Confederate Congress. It is conjectual what would have been the status of this Indian representative had he ever ventured to take his seat. Fortunately, perhaps, for American national equanimity, neither the Delawares nor the Cherokees ever presumed to claim any political privileges under the respective clauses of the treaties mentioned.

[b] Cocke's Report to the House, May 20, 1826, Amer. State Papers, "Indian Affairs," II:667.

[c] Gales and Seaton's Register, III: 537.

[d] 7 United States Statutes at Large, 234.

the Cherokees in 1822 asked to have it marked. Calhoun could not very well refuse the request, so he made, with the help of the southern governors, whose states were involved, a rough guess at the amount of land which the Cherokees had ceded in 1817 and 1819. He then instructed Governor Miller, of Arkansas, to lay off a tract equal to one-third of it.[a] That done, he was again waited upon by the Cherokees. The tract was too small, was not of the right shape, and did not include the outlet which the Government had verbally promised. Nothing would satisfy them but an actual survey of the eastern lands, especially as Governor Miller was intent upon giving them as little as possible. Then there came up the awkward question of the outlet. From the time of its cession by the Osages, it had been known as Lovely's Purchase. The Cherokees had no written title to it, and settlers took advantage of that fact to creep in and occupy it. Things went on from bad to worse until the Government was obliged to treat with the Cherokees for their removal from Arkansas. The negotiations were begun in 1825,[b] but were not concluded until 1828. The Cherokees were then reduced to make their second removal. Was it any wonder that their brethren in the East held aloof from treaty makers?

Late in the summer of 1827, as has been already remarked, Thomas L. McKenney, chief of the Indian Bureau, was sent on a mission through the Southern States in the special interest of removal. He came back fully convinced that three at least of the great tribes would emigrate if only they could be sure of what the Government intended to do for them and that it was acting in good faith. Barbour pleaded again for the adoption " of a general system," [c] and all the winter Isaac McCoy lobbied for an Indian Territory—for just such a one as a House resolution of December 17th provided.[d] State jealousy again intervened. Georgia would have nothing to do with removal unless her Indians were specifically mentioned, and Mississippi could see no reason for including Creeks and Cherokees who did not want to remove in a bill intended to aid Choctaws and Chickasaws who did. With divided energies, the Government could do nothing except provide in the old irregular fashion for special tribes and special sections.

The last annual report proceeding from the Department of War during Adams's Administration was transitional in its nature. It was to constitute a bridge between two policies diametrically opposed—the voluntary removals of Monroe and of Adams and the coercive of Jackson. Barbour had left the Cabinet and his place had

---

[a] Calhoun to Miller, March 4, 1823, " Indian Office Letter Books," Series I, E, p. 396.
[b] Barbour to Izard, April 16, 1825, Ibid., Series II, No. 1, p. 450.
[c] Report, November 26, 1827, " Gales and Seaton's Register," IV, Part 2, Appendix, p. 2789.
[d] " Gales and Seaton's Register," IV, Part 1, p. 820.

been taken by Peter B. Porter, of New York. That was enough to account for the change without ascribing any base political motive to the President. The year before, a joint committee of the Georgia legislature had reported against the civilization of the Indians because its tendencies were to make them opposed to emigration.[a] Porter's suggestions were in the same vein. He advised withdrawing all national support from Indian missionary establishments in the East and expending it in the West. The missionaries, argued he, are personally interested in keeping the Indians where they are and they, therefore, counteract the influence of Government agents. Aside from this fact the report of December 2, 1828,[b] is interesting because of its anticipation of very recent methods, such as the sort of reservation system that prevailed in the West, viz, a tract in common, and tracts in severalty with restricted alienation. In all other respects it followed Barbour's and was just as ineffective as far as Congress was concerned.

---

[a] " Niles's Register," XXXV : 292.
[b] " Gales and Seaton's Register," V, Appendix, pp. 7–10.

16827—08——24

THE REMOVAL BILL AND ITS MORE IMMEDIATE CONSEQUENCES.

Though J. Q. Adams left it to other men to advocate officially Indian removal, there is no question that he was in sympathy with the measure. Why, then, did the Congresses of his day never quite get to the point of passing a bill that would legitimatize exchange on a large scale?[a] Was it because the anti-Indian politicians lived in hopes of securing a greater triumph under his successor? There was much of the bully in Andrew Jackson's make-up and his dealings with the Indians had always been coercive. Consequently, the South and West had every reason to expect a change of tactics as soon as he came into power. Strange, however, to relate, the Indians likewise looked for something from him[b]; for was not justice his cardinal doctrine?

Within a fortnight after his inauguration Jackson showed his true colors, and the Indian hopes were blighted. On the 23d of March he personally addressed the Creeks, through their agent, pointing out the necessity of removal.[c] A little later, April 18, Secretary Eaton talked in the same strain to a Cherokee deputation.[d] Both tribes were given distinctly to understand that the United States could not and would not interfere with the legitimate authority of a State within her own limits. There was no remedy for such except removal, and if they wanted a home that they could call their own they must go West, for there the President could guarantee that the soil should be theirs "as long as the trees grow and the waters run."[e] The Indians were "incredulous" that such sentiments could proceed from their "Great Father,"[f] so, to convince

---

[a] Adams's Administration was open to attack from his enemies because of the practice that had grown up of negotiating treaties of exchange without first seeking the sanction of Congress in the matter of appropriations.

[b] A passage in Jackson's first inaugural speech justified their trust, for he said, "It will be my sincere and constant desire to observe toward the Indian tribes within our limits a just and liberal policy, and to give that humane and considerate attention to their rights and their wants which is consistent with the habits of our Government and the feelings of our people * * *." ("Statesman's Manual" I:696; Richardson, II: 438.)

[c] "Indian Office Letter Books," Series II, No. 5, pp. 373–375; "Niles' Register," XXXVI: 257.

[d] "Indian Office Letter Books," Series II, No. 5, pp. 408–412.

[e] These talks were published at Natchez in the "Statesman and Gazette," June 27, 1829.

[f] Jackson's conversation with Wiley Thompson ("Niles's Register," XXXVI: 231), who went to him for some assurance that Georgia could look to him in confidence for a redress of her Indian grievance, shows that the Administration was not yet very sure of its ground. It had not yet gauged the depth of public opinion.

them, Jackson thought it prudent to send among them a confidential agent,[a] whose mission should be kept absolutely secret, the object being to secure individual acquiesence.[b]

Measures directed toward the same end were taken for the Choctaws and Chickasaws. At the beginning of the year the Mississippi legislature had enacted that the Indian country should be subject to legal process,[c] and there was every indication that the Indians would, at the ensuing term, be themselves rendered amenable to State law. Eaton, therefore, advised them to go to a land that would be theirs and their children's for all time;[d] inasmuch as the General Government had not the constitutional power to prevent the extension of State authority; "but beyond the Mississippi (it) will possess the power and can exercise it. It will be disposed when there settled to molest or disturb them no more, but leave them and their children at peace and in repose forever."[e] Colonel Ward,[f] who had been retained in the service as Choctaw agent, even though the Indians had in 1828

---

[a] Gen. William Carroll, then a candidate for the governorship of Tennessee, was selected for this delicate mission. His compensation was to be $8 for every day of service within the nation and $8 for every 20 miles of travel to and from. An assistant was given him in the person of General Coffee, and together these two political friends of Jackson did good service for removal among the common Indians. Later on a second commission was sent out, composed " of Humphrey Posey, and a Mr. Saunders, having in view the purchase " of Cherokee lands in North Carolina. (Royce, p. 260.)

[b] The object of the Administration is fully disclosed in Eaton's letter of instructions to Carroll, May 30, 1829, but from which illustrative extracts only have been taken, the connection being supplied, when necessary, by a paraphrase of the omitted parts: "A crisis in our Indian Affairs has arrived. Strong indications are seen of this in the circumstance of the Legislatures of Georgia and Alabama, extending their laws * * * These acts, it is reasonable to presume, will be followed by the other States interested * * * to exercise such jurisdiction * * *." Emigration is the only relief for the Indians. The President is "of opinion" that, if they "can be approached in any way that shall elude their prejudices, and be enlightened as to their true relations to the States," they will consent to remove. He therefore desires that you will undertake to enlighten the Creeks and Cherokees, since he does not think " the form of a Council " will take with them any longer. " The past has demonstrated their utter aversion to this mode while it has been made equally clear that another mode promises greater success * * *."

"Nothing is more certain than that, if the Chiefs and influential men could be brought into the measure, the rest would implicitly follow. It becomes, therefore, a matter of necessity, if the General Government would benefit these people, that it move upon them, in the line of their own prejudices; and by the adoption of any proper means, break the power that is warring with their best interests * * *." This cannot be done by " a General Council." It must be done by " an appeal to the Chiefs and influential men." " Your first business, should you consent to engage in this work of mercy to the Indians, would be to ascertain upon whom, as pivots, the will of the Cherokees and Creeks turns."

" It is believed that the more careful you are to secure from even the Chiefs the official character you carry with you, the better—Since no circumstance is too slight to excite their suspicion or awaken their jealousy; Presents in your discretion to the amount of not more than 2000$ might be made with effect, by attaching to you the poorer Indians, as you pass through their Country, given as their friend; and the same to the Children of the Chiefs, and the Chiefs themselves, in clothes, or otherwise * * *." ' (Indian Office Letter Books," Series II, No. 5, pp. 456–459.)

[c] Act of February 4, 1829, "Knoxville Register," March 3, 1830.

[d] Eaton to Folsom, July 30, 1829, "Indian Office Letter Books," Series II, No. 6, pp. 56–57.

[e] Eaton to Ward, July 31, 1829, ibid., pp. 58–59.

[f] Much that was derogatory to the character of Ward came out in the evidence furnished in the case of the Choctaw Nation v. the United States.

petitioned for his removal because of embezzlement of annuity funds,[a] communicated these sentiments to the Choctaws in general council September 17, 1829, and on the 7th of November Colonel Folsom, mingo of the northeastern district,[b] replied on behalf of the whole tribe.[c] He repudiated an idea advanced that white men influenced them against removal and proudly asserted that the Choctaws, being a nation by themselves, acted for themselves. Moreover, they could not understand how there could be any question that they in their own land were independent of Mississippi laws.

"We have no expectation," wrote Folsom, "that, if we should remove to the west of the Mississippi, any treaties would be made with us, that could secure greater benefits to us and our children, than those which are already made. The red people are of the opinion, that, in a few years the Americans will also wish to possess the land west of the Mississippi. Should we remove, we should again soon be removed by white men. We have no wish to sell our country and remove to one that is not fertile and good, wherever it is situated. It is not our wish that a great man, although our friend, should visit us to counsel with us, about selling our beloved country, and removing to another far off. We desire no such visit.

"As the agent of the United States' government, you speak to us and tell us of another country west of the great river Mississippi, that is good, and where we and our children may have a long and quiet home, and enjoy many blessings. In all this you would act as a faithful officer under your superior. But here is our home, our dwelling places, our fields, and our schools, and all our friends; and under us are the dust and the bones of our forefathers. This land is dearer to us than any other. Why talk to us about removing? We always hear such counsel with deep grief in our hearts.

"During your residence in our nation as United States agent, you have seen what improvement we have made in those things which are for our good and the good of our children. And here it is, in this very land that we wish to reside and make greater improvement till we become a happy people. Our hearts cleave to our own country. We have no wish to sell * * *."

Whether the Choctaws wanted a private agent to counsel them or not, President Jackson was bent upon furnishing one, and he found an individual ready at hand in the person of Major David Haley, of Mississippi, who, being about to pass through the Choctaw country, offered to be the bearer of any communication the President might

[a] McKenney to Porter, November 3, 1828, ibid. No. 5, pp. 170–172.

[b] "The Choctaw nation is divided into three parts, or districts, supposed to contain seven or eight thousand inhabitants in each. For some time past, (perhaps from time immemorial) a high chief, called a Mingo, often translated *king*, presided over each district. These three mingos appear to have been equal in power and rank. So far as can be learned, they rose gradually to this station by the consent of other leading men, but without any formal election. In each village, or settlement, a head man was appointed, whose rank is indicated, in our language, by the word *captain*. There are about thirty of these in the northeast district; and perhaps nearly the same number in each of the others. The captains were raised to this office by the consent of their neighbors and of the Mingo; but all appointments appear to have been confirmed in a council of chief, captains, and warriors; meaning by the word *warriors,* all the common men. The councils were held at irregular periods, and were usually called by the chief * * *." ("Missionary Herald," August, 1830, p. 251.)

[c] Folsom to Ward, November 7, 1829, "Missionary Herald," 1830, pp. 82–83.

wish to send.[a] Jackson intrusted him with some documents which Haley, upon his arrival in the Choctaw country, inclosed in a letter of his own to Folsom, November 24, 1829, with the suggestion that he be permitted to interview the Indians himself and " aid the chiefs in obtaining the consent of the people to a removal." [b] Folsom read the letter in council at a time when Colonel Garland, mingo of the southeastern district, and other leading men of the Choctaw Nation were present, and then, under their sanction, replied to Haley, calling him as a neighbor to witness that the Choctaws were already an agricultural people and had always been opposed to removal. Moreover, if he (Haley) did come into the nation, Folsom wanted him to bring with him the treaties of Doak's Stand and Washington and explain their meaning.[c] The scorn and censure implied in this

[a] WASHINGTON, *October 15th, 1829.*

SIR:

You have kindly offered to be the bearer of any communications to the Indians amongst whom you pass on your return home. I place in your hands, copies of a talk made by me last Spring to the Creeks; I wish you to shew them to the Chiefs of the Choctaws, as you pass and say to them, as far as this talk relates to their situation with their white brothers and my wishes for them to remove beyond the Mississippi, it contains my sentiments towards the Choctaws and Chickasaw Indians, and if they wish to be happy and to live in quiett and preserve their Nation, they will take my advice and remove beyond the Mississippi.

Say to them as friends & brothers to listen to the voice of their father, and their friend. Where they now are they and my white children are too near to each other to live in harmony and peace. Their game is destroyed & many of their people will not work, & till the earth. Beyond the Great river Mississippi, where a part of their nation have gone, their father has provided a country, large enough for them all, and he advises them to remove to it. There their white brethren will not trouble them, they will have no claim to the land, and they can live upon it, they and all their children, as long as grass grows or water runs, in peace and plenty. It will be theirs forever. For any improvements in the country where they now live, and for any stock which they cannot take with them, their father will stipulate, in a treaty to be holden with them, to pay them a fair price.

Say to my red Choctaw children, and my Chickasaw children to listen—my white children of Mississippi have extended their laws over their country. If they remain where they now are they will be subject to those laws. If they remove across the Mississippi river they will be free from those laws of the state, and only subject to their own laws, and be under the care of their father the President of the United States. Where they now are, say to them, their father cannot prevent them from being subject to the laws of the state of Mississippi. They are within its limits, and I pray you to explain to them, that so far from the United States having the right to question the authority of any State, to regulate its affairs within their own limits, the general government will be obliged to sustain the States in the exercise of their right. Say to the chiefs and warriors that I am their friend, that I wish to act as their friend but they must, by removing from the limits of the States of Mississippi and Alabama and by being settled on the lands I offer them, put it in my power to be such,—There, beyond the limits of any State, in possession of land of their own, which they shall possess as long as Grass grows or water runs, I can and will protect them and be their friend & father.

That the chiefs and warriors may fully understand this talk, you will please go amongst, & read it to, and fully explain it to them. Tell them it is from my own mouth you have rec'd it and that I never speak with a forked tongue * * *. Again I beg you to tell them to listen. The plan proposed is the only one, by which they can be perpetuated as nations & where can be extended to them, the right of living under their own laws.

I am very respectfully, your friend & the friend of my Choctaw and Chickasaw brethren,

ANDREW JACKSON

Major DAVID HALEY.
(Jackson Papers, 1829.)

[b] " Missionary Herald," 1830, p. 83.
[c] Ibid., pp. 83–84.

request could not have been lost upon Jackson did he hear of it; for he had, in conjunction with General Hinds, himself negotiated the former of these two treaties, and, therefore, had personally subscribed to the express stipulation that the boundaries therein arranged for should not be altered except " in a certain contingency and under the direction of Congress." The subsequent treaty of Washington revoked the conditional rights given Congress, and particularly declared " that the power of bringing the Indians under the laws of the United States should not be exercised but with the consent of the Choctaw Nation." [a]

It is not to be supposed that the Choctaws were a unit in their sentiments regarding removal. Mooshoolatubbe [Mushulatubbe], Folsom's predecessor and later successor in the mingoship of the northeastern district, was the leader of a disaffected band opposed to the missionaries, their work, and improvement generally. These men had come to a decision that, unless they moved westward, they could not hope to retain their primitive customs.[b] They were believed to be influenced in this by certain Indian youths who were being educated in Kentucky. Colonel Leflore, the mingo of the western district, was at first in sympathy with his fellow chiefs, Folsom and Garland; but in the winter of 1829–30 he paid a visit to Tennessee and, although he then declared to the Cherokees that he was unalterably opposed to removal, he came back with his views changed.[c]

This change of feeling was very evident at a general council which was called in March and which was attended largely by Leflore's constituents and very sparsely by those of Garland and Folsom. During the early part of the meeting these two mingos, frightened, it was conjectured, by a law of Mississippi imposing a fine of a thousand dollars and imprisonment for one year upon any Choctaw who should exercise the authority of a chief, resigned their offices; and Leflore, who did not resign his, because, being prepared to advocate a departure of his tribe from Mississippi, he expected to gain the indulgence of the State, was made in this assembly, so noticeably composed of his own personal followers, the sole chief of the Choctaws. In that capacity, he proceeded to serious business and informed his audience that the tribe must do one of three things: " Fight the United States, submit to the laws of Mississippi, or remove." Thoroughly alarmed or else primed beforehand the people answered in substance, " We are distressed, we can not endure the laws of Mississippi; we do not think our great father, the President, loves us; we must go, as he will not protect us here." [d]

---

[a] " Missionary Herald," 1830, p. 251.
[b] Ibid., August, 1830, pp. 251–252.
[c] Ibid., p. 243.
[d] Ibid.

The United States had not yet, be it remembered, appointed commissioners to negotiate with the Choctaws; yet, in some mysterious way, the wily Leflore was able to produce at this stage of the council proceedings a document of cession fully drafted. It was reported by a contemporary to occupy " sixteen sheets of foolscap paper " and to be " in the handwriting of Dr. Tally, the most prominent of the Methodist missionaries," all but one of whom were present. It was read to the people and declared approved, even by Folsom and Garland, who indorsed it as private individuals.[a] Its terms were rather unique and evidently emanated from the Indians themselves.[b] They offered to surrender their land for $1,000,000, provided each man be granted out of it 640 acres, with power of alienation, compensation be given for all domestic animals, provision be made for the journey and for one year after arrival, and, finally, the new land in the West be guaranteed to them as a State with the promise of ultimate admittance to the Union on equal terms with other States.[c]

Scarcely had the doings of the Choctaw Council become generally known than Mooshoolatubbe raised an uproar against the illegality of the proposed treaty. His contention was, that it had not been agreed to in a national council, since few representatives from the northeast and southeast districts were present. He also raised a hue and cry against the missionaries, the prominence of the Methodists at the convention being taken as indicative of the general bad effect of religious influences.[d] All through the spring and early summer a great commotion prevailed in the Choctaw country. In some cases despair and in others indignation gave a loose rein to vice and intemperance. The excitement was not even allayed when it became known that the United States Senate had rejected the treaty; for everyone knew that negotiations would be resumed as soon as possible and an attempt be made to secure the land on terms more favorable to the oppressor.[e]

Among the Creeks and Cherokees the prospect of removal, thanks to Carroll and Coffee, was gradually brightening,[f] so that, by the middle of November, McKenney was able to report that Colonel Crowell had sent off 1,200 of the former and Colonel Montgomery 431 of the latter.[g] Events, however, could not move fast enough to suit the white people. In the course of a few months, the prospective

---

[a] " Missionary Herald," August, 1830, p. 253.

[b] " These people appear to have thus run ahead of the Gov't. Since no commissioners have been appointed to negotiate with them, what is meant by a Treaty is, I presume, the basis of one." (McKenney to Hon. H. L. White, April 9, 1830, " Indian Office Letter Books," Series II, No. 6, p. 381.)

[c] " Niles Register," XXXIX : 19.

[d] " Missionary Herald," August, 1830, p. 254.

[e] " Missionary Herald," December, 1830, p. 384.

[f] This must not be taken to imply that the Cherokees as a nation were becoming compliant. (Royce, p. 260.)

[g] " Indian Office Letter Books," Series II, No. 6, p. 163.

value of the Cherokee lands had increased immeasurably. It was a repetition of the Creek case of 1825, except that there silver[a] had been the lode stone and here it was gold.[b] Diggers flocked to the mines from all directions,[c] and, in utter defiance of the Federal intercourse laws, took up their station in the Indian country, just at a time, too, when the Administration, in its own interest, was considering the project of bringing those same laws to operate upon missionaries and half-breeds. It was a period of lawlessness, and even the War Department lost patience with the Georgians, many of whom thought that the present attack upon the Indians was a good opportunity for the advancement of the most extravagant claims, and Governor Forsyth supported them.[d] Eaton took a more sensible view and hinted that,

---

[a] "Niles's Register," XXIX : 228.

[b] "Knoxville Register," August 11, 1830, September 29, 1830; "Nashville Republican and State Gazette," October 20, 1830; "Niles' Register," XXXVII : 213.

[c] HEAD OF PIGEON ROOST, *27th January, 1830.*

SIR.

We the citizens of Georgia who are engaged in the gold digging business in the Cherokee Nation beg leave to make the following communication (to wit) We are well aware that it is wrong for us to intrude upon the rights of Georgia by digging for gold upon her unappropriated & unsurveyed lands, as we have been doing for some time past & that we of right ought to be stoped. Therefore at the time you visited us, in June last (at your request) we abandoned our Searches for gold in the nation and returned to our homes. But finding that your reasonable request and the exertions of Capt. Brady had not induced the citizens of other States to abandon their Searches we again returned to the Nation. And our excuse for thus acting may be found in this That we believe the Soil of this Nation and the minerals therein contained belong to Georgia and that we have a prospective interest in the same, and that we are more excusable than the citizens from other states or the people of the Nation. Therefore we thought while others were grasping after the wealth of our State that we would strive for a part. But Sir notwithstanding all this, we are now willing to abandon our Searches for gold again, provided all other persons are compeled to do so—But let it be distinctly understood that if affective means are not adopted to restrain & prohibit all other persons from digging that we will again return with the full determination of being the last to quit the mines upon any subsequent occasion.

It is unanimously Resolved that the foregoing Communication be signed by the Chairman in behalf of the Citizens of Georgia present and countersigned by the Secretary and forwarded to Col. Hugh Montgomery.

                                                           B. L. GOODMAN *Chairman*
"Jackson Papers.")   M. H. GUTHRIGHT (?) *Secy.*

[d] Governor Gilmer did put forth an effort to restrain the gold-diggers, but he restrained or tried to restrain both red and white men. On the 3d of July, 1830, he issued two proclamations, the one declaring the laws of Georgia to be in full force over the Cherokees, " the other forbidding the whites as well as the Indians from digging for Gold in the Cherokee Nation." ("Knoxville Register," July 7, 1830.) Later on, he convened the legislature, very largely for the purpose of securing legislation that would prevent trespass upon the gold lands. ("Knoxville Register," October 6, 1830.) Colonel Montgomery exerted himself to protect the Cherokees from intrusion and gave notice to the gold diggers to remove, early in June, 1830. (Cherokee Emigration Papers, Indian Office MS. Records.) He was not, however, supported by the Government. Indeed, S. S. Hamilton wrote to him from the Indian Office, June 7, 1831 : " It is proper to add that with Intruders on the Indian lands within the limits of those states which have assumed jurisdiction over the country, it has been determined (as I believe you are already apprized) that the General Government has not the power to interfere, particularly by military force, for their removal." ("Indian Office Letter Books," Series II, No. 7, pp. 267–268.) Robb modified this statement a little later (Robb to Montgomery, July 31, 1832, "Indian Office Letter Books," Series II, No. 9, p. 107), and United States troops, when sent, appear to have treated the whites much more roughly than they did the Indians. ("Nashville Republican and State Gazette," October 23, 1830; Letter of January 17, 1831, to Col. Hugh Montgomery, "Cherokee Emigration Papers," Indian Office MS. Records.)

since the " aggrieved " persons were frontiersmen, it was " just possible the Indians were not the aggressors." At any rate, the Government could do nothing in the matter of awarding damages out of tribal funds until the Indians as aggressors were regularly convicted and identified, and on something other than interested testimony.[a] Much of the evidence was circumstantial, much of it of a kind wholly inadmissible in a court of law. Hogs missed and no bones found in the woods were not proof that Indians had done the mischief.[b]

With the development of Jackson's " force " policy, Indian removal became a party question, something that it never, strictly speaking, was before, and many religious denominations in the country ranged themselves against it. The Baptists, at least certain missionaries of that persuasion in the North, were a great exception. Under the leadership of Isaac McCoy, they were still dreaming of an Indian State, arguing very sensibly that nothing could be worse for the aborigines than the excitement under which they were then laboring. The old-time trust could never be restored so long as they were daily subjected to new instances of insincerity. The Episcopalians and the Presbyterians, as church organizations, kept well out of the matter, the Methodists were divided, but the Quakers and the Congregationalists stood forth bravely as the champions of Indian rights. Self-interested to a degree they may have been, to be sure, since it was to their advantage to keep the footing already established in the Indian country; yet it stands to reason that much of the feeling was altruistic. Suspicion of having plans diametrically opposed to those of the Government was first directed against their missionaries during the closing years of Adams's Administration,[c] and it increased with time, becoming, indeed, so strong that even a New York society,[d] organized in the summer of 1829 to support the removal policy and with ecclesiastics [e] among its members,[f] was not able, as McKenney anticipated when he gave it his support,[g] to " counteract " it.

[a] Eaton to Forsyth, September 19, 1829, " Indian Office Letter Books," Series II, No. 6, pp. 89–90.

[b] S. S. Hamilton to E. H. Pierce, July 25, 1829, ibid. p. 54.

[c] Report of Secretary Peter B. Porter, November 24, 1828, American State Papers, " Military Affairs," IV : 3.

[d] This society was organized under the name of " The Indian Board for the Emigration, Preservation, and Improvement of the Aborigines of America," and its principal members were the Hon. Stephen Van Rensselaer and the Rev. Eli Baldwin. It worked with the avowed object of supporting the Government in this one phase of its policy— removal. The American Board of Foreign Missions, whose corresponding secretary at the time was the Rev. Jeremiah Evarts, of Boston, was invited to cooperate, but refused. (McKenney to Rev. Eli Baldwin, July 13, 1829, " Indian Office Letter Books," Series II, No. 6, pp. 46–48.)

[e] McKenney reported Bishop Hobart in sympathy with the movement but prevented from taking actual membership by " insuperable difficulties." (McKenney to Baldwin, June 27, 1829, " Indian Office Letter Books," Series II, No. 6, pp. 30–32.)

[f] Baldwin proposed admitting Congressmen as honorary members of the board, but McKenney thought that might be considered " indelicate." (McKenney to Baldwin, October 27, 1829, " Indian Office Letter Books," Series II, No. 6, p. 138.)

[g] McKenney to Baldwin, June 27, 1829, ibid. pp. 30–32 ; Eaton to Forsyth, September 15, 1829, ibid., p. 86.

The Twenty-first Congress met December 7, 1829, and on the day following received the first annual message of Andrew Jackson which, as everyone expected, advised removal, and this it did mainly because the rights of sovereign States were being interfered with.[a] Each House referred the matter to its Committee on Indian Affairs.[b] On the 22d of February, Senator White reported a bill calling for an exchange of lands with the eastern tribes; and on the 24th, Representative Bell, one for removal. The report that accompanied each is well summed up by an editorial in " Niles' Register " as an argument that " seems to begin and end with POWER—originally to claim, and now to possess the right of the soil."[c] Both bills were substantially the same in principle, and the House, recognizing that fact, eventually substituted the Senate bill for its own.

The progress of these two bills in Congress called out much party feeling; for, in spite of what Jackson had said in his message as to his intention not to use force, the whole country knew that every measure yet taken gave it the lie. Removal under the direction of the Georgians and the Jackson party generally could be nothing more or less than compulsory. Therefore philanthropists and the friends of Adams took issue against it. It was pretty nearly a case of North against South, but not quite. Petitions to Congress, praying for a recognition of Indian rights, were almost innumerable,[d] and they came from colleges such as Amherst, from religious and benevolent societies, from the whole State of Massachusetts,[e] and from communities in Ohio, New Jersey, Pennsylvania, Virginia, New York, and Maryland. Counter petitions, considerably fewer in number, came from the Baptists, from the New York board, and from communities in Ohio, Indiana,[f] and Pennsylvania.

The Senate bill came up for debate the 6th of April, and almost daily thereafter, until its passage on the 26th, was the main topic of discussion in Committee of the Whole. Frelinghuysen, of New Jersey, and Sprague, of Maine, were its great opponents; White, of

[a] Richardson, II : 456–459.

[b] The Senate committee consisted of White of Tennessee, Troup of Georgia, Hendricks of Indiana, Dudley of New York, and Benton of Missouri; the House, of Bell of Tennessee, Lumpkin of Georgia, Hinds of Mississippi, Storrs of Connecticut, Hubbard of New Hampshire, Gaither of Kentucky, and Lewis of Alabama.

[c] " Niles's Register," XXXVIII : 67.

[d] Index to Senate and House Journals, Twenty-first Congress, First Session.

[e] The Administration papers in the South took great exception to this unwonted zeal of Massachusetts, and even the " Boston Statesman " rebuked her, suggesting that " the ladies and gentlemen," who met first at the State House and then at Faneuil Hall to protest against the injustice of Georgia, should " look at home, at their own doors, if they " wished " to find opportunities for the exercise of their humanity, and to do justice to the ' small remnant ' left of those they themselves have so deeply wronged, before they " traveled " to Georgia to dispense their favors."

[f] A separate bill for the removal of Indiana tribes was before Congress, consequently one would expect that State to favor the Government policy.

Tennessee; McKinley, of Alabama, and Forsyth, of Georgia, its advocates. The whole range of Indian history was covered. Once in a while sectional feeling crept in, as when a doubt arose as to whether consolidation west of the Mississippi would not necessarily involve a violation of the compromise of 1820, unless, indeed, the southern tribes with their slaves were removed with strict reference to parallel lines of latitude, a thing which had not previously been the case.[a] Most of the arguments, however, turned on State sovereignty, and were strongly reasoned. There was much to be said for Georgia. Her course was violently aggressive; but at bottom it proceeded from the same causes that had eventuated in the extermination of the New England and in the expulsion of the several northwestern tribes. The resisting power of the Cherokees was, however, greater than that of the Narragansetts. Without going further into details, we may conclude with Benton that Indian exchange was in the Senate " one of the closest and most earnestly contested questions of the session, and was finally carried by an inconsiderable majority." [b]

The House bill, which contemplated, not simply exchange, but removal in express terms, went to a Committee of the Whole on the state of the Union, and was not reached on the Calendar until the Senate bill had come to the House for concurrence. It was soon dropped by common consent and a debate started on the other, May 13, 1830, which was, perhaps, even more exciting than its predecessor in the upper House. With admirable forensic power, Storrs, of New York, exposed the fallacy of pretending to remove the Indians for their own good from a community where they had pleasant homes, churches, and schools, to a wilderness where roamed hostile tribes scarcely emerged from savagery.[c] He next attacked the President for embarrassing Congress by presuming to deliver an opinion

---

[a] This argument had come up at intervals during the years since Monroe first advocated consolidation in the Southwest.

[b] "Thirty Years' View," I : 164.

[c] The drift of southern argument in both Houses, aside from asserting the supremacy of the State, was to convince the popular mind that removal was the best thing for the eastern tribes, and the Administration supported the view. Indeed, McKenney's report on Indian civilization (" Indian Office Letter Books," Series II, No. 6, March 22, 1830), sent to the Senate in compliance with the resolution moved by Frelinghuysen on the 25th of January (Senate Journal, p. 101), was evidently intended to minimize the progress of those East and exaggerate that of those West, and this in spite of the fact that McKenney had secured information to the contrary from such men as the Rev. Cyrus Kingsbury, February 8, 1830, and had seemed to concur in it. (McKenney to Kingsbury, March 8, 1830, " Indian Office Letter Books," Series II, No. 6, pp. 315–316.) The Senate compared McKenney's report of March 22 with earlier reports from his pen and mercilessly exposed the inconsistencies and contradictions. (McKenney to Forsyth, April 1, 1830, " Indian Office Letter Books," Series II, No. 6, p. 361.) The charge of misrepresentation made by the Cherokee "Phoenix," June 10, 1829, was just as applicable in the spring of 1830 as it was at the date of publication. The statistics that appeared in the " Missionary Herald," XXIII : 116, are probably more reliable than McKenney's, because based upon data that were furnished in 1826, before the conduct of the missionaries had become the subject of criticism.

as to the extent of State authority before the nation, through its representatives, had been consulted—thus rendering the intercourse laws a dead letter on the statute books and virtually annulling Indian treaties, some of which he had persónally negotiated. He had arrogated to himself, said Storrs, power that had never been conceded to the Executive; for when once a treaty is fixed and adopted as the supreme law of the land the President has no dispensing power over it. He can not override it by an " order in council " or supersede it by giving to his own proclamation the force of law.[a] Lumpkin's attempt at rebuttal was a failure. In a speech, marked by much false sentiment, he appealed to sectional prejudices, attacked religious denominations of the East, and made a most absurd profession of regard for the red race. Ellsworth, of Connecticut, took a stand on the old position. He was not opposed to removal per se, but he was opposed to the present method of enforcing it. It was very plain, their own statements to the contrary notwithstanding, that the South and Southwest were actuated by mercenary motives, and that this bill was but a part of a united effort to expel the aborigines from their possessions. It was advocated upon principles at war with the national policy, for usage had fixed the Indian status, and it was not within the province of the President to change it.

These three speeches were typical of the many that were given in the House as long as the debate lasted, which was until the 18th of May, when Wickliffe, from the Committee of the Whole, reported the bill with amendments. These were accepted on the 24th. On the 25th, the bill was called up for its third reading, and Hemphill, of Pennsylvania, moved that it be recommitted to the Committee of the Whole, with instructions to strike out all but the enacting clause and substitute provisions insuring a voluntary removal only.[b] Trouble then arose over the call for the previous question which, by the casting vote of the Speaker, prevented further action for that day. On the 26th, the vote on the passage was taken and stood in favor of the affirmative, 102 to 97.

The bill was immediately returned to the Senate for concurrence in the House amendments. Frelinghuysen seized the opportunity to offer an additional one in the shape of protection from the States until removal. It was lost. He then asked that treaty rights be respected until removal, and lost again. Sprague next took up the cudgel to insist that treaties be executed according to the true intent and meaning thereof, and was voted down, as was also Clayton, of Delaware, who wanted the new act to apply to Georgia only.[c] With-

[a] " Gales and Seaton's Register," vol. VI, Part 2, pp. 996–1003.,
[b] " House Journal," p. 716.
[c] Senate Journal, pp. 328–329.

out more ado, the Senate agreed to the amended bill,[a] and on the 28th it was approved by the President.

From a textual point of view, the act [b] just passed was a very ordinary affair. It implied no new departure from the policy that had been pursued for years, except that there would be no longer any necessity for individual communities to apply for an extinguishment of Indian titles, since the President was authorized to offer an exchange of lands to any of the tribes " now residing within the limits of the states or territories." There was not the slightest hint at a compulsory removal. Why, then, the bitter disputes in Congress and why the alarm among the Indians? We shall soon see.

In the course of the winter, both the Creeks and the Cherokees had memorialized Congress in defense of their treaty rights as against the extension of State laws, but without effect. Jackson and the Georgians had triumphed. The object of extension was to force removal,[c] and Jackson's attitude toward extension was so well known that there was not the slightest doubt as to the way he would execute the new law. As soon as it was passed, therefore, the Cherokee delegation in Washington listened to the advice of such men as Webster and Frelinghuysen [d] and prepared to seek redress in the Federal courts. They employed Ex-Attorney-General William Wirt as chief counsel, who began action by suggesting to Governor Gilmer, his relative by marriage, the making of a test case to be heard in the Supreme Court that should determine the constitutionality of the Georgian procedure.[e] The idea was rejected with scorn.[f] Left to his own devices and hesitating much about assuming so great a responsibility, Wirt resolved to move the Supreme Court for an injunction, restraining the execution of State laws within the Indian country.[g]

Meanwhile Jackson and Eaton devised a plan of their own for an immediate execution of the law of May 28. Their holidays were to be spent in Tennessee, and they notified each of the four great southern tribes that they would confer with delegates there. The Creeks and Cherokees were not ready to treat, for their hopes were fixed

---

[a] Pryor Lea, writing May 27, 1830, thus reflects the interest felt in a measure toward which events had so long been tending; " The Indian Bill finally passed both Houses—, after one of the severest struggles that I have ever witnessed in Congress * * *. All the avowed opponents of this Administration in the House, with one honorable exception, Colonel Dwight of Massachusetts, united against the bill. The bill finally passed the House by a majority of five; but on preliminary questions we were tied three times, and the Speaker decided in our favor. On the decision of this question depended some consequences of awful importance * * *." (" Knoxville Register," June 9, 1830.)

[b] 4 United States Statutes at Large, 411.

[c] Governor Gilmer confessed as much in a letter to Judge Clayton, June 7, 1830, Gilmer's " Georgians," p. 355.

[d] Kennedy's " Wirt," II : 254.

[e] Wirt to Gilmer, June 4, 1830, Gilmer's " Georgians," p. 347.

[f] Gilmer to Wirt, June 19, 1830, ibid., p. 350.

[g] Wirt to Judge Carr, June 21, 1830, Kennedy's " Wirt," II : 253–258. Madison to Wirt, October 1, 1830, ibid., p. 260.

upon Wirt and the Supreme Court.[a] The Chickasaws appeared in due season, and Jackson,[b] together with Eaton and Coffee, whom he had commissioned for the purpose, personally addressed them,[c] emphasizing the Federal inability to prevent the extension of State laws. This was their last chance. If they refused the Government offer now, their Great Father would leave them to shift for themselves; and if they found it impossible to exist under the municipal laws of Mississippi, they would have to seek a new home in their own way and at their own expense. The Chickasaws had professed some months before a willingness to emigrate, provided they could find a suitable country,[d] and, upon that contingency, they consented August 31–September 1, 1830, to a provisional treaty of removal.

Tribal differences and the inattention to duty of Agent Ward prevented the Choctaws from appointing delegates in time to meet Jackson at Franklin.[e] Eaton, therefore, in defiance of the criticism that was being hurled at "the strolling Cabinet," repaired to Mississippi, where, "after thirteen days of the most fatiguing duty,"[f] he and Coffee managed [g] to bring the Choctaws to terms in the treaty of Dancing Rabbit Creek, September 27, 1830.[h] The Choctaws ceded all their eastern lands except such small reservations [i] as might be selected [j] by individuals who preferred citizenship to emigration, and

---

[a] Eaton to Jackson, August 18, 1830, "Jackson Papers."

[b] Jackson was much criticised in Opposition prints for thus negotiating in person, it being pertinently asked whether he were acting as President or as Indian commissioner.

[c] "Jackson Papers," August 23, 1830; "MS. Journal of the Commissioners," pp. 3–7; Indian Office MS. Records.

[d] "MS. Journal of the Commissioners," "Indian Office MS. Records." For the original unratified document see "Treaty Files," 1802–1853, "Indian Office MS. Records."

[e] They were advised the first of June that if they wanted to make a treaty they should send a deputation to Tennessee to meet their "Great Father." (Eaton to Choctaws, June 1, 1830, "Indian Office Letter Books," Series II, No. 6, pp. 439–441.)

[f] "Nashville Republican and State Gazette," October 6, 1830.

[g] The missionaries were denied admission to the treaty councils, "MS. Journal of the Commissioners," Indian Office MS. Records.

[h] 7 United States Statutes at Large, 333.

[i] "Indian Land Cessions in the United States," p. 727.

[j] This provision was the substance of the notorious fourteenth article, concerning which Greenwood Leflore, in 1843, made the following deposition before the commissioners, John F. H. Claiborne and Ralph Graves, appointed by the United States to investigate the alleged frauds against the Choctaw Nation:

"To the 5th interrogatory, I answer that I was one of the chiefs who negotiated this treaty on the part of the Choctaws, and am sorry to say that the benefits realized from it by my people were by no means equal to what I had a right to expect, nor to what they were justly entitled by the stipulations of the treaty on the part of government. The treaty was made at the urgent solicitations of the commissioners of government, and upon their abundant assurances that its stipulations would be faithfully carried out. Confiding in these assurances and in the honor of government to comply with the treaty, if it should be ratified at Washington, and conceiving it, under the circumstances, a measure of policy, if not of necessity, so far as the Choctaws were concerned, I urged it upon my people, in the face of a strong opposition, which I finally determined, if possible, to remove by suggesting the insertion of the 14th article. This article was accordingly inserted, and believing it removed the principal objection to the treaty, I signed it myself, and procured for it the support of many who were previously hesitating and undetermined. After the treaty was ratified I was active in urging forward the emigration of the people, and induced most of those in the part of my district where I resided

in return gained not a single acre of western territory over and above that which their tribe already possessed; but they did gain what was of infinitely greater moment just then, though experience ought to have warned them that it was worthless, a promise that no State or Territory should ever circumscribe them again.[a]

The appointment of Col. James B. Gardiner as special agent to treat with the tribes of Ohio was the initiatory step in the execution of the Removal Act outside the southern belt.[b] The results of his mission came out for the most part in the spring and summer of 1831.

to remove west. I think there were very few in the vicinity of my residence who applied for the benefit of the 14th article, and the most of them, I think, were duly registered and got their lands reserved. This article was inserted to satisfy those in the southern part of my district and other parts of the Choctaw country who were opposed to the treaty and were inimical to me, from an impression which prevailed among them that I wished to sell their country and force them to go west. After the treaty I did not consider myself any longer chief, and as I was engaged in preparing the people for the first emigration, and actually accompanied it, my intercourse with the Indians was confined to those in my part of the country who sustained me in my course & were preparing to remove west, & I never troubled myself about the course pursued by those who had been opposed to my measures—had rejected my advice—and were determined to remain in the ceded country. I do not, of course, know how many of them applied for the benefit of the 14th article. Before closing my answer to this interrogatory I think it proper to state that about three years after the treaty I was present at Columbus during the excitement which arose there at the time of the land sales about the contingent locations of the 14th article claimants & hearing a remark made by one of the agents of these claimants in a public speech to a large assembly of people charging the chiefs who had made this treaty with bribery & corruption, I rose after he sat down & retorted the charge of fraud in as severe language as I could command. I was excited, & might have said more than was proper, but I felt, in the absence of any positive knowledge on the subject, that I had a right to impute any motives to one who could make such a serious & unfounded charge affecting my character as one of the chiefs who had been mainly instrumental in making the treaty. I knew that the locating agent who lived in my section of country had been furnished with a list containing but few names of persons registered under the 14th art. of the treaty, but did not at that time know that many had applied to the registering agent for the benefit of this article whose applications had been rejected. I have never since then taken any pains to inform myself particularly about their claims, & do not know how many received the benefit of this article or being entitled to the benefit of it failed to realize it. I would also add that the commissioners on the part of the United States went to the ground, at Dancing Rabbit Creek, much prejudiced against me, & would have no intercourse with me. They believed they could make a treaty with the other chiefs, without my aid, and attempted to do so. After ten or twelve days of fruitless negotiations with them failed entirely to make any treaty. The commissioners then came to me, & made many apologies for their neglect of me, saying they had been deceived and misled in regard to me, by many misrepresentations, & then solicited me to enter into negotiations with them. I then told if they would embrace in the treaty such provisions and articles which I suggested, the fourteenth article being one of them, I would undertake to make a treaty in two days. They agreed to the articles I suggested, and in twenty-four hours I had the treaty made." (Case of Choctaw Nation *v.* the United States, pp. 430–431.)

[a] Art. IV. " The Government and people of the United States are hereby obliged to secure to the said Choctaw Nation of Red People the jurisdiction and government of all the persons and property that may be within their limits west, so that no Territory or State shall ever have a right to pass laws for the government of the Choctaw Nation of Red People and their descendants; and that no part of the land granted them shall ever be embraced in any Territory or State. * * * ."

[b] It will be remembered that the only Indian lands remaining within Ohio were comprehended within detached reservations, and the desire to have the title to these extinguished seems to have come not so much from the white people as from the Indians themselves. McKenney in 1829 tried to draw a general inference from this that the common Indians everywhere east of the Mississippi were anxious to remove. (McKenney to Rev. Eli Baldwin, October 23, 1829, " Indian Office Letter Books," Series II, No. 6, pp. 132–136.)

In all he negotiated, sometimes with the assistance of Agent McElvain, five treaties of exchange; [a] but in connection with the last four his character and methods were so open to question that Ewing, of Ohio, moved in the Senate for an inquiry into the genuineness of the documents presented for ratification.[b] The Quakers were the chief accusers. Sub-agent David Robb was interrogated by the Committee on Indian Affairs,[c] but nothing more could be gleaned from him than that

[a](1) Treaty of Washington with Senecas living within the counties of Seneca and Sandusky, February 28, 1831, 7 U. S. Stat. at L., 348.

(2) Treaty of Lewistown with Wyandots, Senecas, and Shawnees, living within the county of Logan, July 20, 1831, ibid., p. 351.

(3) Treaty of Wapaghkonnetta with the Shawnees in Allen County, August 8, 1831, ibid., p. 355.

(4) Treaty with the several Ottawa bands of Blanchard's Fork, Oquanoxa's Village, Roche de Boeuf, and Wolf Rapids, August 30, 1831, ibid., p. 359. Concerning this treaty Gardiner sent in the following brief report to the Secretary of War:

TIFFIN, OHIO, Sept. 2d, 1831.

SIR:

I have the gratification to accompany this letter with the "Articles of Agreement and Convention" concluded at Miami Bay, in Michigan Territory, on the 30th ultimo, with the *Ottawa* Indians, residing in this State, for a cession of all the lands owned by them in Ohio, amounting to nearly 50,000 acres.

I will make another and more detailed official communication on this subject, so soon as the impaired state of my health will permit.

I have the honor to be, with great respect,

Yr. mo. obt. Servt.

JAMES B. GARDINER.

Hon. LEWIS CASS,
    Secy. of War.

("Treaty Files," 1802–1853, Indian Office MS. Records.)

(5) Treaty of McCutcheonsville with the Big Spring Wyandots, living within Crawford County, January 16, 1832, 7 U. S. Stat. at L., p. 364.

[b] "Jackson Papers," January 16, 1832.

[c] David Robb's communication to H. L. White, chairman of the Committee on Indian Affairs in the United States Senate, embodying his replies to the questions put to him, was transmitted by Mr. Haywards to Jackson, February 7, 1832, and is to be found among the Jackson Papers of that date. Jackson thought Robb's answers placed Ewing in a disgraceful situation; but the missionary reports of the time would indicate that Gardiner's methods were really blameworthy and that the Ohio Indians were far from being as ready to emigrate as McKenney informed Baldwin they were. This is what he wrote under date of October 23, 1829: "The State urges not their removal—indeed great efforts were made in Congress by representatives of this State to keep away every sort of influence from operating upon the Indians within it, tending *in the slightest degree*, to their emigration. There, too, they are really comfortable. The Wyandots are well off—and most of them would make good Citizens. It is fair to presume therefore that these Indians are satisfied and will remain. But it is not so. They are now, the Delawares and Shawnese, seeking for the ways and means to go; and even the Wyandotts, it is the opinion of the Agent, (McElvain) are inclined to go also; and in five years, he believes, there will not be one Indian in Ohio! Whence comes this? Of that unconquerable antipathy, I answer, of the red to the near neighborhood of the white men. And much of this arises from that conscious inferiority of which the former is never, for a moment, relieved * * *." ("Indian Office Letter Books," Series II, No. 6, pp. 132–136.)

The missionary reports were quite different. "The prospect of doing good," said one, "at this place [Wauppaughkaunetta] was soon after [i. e. after Miss Newell established her school at Shawnee request] blighted by an attempt to purchase their land, and induce the Indians to remove to a country west of the Mississippi river. The agent, who was commissioned to conduct the negociation, after rehearsing to the Shawnees the fate of the Cherokees, and stating that these were the last proposals the government of the United States would ever make to them, and presenting various other motives, at last obtained their assent to the proposed treaty. Miss Newell, who was present at the

Gardiner greatly enlarged upon the danger of staying within the limits of Ohio. He was not prepared to vouch for the authenticity of the treaties, because he was not acquainted with the Seneca and Shawnee tongues. The treaties were duly proclaimed April 6, 1832, and Gardiner was reassured of Jackson's trust by being appointed [a] superintendent of the removals that were to take place under them.[b]

---

council, and witnessed all the proceedings, gives the following account of the distressing despondency manifested by the headmen. The date is June 29 (1831). 'One of the chiefs said it was a tough, hard case, to give his people up to come under state laws without being permitted to vote, or having their civil oaths regarded before a magistrate; it would be as bad as to give themselves up to have their throats cut; for he could easily conceive of their being driven to desperation, and immediately committing outrage that would bring them to the gallows; and it was a tough, hard case, to decide to go, but as there was no alternative, they had better be reconciled to go. * * *

" 'The old men sat in council, looking each other in the face, and mourning over their fate from Monday morning until Tuesday night. They sat and talked all night long, and parted with no better state of feeling than when they came together. * * * They had thought for years past, that there would be no hope for them; only by their conduct pleasing the white people so well, that they would not wish them to move away. This they had endeavored to do, had made up their minds to encourage schools, attend to agriculture, and examine the religion of the bible; but they now saw it would be all in vain. * * * They said the president had offered to build them school-houses and a meeting-house beyond the Mississippi, but if they went, they should abandon the whole, build their own council-house, and worship the great spirit in their own way.'" (" Missionary Herald," December, 1831, XXVII : 387–388.)

Another report was: " But after the negociation with the Shawnees (1831) had been completed, overtures of a similar character were made by the same agent to the Ottawas. At the first council of the Indians held for this purpose, they appeared determined to retain their land and remain where they were, and decidedly refused the offers made them. Another council was, however, called, and after having been continued a number of days, a portion of the Indians were induced to assemble in general council on the Sabbath, and sign a treaty by which they sold all their land in Ohio. Many protested against the treaty, but without effect." (" Missionary Herald," December, 1831, XXVII : 338.

And still another, this from Mr. Van Tassel, September 29, 1831 : "At the time of the treaty, they prevailed on about half of those at Blanchard's Fork and a small party on the Oglaze to go west of the Mississippi, in all about fifty men. The others refused to go, and will probably remain here for the present * * * since they have had time to reflect upon what they have done, they appear to be very much cast down. * * * Since the treaty, some of the Indians have said they will never leave this country; if they can find no place to stay, they will spend the rest of their days in walking up and down the Maumee, mourning over the wretched state of their people. Some have said they would place themselves under our protection, and stay by us as long as we remain * * *." (" Missionary Herald," December, 1831, XXVII : 388.)

[a] Cass to James B. Gardiner, May 17, 1832, " Indian Office Letter Books," Series II, No. 8, pp. 397–398.

[b] The Big Spring Wyandots did not accept an exchange of land west of the Mississippi, but declared their intention of going northward, perhaps to Canada. Gardiner, therefore, had nothing to do with their removal. Two-thirds of the original Wapaghkonetta band of Shawnees had already removed from Ohio by 1829. (McKenney to John Johnston, April 29, 1829, " Indian Office Letter Books," Series II, No. 5, p. 425.) An act of Congress of March 2, 1829, appropriated $600 for negotiating with the Delawares of Ohio (McKenney to John McElvain, June 8, 1829, ibid., No. 6), and a treaty was concluded at Little Sandusky August 3rd of the same year. (7 U. S. Stat. at L., 326.) The unexpended portion of the appropriation was used to defray the costs of their removal. (McKenney to McElvain, August 29, 1829, " Indian Office Letter Books," Series II, No. 6, p. 75.) The Jackson Papers show that a good deal of discussion took place over the best way to remove the various Ohio bands. During the progress of the treaty negotiations, the Indians were promised transportation in wagons; but Gardiner preferred their going on horseback (Gardiner to Gen. George Gibson, July 31, 1832; Lieut. J. F. Lane to Gen. George Gibson, July 31, 1832) ; while economy argued for a water route, to which the Indians were unalterably opposed. A few score of Indians remained in Ohio. (W. K. Moorehead, " The Indian Tribes of Ohio " in " Ohio Arch. and Hist. Soc. Quar., VII : 108.)

Wirt's motion for an injunction came up for a hearing before the Supreme Court on the 5th of March,[a] and, to the discomfiture of the Cherokees and gratification of the Southerners,[b] was dismissed for want of jurisdiction, it being the opinion of the bench, Justices Story and Thompsan dissenting, that an Indian Nation was not a

---

[a] Cherokee Nation v. Georgia, 5 Peters, 1–80.

[b] "The Knoxville Register," July 21, 1830, and August 18, 1830, quoting from "The Louisville Public Advertiser," gives a good idea of the way in which Wirt's "wicked and unprincipled project" was regarded in the South. "We are thus convinced that Mr. Wirt and his employers can have but one object in view—and that is, to increase the excitement that has been got up on the Indian Question. They may hope to enlist the Supreme Court in their behalf, and to procure a decision adverse to the sovereignty of Ga. and to effect thereby, in the sequel, a severance of the Union. They are aware that Ga. will not surrender her rights as a State without making a manly and patriotic effort to defend them, and that, should they be forced to resist a decree of the federal judiciary, they would not stand alone in the conflict. Thus under pretense of sustaining the pretension of the Cherokees to sovereignty and independence, the opposition are obviously striving to overthrow the State governments or to dissolve the Union. The treason of Arnold, though more palpable, was not more reprehensible or base." The "Kentucky Gazette" offered something of the same tenor when it said that the idea of Indian sovereignty was in every sense a "new-fangled doctrine" and had never been contended for until the law for the removal of the Indian tribes was made a pretext for opposing the Administration. ("Nashville Republican and State Gazette," November 13, 1830.)

Jackson's personal views were expressed in a memorandum to Cass as follows: "The case of Johnston & McIntosh (8 Wheaton) has settled, that the North American Indian tribes, east the Mississippi are a conquered & dependent people—that their hunting grounds were subject to be granted and that the Indian tribes had no right to grant to Individuals. There they are dependent, not on the Federal power in exclusion to the State authority where they reside within the limits of a State, but to the sovereign power of the State within whose sovereign limits they reside. No feature in the Federal constitution is more prominent, than that the general powers confered on congress, can only be enforced, & executed upon the people of the union. This is a government of the people. 1st. The House of Representatives are their immediate representative or agent. 2nd. The senate is their agent elected in the sovereign State assemblies. 3rd. The President is their agent elected by their immediate agents, the Electors. Who does these represent? The people of the *Union* as law makers—over whom does their jurisdiction extend? *Over the people of the union.* Who are the people of the union? All those subject to the jurisdiction of the sovereign States. None else, and it is an idle feeling that can advocate any other doctrine—or a total ignorance of the real principles upon which our federal union is *based.* An absolute independence of the Indian tribes from State authority can never bear an intelligent investigation and a quasi-independence of State authority when located within its Territorial limits is *absurd.*

"If the Indians were not subjects of the State within whose Territorial limits they were, what right had the General Government to accept cessions of Territory that the States had no right to? What right had Virginia nor Carolina &c to pay part of the claims which was encurred in the revolution struggle by grants of land within her territorial limits & in the actual occupancy of the Indians & afterwards cede the same country to the United States—If the Indians were an independent people, then these grants are void, & the titles granted in Kent[y], Tennessee & parts of Ohio are void— Such a doctrine would not be well relished in the west by those who suffered & bled so freely by being the first pioneers to enjoy the land so dearly bought by their privations in the revolutionary struggle.

"I have rose from my couch to give you these crude & undigested thoughts, that if you see Mr. Bell you may give him the ideas tho crude, he can digest them—We have acted upon these principles, they are *sound* and are such upon which our confederated *union* rests—I cannot abandon them. I will thank you to preserve this and return it to me— it may be of use hereafter to guard my consistency.

"Very respectfully yours

"ANDREW JACKSON

"Gov[r]. CASS,
    "*Secretary of War.*"
("Jackson Papers," 1831.)

foreign State within the meaning of the Constitution, and therefore could not bring a suit that would be cognizable by the Supreme Court. Governor Gilmer viewed the whole proceeding with the contempt he thought it deserved. Even had judgment been rendered, unless, perchance, it were not adverse to Georgia, it is not likely he would have concerned himself with it, since only two months before, sustained by the legislature, he had ignored a citation to appear before the same tribunal and show cause why a sentence delivered by a Georgian court against a Cherokee Indian should not be reversed.[a]

The dismissal of Wirt's case was a great disappointment to others besides the Cherokees.[b] The Creeks were utterly discouraged. Then falling back once more upon treaty guaranties they renewed their plea for protection and were told, " You are within the limits of Alabama which is an independent State, and which is not answerable to your Great Father, for the exercise of her jurisdiction over the people who reside within her limits." [c] Still persistent, they asked to be allowed to send a delegation to Washington. Many of their people were starving. The method of distributing their annuities had been changed without consulting them,[d] and Agent Crowell was holding back a large sum wherewith to pay judgments allowed in Alabama courts in suits brought against the Indians by white people.[e] Permission to come to Washington was granted only on one condition, that the delegation be fully empowered to treat " in conformity with the wishes of the Government." [f] The delegation came,

---

[a] Corn Tassel, a Cherokee, murdered a tribesman within the limits of the Indian country and was taken before the superior court of Hall County, Georgia, for trial. He was found guilty and sentenced to death. The Cherokees appealed the case on a writ of error to the United States Supreme Court—hence the citation to Governor Gilmer; (" Niles's Register," XXXIX : 338) ; but before the case could be reached on the Supreme Court docket the sheriff was instructed to execute the sentence of the local tribunal. (Chappell, p. 297.)

[b] The Chickasaws were particularly disappointed. Scarcely was the treaty of August, 1830, negotiated, than they showed signs of discontent and seemed determined not to remove willingly. (" Missionary Herald," December, 1830, vol. 26, p. 383.) The exploring delegation did, however, start for the West in the autumn (Ibid., January, 1831, vol. 27, p. 45), and in course of time returned with a favorable report of the land visited. (Ibid., November, 1831, p. 352.) Against this, however, were the earlier adverse decisions of individual Chickasaws who had gone West for their own satisfaction. Much undecided as to what course to pursue, the common Indians abandoned themselves to dissipation, and were only restrained by the hope that their land would be saved to them either by the decision of the Supreme Court (" Missionary Herald," October, 1832, 28 : 334) or by the failure of a final delegation to find a suitable country in the West next to that of the Choctaws.

[c] Eaton to Creeks, May 16, 1831, " Indian Office Letter Books," Series II, No. 7, p. 226.

[d] This was done by Executive order, because, as Cass explained, February 10, 1832 (" Indian Office Letter Books," Series II, No. 8, pp. 88–89), it was only fair, if the whole tribe owned the land in common, that chiefs, warriors, and common Indians should all share alike. Wirt was of the opinion that the change was made in order to prevent the chiefs of the southern tribes from having any funds with which to prosecute a suit in the Federal courts.

[e] S. S. Hamilton to Crowell, October 6, 1831, " Indian Office Letter Books," Series II, No. 7, p. 423.

[f] Hamilton to Crowell, October 5, 1831, " Indian Office Letter Books," Series II, No. 7, p. 422.

and Cass had but one answer to their cry of distress—removal.[a] At length he succeeded in negotiating a treaty with them whereby for a pecuniary consideration their tribal rights east of the Mississippi were extinguished.[b] Such as chose might select land in severalty; the others were to take their own time and remove westward at the Government expense. The fourteenth article contained a guaranty of integrity as against the operation of State or Territorial laws similar to that given to the Choctaws.

The reader will begin to think that the execution of the Removal Act was proving to be a very easy matter—not so. In Illinois all was confusion. For many years trouble had been brewing with the Sacs and Foxes of Mississippi, or with such of them as constituted the " British Band of Rock River." In 1804 the confederated tribes had made a treaty [c] of limits with Governor Harrison which they had confirmed in 1816 [d] without making any specific reference to its substance, and again in 1822 and 1825. The white men interpreted those agreements to mean a relinquishment of all territorial claims east of the Mississippi; but the Indians disagreed. Indeed, they denied that the original treaty of 1804, as read to them, had ever contained any such stipulation. They had never sold any land north of the mouth of Rock River.[e] Until about 1827 they were allowed to reside on the disputed tract, for the most part unmolested, a right which could have been counted theirs under all circumstances; for, by a clause in the seventh article of the treaty of 1804, they were to be allowed to live and hunt upon the ceded land as long as the United States held it as public property. Squatters had come at intervals since the summer of 1823 [f] and had made more or less trouble, but there were no bona fide preemptioners. Even as regarded other Indians, the occupation by the Sacs and Foxes was not exclusive, but was shared to a greater or less extent by the Kickapoos, Chippewas, Pottawatomies, and Winnebagos.[g] Governor Edwards was determined to get rid of them all,[h] and, apprehensive of this, the tribes became restless, especially as the white people threatened to take by

---

[a] Cass to Nehoh Mico and other Creek chiefs, November 1, 1821, " Indian Office Letter Books," Series II, No. 7, pp. 446–448 ; Same to Same, January 16, 1832, Ibid., No. 8, pp. 15–17.

[b] March 24, 1832, 7 United States Statutes at Large, 366–368.

[c] 7 United States Statutes at Large, 84–87.

[d] Ibid., pp. 141–142. The Sacs and Foxes who had emigrated to Missouri confirmed it in 1815, ibid., p. 134.

[e] Letter of Forsyth, May 24, 1828, Clark's Report on the Causes of the Black Hawk War, among " Jackson's Papers."

[f] Thwaites, p. 8.

[g] The three tribes last mentioned had doubtless a better claim than the Sacs and Foxes to at least some of the disputed land (treaty of Prairie du Chien, August 19, 1825, 7 U. S. Stat. at L., 272), but the claims of all were equally untenable in the eyes of Governor Edwards.

[h] Superintendent to Forsyth, May 29, 1829, Clark's Report.

force the Cosh-co-cong mines, which belonged unquestionably to the Winnebagos.[a]

Affairs went from bad to worse. Each winter the Sacs and Foxes went off on their annual hunt, and each spring returned to find the unmistakable evidences of some new encroachment. On one occasion a whole village was seized, the cornfields enclosed, and the lodges torn down.[b] Agent Forsyth endeavored to pacify the despoiled owners who, though enraged and fiercely determined to secure their rights in the ejectment of the squatters, attempted as yet no violence. They did, however, boast of what they would do in the event of failure, and declared that other tribes of the Northwest were ready to combine with them against the Americans.[c] From this time on the Sacs and Foxes were divided into two hostile camps, Keokuk's and Black Hawk's. The Keokuk faction was inclined toward peace and promised that it would move West as soon as its individual members had gathered their crops. With this peaceful retirement in prospect, the Department of War requested the leniency of the governor of Illinois for one year more.[d] It was a case, however, of holding out the olive branch with one hand and stabbing with the other; for within a fortnight it had consented to a new plan of irritating the Indians by permitting Clark to instruct Menard[e] "to feel the Sacs and Foxes upon the subject of a cession of their mineral lands west of the Mississippi."[f]

When the year of grace had almost expired, Forsyth again broached the subject of removal.[g] Keokuk said he had done his best "to persuade the mutinous Indians to leave," but they would not. Shortly afterwards they themselves promised that they would give a definite answer as soon as their chiefs and braves, who had gone on a journey to the Winnebagoes, had returned. Forsyth thought this was only a pretext to gain time and urged a display of military force.[h] The Government dilly-dallied and contented itself with threats,[i] meanwhile finishing the negotiations for a cession West.[j] Spring and summer passed, and when autumn came the Indians of the British band went on their winter hunt, intending to return as

---

[a] Superintendent to Forsyth, June 23, 1828, ibid.

[b] Same to same, May 17, 1829, ibid.

[c] Same to same, May 22, 1829, ibid.

[d] McKenney to Clark, June 17, 1829, " Indian Office Letter Books," Series II, No. 6, p. 18.

[e] July 4, 1829, Clark's Report.

[f] These were the Dubuque mines which the General Government was anxious to possess, partly for their own value and partly for the purpose of forcing the Indians back from the river (McKenney to Clark, June 9, 1830, "Indian Office Letter Books," Series II, No. 6, p. 469), out of reach of the illicit traffic in spirituous liquors which had not a little to do with their hostile attitude.

[g] Forsyth to Superintendent, April 28, 1830, Clark's report.

[h] Same to same, April 30, 1830, ibid.

[i] Same to same, May 25, 1830, ibid.

[j] Treaty of July 15, 1830, 7 United States Statutes at Large, p. 328.

usual,[a] which they did; but with at first, as far as the agent could make out, no hostile disposition, except such as might be implied by a determination to keep their territory north of Rock River.[b] Soon, however, they discovered that it had been surveyed and sold during their absence,[c] and they thereupon threatened to form a coalition against the United States and to destroy the settlements from the Detroit to the Sabine.[d] The intruding white men were seriously alarmed, as well they might be, and assailed Governor Edwards's successor, John Reynolds,[e] with petitions for aid, not scrupling to exaggerate the number of the Indians and their past offenses enormously. In answer to this the militia came, and, while it quelled, with the help of regulars under General Gaines, the present disturbance, provoked new disorders by desecrating the Indian burial ground,[f] which the Sacs and Foxes tried to set to rights, but were prevented from so doing by the settlers. To his credit, be it said, Governor Reynolds did not countenance any of these later proceedings;[g] but, whether sanctioned or not, they angered the already excited Indians. For the time being, however, with the help of General Gaines, they were quieted and withdrew to the western bank of the Mississippi, from whence they were shortly summoned and forced to sign a capitulation, June 30, 1831. Then they went back under a solemn promise never again to return to the vicinity of Rock River.

It was not long, as fate would have it, before Black Hawk's thirst for vengeance against some marauding and murdering Sioux and Menominees brought him once more into unpleasant relations with the United States, whose officers tried to restrain his fury. Incensed at the interference, he lent a ready ear to the evil reports of Neapope, his associate in command, that the British at Malden, together with neighboring Indian tribes or parts of tribes, were to cooperate in an attack upon his enemies. Encouraged by this news, false as it was, Black Hawk left Keokuk and the peaceful Sacs and Foxes on the west side of the Mississippi and, in defiance of the capitulation exacted by Gaines, recrossed with his warlike band to the old camping ground. This was the signal for a renewal of hostilities; but per-

---

[a] Felix St. Vrain to Superintendent, October 8, 1830, Clark's Report.

[b] Same to same, May 15, 1831, ibid.

[c] Davidson and Stuvé, p. 375.

[d] Reynold's Report of May 29, 1831.

[e] Reynolds lost no time in threatening retaliation should any outbreak occur. He had already warned the Kickapoos and Pottowatomies that if they did not vacate " the ceded land," and any act of hostility were committed on the frontier, he would not wait for the Federal Government but would remove them upon his own responsibility. (Superintendent to Menard, May 31, 1831, Clark's Report.) The Indians protested, because the treaty of Prairie du Chien, upon which Illinois based her title, had been made with factions only, and they, the actual occupants, had not consented to it. (Talks, accompanying Clark's Report.)

[f] Letter of Felix St. Vrain, July 23, 1831, Clark's Report.

[g] Letter to Clark, August 5, 1831, ibid.

chance they might not have amounted to much, for Black Hawk was soon aware of the falsity of Neapope's report, had not a troop of rangers, under Maj. Isaiah Stillman, violated an Indian flag of truce. The effect was electrical. The maddened Indians routed the half-intoxicated and cowardly aggressors, and then, though handicapped by the presence of wives and children, hurried on, closely pursued by General Atkinson with his regulars, who had come from Jefferson Barracks for the purpose of forcing the surrender of such Sacs as had attacked and murdered the Menominees at Prairie du Chien. Illinois militiamen were also on hand in large numbers. The campaign seemed unduly protracted, and much dissatisfaction with Atkinson's movements was exhibited by the eastern press. Finally, General Scott was ordered to repair to the seat of war; but on the way his army was so ravaged by cholera that the conflict was practically over before he arrived. The glory of victory fell largely to the volunteers. After making more than one brave stand, and leading their pursuers a wearisome chase, the Indians were completely defeated in the memorable battle of Bad Axe, August 2, 1832.[a]

To Governor Reynolds and General Scott was intrusted the task of negotiating the terms of peace, and two treaties resulted, one with the Winnebagoes and one with the Sacs and Foxes. In both cases the entire tribe suffered for the disaffection of the few. The Winnebagoes, who though vacillating and treacherous, had rendered some assistance to Black Hawk, ceded all their claims east of the Mississippi and agreed to retire to the "neutral ground" of Iowa and Minnesota.[b] The Sacs and Foxes, as the greater sinners, were still more harshly dealt with. They surrendered nearly the whole of eastern Iowa, except a comparatively small reserve of 400 square miles, upon which they were henceforth to be concentrated.[c] The exchanges and removals contemplated by these two treaties of Fort Armstrong were to be effected upon the 1st of June, 1833.

With two more tribes disposed of, let us turn to Florida. The execution of the Removal Act was there to result in a far greater war; but there was much to be done before that could be. At the importunity of the Territorial delegate, Joseph M. White,[d] President Jackson commissioned Gadsden to negotiate for the removal of the Seminoles, who were still in dire need and whose wants were to be supplied only on the condition that they would consent to emigrate.[e] Gadsden was to tell them so and that they must unite with the Creeks.[f] A treaty was negotiated at Payne's Landing on the 9th of

---

[a] Reports of the Commanding Generals, "Jackson Papers."

[b] Treaty of September 15, 1832, 7 United States Statutes at Large, 370–373.

[c] Treaty of September 21, 1832, ibid., p. 374–376.

[d] White to Cass, January 23, 1832, "Miscellaneous Files," Indian Office MS. Records.

[e] Cass to H. L. White, January 30, 1832, "Indian Office Letter Books," Series II, No. 8, pp. 46–48.

[f] Instructions, January 30, 1832, ibid., pp. 48–51.

May, 1832; [a] but it was not to be considered binding upon the Indians until the exploring party which they were to send West in search of a home had returned and had reported favorably, so far so good. That much accomplished, Gadsden went on and completed his mission, which was to negotiate for a cession of the Appalachicola reservations.[b]

The design of uniting the Seminoles with the Creeks increased the difficulties already existing in the West. The Quapaws, disappointed in their union with the Caddoes, had returned to Arkansas; the Chickasaws had not yet found a country to suit them except within Choctaw limits or beyond the line, in Texas; [c] the Creek and Cherokee boundaries conflicted, as did also the Delaware and Pawnee. To facilitate the Chickasaw removal, Eaton and Coffee had gone West to confer with the Choctaws; for it was believed that their country was large enough to accommodate both tribes comfortably.[d] To adjust the other difficulties, and this one too, should Eaton and Coffee fail,[e] Jackson appointed, under act of Congress, July 14, 1832, three commissioners—Montfort Stokes, governor of North Carolina; Henry Ellsworth, of Connecticut, and the Rev. J. F. Schermerhorn, of Utica, New York.[f]

The acts of this commission were various. For a time the men worked together, and at Fort Gibson negotiated, in the spring of 1833, some treaties of memorable import—one with the Cherokees,[g] another with the Creeks,[h] and a third with the unaccredited Seminole explorers.[i] The first two do not concern us at present, except in so far as the Creeks—their territorial disputes with the Cherokees amicably adjusted—agreed to permit the Seminoles to unite with themselves and

---

[a] 7 United States Statutes at Large, 368–370.

[b] Treaty of October 11, 1832, and of June 18, 1833, ibid., pp. 377, 427.

[c] The Chickasaw treaty, negotiated in 1830, was to be null and void unless the Indians found a suitable home in the West. That they had not done, and consequently the treaty had not yet been sent to the Senate for ratification. In the spring of 1832 the House of Representatives called upon the President for papers relating to it. (Resolution of February 21, 1832.) It had leaked out that some of Jackson's friends—Coffee, Currin, and Lewis—were beneficiaries under it for a lease of the valuable Salt Lick. Jackson parried the thrust by refusing to produce the papers unless the House intended an impeachment. If Washington could make that an excuse in the case of a ratified treaty, surely he could in the case of an unratified. (Cass to Chas. A. Wickliffe, March, 1, 1832, "Chickasaw Letter Books," Vol. A, p. 3.)

[d] Eaton to Coffee, March 31, 1831, "Indian Office Letter Books," Series II, No. 7, pp. 168–170.

[e] They did fail, but the task did not fall upon the Schermerhorn Commission. So much pressure was brought to bear upon the Administration for a settlement of the Chickasaw lands that it was obliged to commission Coffee to negotiate the treaty of Pontitock Creek, October 20, 1832. (7 U. S. Stat. at L., pp. 380–390.) The Indians sold their lands at a cash valuation and went again in search of a country. It was not until 1837 that the Choctaws consented to receive them. (Choctaw-Chickasaw Convention, January 17, 1837, 7 U. S. Stat. at L., p. 605, Appendix IV.)

[f] It was originally intended to have Governor Carroll, Governor Stokes, and Roberts Vaux, of Pennsylvania.

[g] 7 United States Statutes at Large, 414–416.

[h] Ibid., 417–420.

[i] Ibid., 423–424.

to locate in a body upon their reserve. The third treaty must go down in the annals as the direct cause of the second Seminole war. It was absolutely unauthorized by the Indians whom it professed to bind. The seven chiefs had been sent West to seek a new home and not to conclude an exchange for one until they had reported to their constituents in Florida. Notwithstanding this, the United States commissioners prevailed upon them to sign a treaty which should complete and practically give force to the earlier one of Payne's Landing,[a] whereby the Indians had provisionally promised to remove within three years from the date of ratification; there was to be the rub. The new treaty specified the limits of the new home. Schermerhorn,[b] whose conduct, as long as we know anything of him

---

[a] There is a suspicion that even this treaty was not negotiated in a straightforward manner. According to a story current among old Florida settlers, the chiefs themselves did not sign, but young bucks, dressed to impersonate their elders, did.

[b] A letter, written by the Rev. J. F. Schermerhorn to Joel R. Poinsett, Secretary of War, November 11, 1839 (" Miscellaneous Files," 1839–1841, Indian Office MS. Records), conveys the impression that Schermerhorn may not have been so unprincipled by nature as his actions relative to Indian removal would indicate. This is the letter :

UTICA, *11th Nov. 1839.*

To the Honorable
    JOEL R. POINSETT
        Sec. of War.
SIR.

Having heretofore taken an active, and to me a deeply interesting part, in accomplishing the removal of the Indians from the territorial limits and jurisdiction of the States, and in settling them in a country exclusively their own,—I am exceedingly anxious to see carried into effect those measures for improving their condition and promoting their present and future well being, which were then contemplated by the administration and its friends, and which were held out as inducements to the Indians to remove.

These were to preserve the Red men from further degredation and final extermination and ruin—to secure to them a permanent and peacable home—to deliver them from State oppression & aggressions—to protect them in the enjoyment of all their personal and political rights, which they had lost or could no longer enjoy ; (and in which the U. States could not sustain them) while they continued to reside within the jurisdiction of the states—and finally to civilize and christianise them by every proper means, and as soon as they were qualified for it, to give them a name and rank in our federal Union.

These I have ever understood, were the great objects intended to be promoted and designed to be effected by the emigration of the Indians. These were the objects I had in view, in the part I have acted of this great drama ; and I consider it an object worthy all the toil, labour, expense, sacrifice and suffering it has cost our nation & the Indians. And if the necessary measures to effect these objects are now put in successful operation, it will stop the mouths of opposers, and convince the world that the policy of the Government was dictated by humanity, benevolence, wisdom and justice.

The Indians whom it was contemplated to remove from the east to the west of the Mississippi have now nearly all emigrated, or are under treaty stipulations to emigrate ; and it now becomes necessary to adopt some wise and prudent measures, to advance them in the occupation & pursuits of civilized life ; and to preserve peace among themselves & between them and our own citizens. To effect these objects permit me to suggest a Territorial organization, and the adoption of a plain and simple code of laws for regulating trade and intercourse between the several tribes and between them and our own citizens.

I. The boundaries of the territory should be accurately defined, and the same be set apart for the exclusive occupation of the Indians ; and provision should be made for the enjoyment of real estate in severalty, with the right of inheritance and the powers of alienation, only to citizens of the several tribes.

II. A code of laws should be adopted by congress for the purpose of protecting the persons and property of the members of the several tribes, and for the punishment of all acts of hostility, assault, fraud, theft, robbery, & murder committed in the Indian country by persons of one tribe upon another ; or by the Indians upon our citizens ; or our citizens upon the Indians—and for the adjudication & decision of all conflicting

as a Government commissioner, merits reproach and is such as to
disgrace his cloth, left the Seminoles to return to their expectant

interest & claims between them—we all know that through offences of this kind committed
by individuals or parties of one tribe upon another, or by the Indians upon our citizens,
or our citizens upon the Indians, (because there were no laws or authority in the Indian
country, to punish promptly such offenders) all have practised on·the principles of the
"lex talionis" & have indulged in private reprisals, retaliation & revenge, which have
generally ended in blood & sometimes in Indian wars, accompanied with the most cruel
barbarities & the sacrifice of valuable lives and much treasure.

I know we have some laws to punish certain crimes committed in the Indian country,
but where is the power in the country to try & punish them—There is none—the culprits
if they can be caught, must be drag'ed to Little Rock, Ark.—or some place in Missouri
some hundred miles from the Indian country, & there if he is an Indian, must be tried,
without the benefit of the testimony of his friends, perhaps the only witnesses of the
transaction, and could they be heard might prove his innocence—all must be pursuaded
he has no chance of justice. If the white man is the aggressor, what chance has a poor
Indian on redress to prosecute before the courts of those states?—[?] therefore the
Indian knowing or believing he can have no redress, the white man goes unpunished or
the Indian takes the law in his own hand, & avenges his own wrongs—To remedy this
evil I would propose :—

III. The organization of an Independent Federal court, for the Indian Territory, to
take cognizance of all overt acts committed in the Indian country by individuals of one
tribe upon another, or by Indians upon our people, & our people upon the Indians, and to
adjudicate all claims or demands of Indians of one tribe upon another, or of our citizens
upon Indians or Indians upon our citizens—In the organization of this court provision
should be made for receiving the testimony of Indians as competent witnesses and to act
as jurors & assistant justices, & deputy marshalls. In the first place the Judges, clerks, &
marshalls should be white men, and from their manner of doing business in court, the
Indians will learn how to conduct and carry on their judicial proceedings among themselves, especially if the judges of the Indian courts should sit as associate justices in the
Federal Court in matters appertaining to the people of their own tribes—The marshall
should be required to carry the judgment of the courts into execution ; and if resisted to
be authorized to call upon the constituted authorities of the tribe to aid him in the execution of his duties ; and if refused or insufficient, then to call upon the U. S. troops sta-
tioned in the Indian country to enforce his authority.

IV. The officers of the Territory need be very few—a governor, who should also be
superintendent of Indian Affairs—a secretary who might also be a disbursing officer, to
pay all Indian annuities—-(which might be paid at the seat of Government of the Territory unless otherwise provided for by treaty stipulations)—and as many Judges, clerks &
marshalls as might be found requisite—two or three of each would be the most that
would be required at present—I would have no legislative council, and I question whether
one could be organized without the consent of the Indians—If you deemed it necessary,
you might have an executive council, consisting of the Governor, Secretary & Judges, who
might also be a court of final appeals from the decisions of the district courts.

V. Provision should also be made by Congress, for the choice and reception of a delegate or delegates to represent the Indian Territory according to the just expectations
held up to the Indians in several of the treaties.

There might be three delegates allowed them—one to represent the Southern Indians,
or those from the south of the Ohio River—one to represent the Northern Indians, or
those formerly residing north of the Ohio & on the great Lakes—and one to represent
the indigenous tribes—These might be selected by a certain number of electors to be
chosen by each tribe, according to their relative population—

You will perceive on a careful examination, that the organization of the Indian Territory above proposed, neither interferes with, nor is subversive of any treaty provision
with the Indians. It does not touch the rights of the several tribes to make and execute their own laws, upon their own people and in their own country. Neither does it
include them under the jurisdiction or within the territorial limits or any state or territory—of the citizens of the U. S.—By the constitution of the United States and by
Treaty stipulations, legislation over the Indians is the right of congress—whose duty
it is to preserve and promote peace between the several Indian tribes and between
them and citizens of the United States.

The object of the organization of the territory as above suggested being wholly con-
find to regulating trade, & intercourse between the several tribes ; & between them &
citizens of the United States ; and to promote the peace of the country ; with which is
inseparably connected the improvement of their moral condition, temporal prosperity &

countrymen and himself proceeded to force the refugee Quapaws into the northeastern corner of the Indian Territory.[a]

Missouri, within whose limits so many remnants of the northern tribes had found a temporary asylum, derived great benefit from the Removal Act.[b] Some of her Indians were claimants to lands in Illinois and Indiana, therefore one and the same commission, Messrs. Clark, Allen, and Kouns, was empowered to relieve the three States jointly—in whole or in part. In October, 1832, four treaties were negotiated at Castor Hill; [c] and " remnants " of the Kickapoos, Delawares, Shawnees, Weas, Peorias, Kaskaskias, and Piankeshaws passed over the border. Missouri was free. Meanwhile another commission, headed by Governor Jennings, was negotiating with the Pottawatomies, who were common to Indiana, Illinois, and Michigan. Certain cessions were secured, but the tribe was not yet ready for removal.[d] The subsequent commission of George B. Porter, governor

progress in civilization. With such an arrangement in the Indian territory, you might dispense with a host of Indian agents & subagents who in nine cases out of ten do more evil than good among the Indians—You might also greatly simplify & lessen the labour and expense of the Indian department at Washington—You might more effectively restrain & punish the iniquitous & licentious practices, & frauds committed in the Indian country by our own citizens; from whence come wars and fightings among them—It would also have the tendency to prevent " the hue & cry " which we now hear, ever and anon, about the danger of Indian difficulties, and of Indian Wars, whenever some men on the frontiers want more public money expended among them. Then suddenly a new military post on the Frontier is found to be necessary, or some new companies of dragoons, or mounted militia must be raised.

Indeed I consider that some such organization would do more to preserve the peace & prosperity of the Indian Country than any standing army you could place there; for experience has taught us that these are as often the occasion of broils and Indian Wars, as they prevent them—I see no alternative between governing the Indian country by a few well defined, settled & simple laws, easily to be understood, promptly executed by an efficient & energetic executive officer, to carry the decisions of the court into effect, and to enforce them by the military if necessary—or else to govern it by military orders & rule, as occasions may require, to prevent or put down open hostilities. But this has no tendency to prevent the commission of crimes, or improve the moral condition of a people, which are the great things, that ought to be aimed at—to promote the peace and prosperity of any people—

The only apology I have to make for the liberty I have taken in addressing you on this subject, is the deep interest I feel to promote, the peace prosperity & welfare of the Indians—

If anything I have suggested meets your approbation, and shall lead to any favourable action from Congress on this subject, I shall feel much gratified, & thank God for his goodness & mercies toward the Indians; and if not, I shall have a satisfaction of knowing I have done all in my power to serve and save this once noble but now degraded neglected, & despised race.

    With great respect

        I am your obt. serv[t]—

                    J. F. SCHERMERHORN.

[a] Treaty, May 13, 1833, 7 United States Statutes at Large, 424–426.

[b] Prior to its passage the Delawares had consented to follow the example of the Shawnees and cross the line into the present State of Kansas (Supplementary Article, negotiated by Agent Vashon, September, 24, 1829, 7 U. S. Stat. L., 327), but the agreement was not ratified until 1831.

[c] 7 United States Statutes at Large, 391, 397, 403, 410.

[d] The treaties, negotiated by Messrs. Jennings, Davis, and Crume, provided for a large number of reserved sections, title to which it was the duty of later commissions—William Marshall, 1834, and Abel C. Pepper, 1836—to extinguish. Pepper's last treaty, negotiated at Washington, February 11, 1837, capped the climax. There was a general agreement that the Pottawatomies should, within two years, remove to Osage River. Marshall and Pepper in turn negotiated with the Miamies; but it was not until after the second treaty of the Forks of the Wabash, November 28, 1840, that these Indians gave up their last acre in Indiana and went west.

of Michigan Territory, Col. Thomas J. V. Owen, agent to the Indians interested, and Col. William Weatherford, was decidedly more successful as regarded emigration. It negotiated with the " United Nations of Chippewa, Ottawa, and Pottowatomie Indians," [a] and, after careful warning to the Indians that experience had shown it was " too late to treat at the cannon's mouth,"[b] gained its consent, in the treaty of Chicago, September 26, 1833, to an exchange of territory.[c]

It is now incumbent upon us to return to the Cherokees. Both the State and Federal authorities were desirous of avoiding notoriety by accomplishing removal without provoking a further appeal to the judiciary, but it was not to be. Invasions of the gold country were so numerous that Governor Gilmer was obliged to recommend that

---

[a] Treaty of Chicago, September 26, 1833, 7 United States Statutes at Large, 431.

[b] MS. Journal of the Commissioners, " Treaty Files," 1802–1853.

[c] (1) This does not signify that three whole tribes emigrated. Particular bands of each had confederated together and now negotiated as a " nation." As a matter of fact, nearly all the tribes of the Northwest emigrated in detachments. Henry Schoolcraft brought about the removal of most of the Chippewas. The Swan Creek and Black River bands emigrated under treaty of May 9, 1836. They had the choice of going west of the Mississippi or northwest of St. Anthony's Falls, and they preferred the former. The Saginaw Chippewas, by the treaty of Detroit, January 14, 1837, had a similar privilege ; that is, they might go west of the Mississippi or west of Lake Michigan. The treaty of Flint River, December 20, 1837, substituted the headwaters of Osage River, but the agreement was never carried out.

(2) The following is a copy of a letter from G. B. Porter announcing the successful prosecution of his mission to date :

CHICAGO, *Sep. 28th, 1833*.

SIR :

I have the honor to transmit for your perusal, the better to enable you to decide upon the request that I shall make, the Copy of a Treaty and Supplementary articles, concluded on the 26th & 27th inst. with the United Nations of Chippewa, Potawatamie & Ottawa Indians.

You will perceive the Cession embraces all their land on the West Shore of Lake Michigan, and all owned by them in Michigan Territory South of Grand River, (without a Reservation ! !)—The Treaty will be transmitted as soon as the pressure of my avocations will permit me to close the schedules attached to it.

The Indians are thoroughly imbued with the spirit of emigration. From the issue of this negotiation, and the feeling it has generated, among them, I anticipate confidently, a favorable result to my intended effort with the Miamies, whom I shall meet on the 8th October. The example will, I doubt not, produce an impression upon all the Indians remaining, decidedly advantageous. I am equally confident in the belief that while these impressions are yet fresh, propositions would be readily entertained by the owners of the reservations of land retained by the Tippecanoe Treaties of Oct. 26th and 27th, 1832, to cede them to the United States, & join their brothers in their pilgrimage to the West. Not a foot is reserved to them by the Treaty we have just concluded. Thus this whole Country may probably be altogether relieved from any serious impediment to it's entire settlement, by the removal of a population, which will always embarass & retard it, while at the same time the policy of the Government in respect to it's Indian Intercourse will have been advanced to an important extent.

Under these circumstances I feel impelled by my sense of duty, to submit to the consideration of the Department, the expediency of following up the policy of the Government, while the time is propitious by authorizing an immediate negotiation to be had with these people for their reserves under the two treaties aforesaid. As I shall have these Potawatamies assemble at the Tippecanoe Mills to receive their money & Goods, the attempt to procure a cession of these reservations can be made without any expense to the Government. They embrace almost every valuable spot of land in that Country :— for without these groves of timber and water privileges, what are the prairies worth?

If the views I have taken the liberty to suggest meet the approbation of the Department, I have the honor to request that an authority and instructions to me may be imthe legislature enact a law forbidding white men to reside among the Indians,[a] special exemption to be had, however, where persons were agents of the Federal Government or were of high respectability, willing to take an oath as citizens to support the laws of Georgia. An act of this tenor was approved December 22, 1830. One week later the whole body of missionaries within the Cherokee country took a step that so enraged Governor Gilmer that he decided so to interpret the recent enactment that *they* might be brought within its operation. Their offense was they had held a meeting at New Echota and, while exonerating themselves for meddling in politics, declared their conviction that the Cherokees as a people were averse to emigration and that the extension of Georgian jurisdiction would work " an immense and irreparable injury." [b] Soon they were called upon to retract or remove.[c] Refusal to do either brought about the arrest of three of their number—two ordained missionaries, S. A. Worcester and John Thompson,[d] and one missionary teacher, Isaac Proctor. An application for a writ of habeas corpus was successful, and when the case came up for hearing before the superior court for Gwinnett County, Judge Clayton (another of Wirt's relatives, but a man of confessedly different opinions upon the doctrine of State Rights), ordered the release of the prisoners, not upon the plea of their counsel that the late law was unconstitutional, but upon the assumption that, by the indulgence of Georgia, they were exempt from its operation, because, as dispensers of the civilization fund, they were nominally agents of the United States. Gilmer was of a different opinion, and communicated [e] with Eaton, whence it was

---

mediately prepared & transmitted to the Post Office at Maumee, with directions to the Postmaster to forward them to me by express at the Forks of the Wabash. The Letter can reach me in this way in 8 days after it is mailed at Washington.

   I am in very great haste
      With considerations of
         Much regard, your
            Ob. Serv[t].

                                                            G. B. PORTER.
The Hon. LEWIS CASS,
         Secy. of War.
   (Indian Office MS. Records, " Treaty Files," 1802–1853.

   (3) An interesting incident in connection with the negotiation of this treaty of Chicago was the Indian demand to see the credentials of the Commissioners. (MS. Journal of the Commissioners, " Treaty Files," 1802–1853, Indian Office MS. Records.)

   [a] " Georgians," p. 365.

   [b] " Missionary Herald," March, 1831, Vol. XXVII : 79–84.

   [c] A copy of a newspaper containing the text of the law was sent to them about the middle of January, while " many reports " * * * " were circulated and came to [their] ears * * * , and some of them very directly from the agents and other officers of Georgia, who were charged with carrying the law into effect, which tended to confirm the opinion that the law was designed to apply to them." (" Missionary Herald," May, 1831, Vol. XXVII : 165.)

   [d] The arrests were all made " without a warrant from any magistrate, or any civil precept whatever. The proceedings were entirely of a military character. Upon their arrival at the headquarters, they were marched into camp with drum and fife, and a good deal of military pomp was displayed. * * * " (Ibid., p. 166.)

   [e] Gilmer to Eaton, April 20, 1831, " Georgians," p. 389.

divulged that seven out of nine of the regular missionaries within the Cherokee country, and those the most offending, were supported entirely by the resources of the American board.[a]   The Government was not prepared to count any of them its agents, except, perhaps, Mr. Worcester, who was postmaster at New Echota as well as missionary, and who, in order that he might be rendered fully answerable to Georgia for his conduct, was at once to be deprived of his secular office.

Thus stranded, the missionaries were again attacked and warned by Gilmer.[b]   Some of them still refused to comply with the legal

---

[a] Eaton to Gilmer, May 4, 1831, " Indian Office Letter Books," Series II, No. 7, p. 208.

[b] (1) " Sir—Sufficient evidence has been obtained from the government of the United States to convince the courts of this state that the missionaries employed among the Cherokees by the American Board of Foreign Missions, are not its agents, and therefore not exempted from the operation of the law forbidding white persons to reside among the Cherokees without license.   In continuing so to reside, you must have known that you were acting in violation of the laws of the state.   The mistaken decision of the superior court upon this subject, in the late case determined in Gwinett county, has enabled you for a time to persist in your opposition to the humane policy which the general government has adopted for the civilization of the Indians, and in your efforts to prevent their submission to the laws of Georgia.   However criminal your conduct in this respect may have been, I am still desirous that you should have an opportunity of avoiding the punishment which will certainly follow the continuance of your present residence.   You are therefore advised to quit it with as little delay as possible.   Col. Sanford, the commander of the Guard, will be directed to cause to be delivered to you this letter, and to enforce the laws if you should persist in your disobedience.

    Very respectfully, yours, &c

George R. Gilmer."

[Messrs. Butrick, Proctor, and Thompson, May 16, 1831.]
(Missionary Herald, August 1831, Vol. XXVII : p. 249.)

(2) " Sir—It is a part of my official duty to cause all white persons residing within the territory of the state, occupied by the Cherokees to be removed therefrom, who refuse to take the oath to support the constitution and laws of the state.   Information has been received of your continued residence within that territory, without complying with the requisites of the law, and of your claim to be exempted from its operation, on account of your holding the office of postmaster of New Echota.

You have no doubt been informed of your dismissal from that office.   That you may be under no mistake as to this matter, you are also informed that the government of the United States does not recognize as its agents the missionaries acting under the direction of the American Board of Foreign Missions.   Whatever may have been your conduct in opposing the humane policy of the general government, or exciting the Indians to oppose the jurisdiction of the state, I am still desirous of giving you and all others similarly situated, an opportunity of avoiding the punishment which will certanly follow your further residence within the state contrary to its laws.   You are, therefore, advised to remove from the territory of Georgia, occupied by the Cherokees.   Col. Sanford, the commander of the Guard, will be requested to have this letter delivered to you, and to delay your arrest until you shall have had an opportunity of leaving the state.

    Very respectfully, yours, &c.

George R. Gilmer."

[Mr. Worcester]
(" Missionary Herald," August, 1831, Vol. XXVII : p. 248.")

(3) The letters of Governor Gilmer " were forwarded to the missionaries by Colonel Sanford, the commander of the military corps called the Georgia guard, employed in the Cherokee nation ; and were accompanied by a note from himself, stating that ten days would be allowed them to remove ; and that if found residing in the nation after the expiration of that period, the law would certainly be executed upon them.

" It is hardly possible to avoid remarking, that in these letters the criminality of the missionaries is made to consist principally, if not wholly, in the influence which they are charged with having exerted on the Cherokees, unfavorable to their removal, and to the policy of the general government ; while the law makes their criminality to consist solely in being found residing within the Cherokee country on or after the first day of March, without having taken a prescribed oath, and obtained a license from the governor of Georgia   *   *   *."   (" Missionary Herald," August, 1831, Vol. XXVII : p. 249.)

requirements,[a] so were arrested,[*] brought to trial along with other

* 1. "After his (Mr. Thompson's) acquittal by the court, he returned to the station [Hightower] and pursued his labors as usual, until he received a letter from the governor of Georgia, threatening a second arrest. He then thought it best to remove his family to Brainerd, a station without the limits of that portion of the Cherokee country claimed by Georgia, intending, while he made that station his home, to itinerate among the Cherokees * * *. Miss Fuller was left at the station to continue the school. Such an arrangement, he supposed would be a compliance with the law of Georgia, requiring his removal * * * ." ("Missionary Herald," August, 1831, Vol. XXVII : 252-253.)

It seems from a letter written by Miss Fuller to Mr. Worcester, June 23, 1831 (ibid., p. 253), that while Thompson was absent Colonel Chas. H. Nelson called at Hightower and gave Miss Fuller warning that he and his men would occupy the mission premises the succeeding night. Thompson returned and hearing of the intentions of Nelson, addressed a letter to him (ibid., p. 253) refusing the hospitality of the mission house. The result was Thompson's second arrest. He was taken to headquarters about fifty miles distant and then set at liberty—no apology or explanation being given. (Letter from Thompson, July 1, 1831, "Missionary Herald," September, 1831, Vol. XXVII : 282.)

2. Dr. Elizur Butler, an assistant missionary residing at Haweis, had not been "arrested with the others in March, but remained unmolested till the 7th of May, when a detachment of the Georgia guard came to the station and made him their prisoner. After carrying him about twelve miles, and he having told the commanding officer of the critical state of his family, the officer released him, on condition that he would come to the headquarters and surrender himself, as soon as the circumstances of his family would permit. Dr. B. afterwards received a letter from the governor of Georgia, similar to those quoted * * *; and information has been received that on the 6th of June he was on the point of starting for the headquarters of the guard to surrender himself. On the 7th, he addressed a letter to the governor of Georgia ("Missionary Herald," August, 1831, Vol. XXVII : 252) denying that he had attempted to prevent the Indians removing or submitting to the jurisdiction of Georgia, as was insinuated in the letter of the governor to him, and stating explicitly the object for which he was laboring among the Cherokees, and the principles which had governed his conduct, and what were his present views of duty in respect to continuing his labors." ("Missionary Herald," XXVII : 251-252.)

Dr. Butler, surrendered himself to Colonel Sanford, July 1, 1831. (Letter, Ibid, September, 1831, Vol. XXVII : 283.)

3. Two Methodist missionaries, Messrs. Trott and M'Leod, were also arrested, though the latter was soon released.

a(1) In reply to the letters which he received, Mr. Worcester wrote a brief note to Colonel Sanford, informing him that Mrs. Worcester was closely confined to her bed, and from the nature of the disease she was likely to be confined so for some time to come; that, as she could not be removed, except at the almost certain loss of her life, and there was no person in whose care he could properly commit her, he could not regard it as his duty to leave his station. Ten days afterwards, he wrote the following letter to the governor of Georgia which clearly presents his view of the case, and the reasons which governed his conduct:

NEW ECHOTA, CHER. NA. *June 10, 1831.*

To His Excellency, George R. Gilmer, governor of the state of Georgia.

Sir—Your communication of the 15th ult. was put into my hand on the 31st by an express from Col. Sanford, accompanied with a notice from him, that I should become liable to arrest, if after ten days, I should still be found residing within the unsettled limits of the state.

I am under obligation to your excellency for the information, which I believe I am justified in deriving by inference from your letter, that it is through your influence, that I am about to be removed from the office of postmaster at this place; inasmuch that it gives me the satisfaction of knowing that I am not removed on the ground of any real or supposed unfaithfulness in the performance of the duties of that office.

Your excellency is pleased to intimate that I have been guilty of a criminal opposition to the humane policy of the general government. I cannot suppose that your excellency refers to those efforts for the advancement of the Indians in knowledge, and in the arts of civilized life, which the general government has pursued ever since the days of Washington, because I am sure that no person can have so entirely misrepresented the course which I have pursued during my residence with the Cherokee people. If by the humane policy of the government, are intended those measures which have been recently pursued for the removal of this and other tribes, and if the opposition is no more than that I have had the misfortune to differ in judgment with the executive of the United States, in regard to the tendency of those measures, and that I have freely expressed my opinion, I cheerfully acknowledge the fact, and can only add that this expression of

offending white men,[a] convicted, and sentenced; but not without a recommendation to executive clemency. The punishment was four years in the penitentiary at hard labor. All but two of the prisoners, Worcester and Butler, preferred to accept the governor's pardon by taking the oath of citizenship.[b] Worcester and Butler appealed to

---

opinion has been unattended with the consciousness of guilt. If any other opposition is intended, as that I have endeavored to bias the judgment, or influence the conduct of the Indians themselves, I am constrained to deny the charge, and beg that your excellency will not give credit to it, until it shall be sustained by evidence.

Your excellency is pleased further to intimate that I have excited the Indians to oppose the jurisdiction of the state. In relation to this subject, also, permit me to say, your excellency has been misinformed. Neither in this particular am I conscious of having influenced, or attempted to influence the Indians among whom I reside. At the same time, I am far from wishing to conceal the fact, that, in my apprehension, the circumstances in which providence has placed me, have rendered it my duty to inquire whose is the rightful jurisdiction over the territory in which I reside; and that this inquiry has led me to a conclusion adverse to the claims of the state of Georgia. This opinion, also, has been expressed—to white men with the greatest freedom; and to Indians, when circumstances elicited my sentiments.

I need not, however, enlarge upon these topics. I thought it proper to notice them in a few words, because I understood your excellency to intimate that, in these respects, I had been guilty of a criminal course of conduct. If for these things I were arraigned before a court of justice, I believe I might safely challenge my accusers to adduce proof of anything beyond that freedom in the expression of opinions, against which, under the constitution of our country, there is no law. But as it is, the most convincing evidence of perfect innocence on these points would not screen me from the penalty of the law, which construes a mere residence here, without having taken a prescribed oath, into a high misdemeanor. On this point, therefore, I hope to be indulged a few words in explanation of my motives.

After the expression of my sentiments, which I have already made, your excellency cannot fail to perceive, that I could not conscientiously take the oath which the law requires. That oath implies an acknowledgment of myself as a citizen of the state of Georgia, which might be innocent enough for one who believes himself to be such, but must be perjury in one who is of the opposite opinion. I may add, that such a course, even if it were innocent of itself, would in the present state of feeling among the Indians, greatly impair or entirely destroy my usefulness as a minister of the gospel among them. It were better, in my judgment, entirely to abandon my work, than so to arm the prejudices of the whole people against me.

Shall I then abandon the work in which I have engaged? Your excellency is already acquainted, in general, with the nature of my object, and my employment, which consist in preaching the gospel, and making known the word of God among the Cherokee people. As to the means used for this end, aside from the regular preaching of the word, I have had the honor to commence the work of publishing portions of the holy scriptures, and other religious books, in the language of the people. * * * This work it would be impossible for me to prosecute at any other place than this, not only on account of the location of the Cherokee press, but because Mr. Boudinott, whose editorial labors require his residence at this place, is the only translator whom I could procure, and who is competent to the task. My own view of duty is, that I ought to remain, and quietly pursue my labors for the spiritual welfare of the Cherokee people until I am forcibly removed. If I am correct in the apprehension that the state of Georgia has no rightful jurisdiction over the territory where I reside, then it follows that I am under no moral obligation to remove, in compliance with her enactments; and if I suffer in consequence of continuing to preach the gospel and diffuse the written word of God among this people, I trust that I shall be sustained by a conscience void of offence, and by the anticipation of a righteous decision at that tribunal from which there is no appeal.

Your excellency will accept the assurance of my sincere respect.

S. A. WORCESTER.

("Missionary Herald," August, 1831, Vol. XXVII: 250–251.)

[a] "There are eleven of us in all. ('Rev. Samuel A. Worcester, Rev. J. J. Trott, Doct. Elizur Butler, Messrs. J. F. Wheeler, T. Gann, J. A. Thompson, B. F. Thompson, S. Mayes, A. Copeland, and E. Delozier, and Mr. Eaton—Ed. p. 363, note.') One besides myself, Rev. Mr. Trott, of the Methodist church, is a preacher of the gospel; and six, I believe, including us, are professors of religion * * *." (Letter from Worcester, September 16, 1831, "Missionary Herald," XXVII: 363.)

[b] "Missionary Herald," November, 1831, Vol. XXVII: 364.

the Supreme Court, with Wirt as their chief counsel. The case was tried in 1832,[a] and a decision rendered adverse to the Georgian assumption of jurisdiction over the Cherokee country; but both Jackson [b] and Lumpkin [c] who had then succeeded Gilmer, ignored it. In September of 1831 * additional machinery was put in operation

---

* Col. John Lowry had been sent on a special mission to the Cherokees, emigration being of course the object, in the early autumn of 1830, but had failed. (Royce, p. 262.)

[a] Worcester v. Georgia, 6 Peters, 515–597; Marshall's "Writings on the Constitution," p. 419.

[b] Note Jackson's alleged remark to the effect that Marshall might execute his own decision, Greeley I: 106, and note 27.

[c] " Immediately after the decision of the Supreme Court of the United States " (had been rendered) * * * " the mandate of that Court was * * * laid before the court of Georgia, by which they [the missionaries] had been tried and sentenced, and a motion made by the counsel for the missionaries' that the court reverse its decision. But after the case had been argued at length, the motion was rejected. The court also refused to permit the motion, or its own decision upon it, or anything by which it might appear that such a motion had ever been made, to be entered on its records. The counsel then made an affidavit, stating that the mandate of the Supreme Court had been presented to the court in Georgia, and the motion made to reverse the decision of the latter, in obedience to the mandate. This affidavit was signed by the counsel for the missionaries, and acknowledged by the judge, and would have been used before the Supreme Court of the United States, instead of the record of the court in Georgia, had a motion been made there for further proceedings at its present session.

On the 4th of April last, immediately subsequent to this refusal of the Court in Georgia to obey the mandate of the Supreme Court, the counsel for the prisoners presented a memorial in their behalf to his excellency Wilson Lumpkin, governor of that state, showing in what manner the mandate of the Supreme Court had been rejected by the state court, and praying him to use the executive power intrusted to him, and discharge the prisoners. To this the governor refused to give any written reply, but stated verbally that the prayer of the memorialists would not be complied with.

In this state, so far as any legal proceedings are concerned, the case remained until the 27th of November, when Messrs. Worcester and Butler were informed that, if any motion were to be made before the Supreme Court of the United States for further proceedings in their case at its next approaching session, notice to that effect must be served on the governor and attorney general of Georgia without delay. They had no time to deliberate or consult their patrons on the subject. Knowing, however, that, if the notice should be served, and they should afterwards decide that it was inexpedient to prosecute their case further, the notice could be withdrawn, and the process arrested; while, if they neglected to serve the notice till it should be too late, the motion in their behalf before the Supreme Court could not be sustained, however desirable it might seem, but must be deferred another year. Placed in this predicament, they decided to give notice of the intended motion, leaving the question whether that motion should be actually made open to further consideration.

Messrs. Worcester and Butler immediately informed the Prudential Committee (of the American Board) of what they had done, and requested their advice on the point, whether they should prosecute their case further before the Supreme Court of the United States or not.

Here it should be remarked that, from the time that the missionaries were first informed of the law enacted by the legislature of the state of Georgia * * * they have had a constant and free interchange of views with the Committee respecting the course to be pursued by themselves; and while the Committee have forborne to direct or even advise them, they have still expressed their views freely, relative to what was right and expedient, in these trying circumstances, * * * and have uniformly enjoined it upon the missionaries to act upon their own responsibility as citizens, and especially as ministers of our Lord Jesus Christ. This, it is believed, they have uniformly done; and while the Committee have acted with entire unanimity, it is not known that, at any stage of this business, their judgment has differed from that of the missionaries.

It should also be remarked, before proceeding further with this statement, that Messrs. Worcester and Butler, very soon after they were placed in the penitentiary, were visited by a number of highly respectable gentlemen, who urged them, not to appeal to the Supreme Court of the United States, but to accept of a pardon from the governor of the state, and promise not to return to the Cherokee nation—the condition on which pardon was offered them immediately after their sentence was pronounced. This they steadily

for the compulsory removal of the Cherokees. Under the superintendency of Benjamin F. Curry, and at the dictation of Georgia,
enrolling agencies were opened within the nation that stopped short

refused to do, deeming it of great importance, in its bearing on their own characters and
the cause in which they were engaged, to obtain the opinion of that Court whether the
law of the state of Georgia, extending her jurisdiction over the Cherokee country, was
or was not contrary to the constitution, laws, and treaties of the United States: and
whether they had or had not been lawfully arrested and subjected to an ignominious
punishment for disregarding that law. Among the gentlemen who repeatedly visited
them on this errand, were Mr. Berrien, late attorney general of the United States, and
Rev. President Church of the Georgia University. After the decision of the Supreme
Court, given in March last, and especially after they had given notice of their intention
to move the Court for further proceedings in their case, Messrs. Worcester and Butler
were again urged by gentlemen who visited them, and by others who communicated their
views in writing, to withdraw their suit and accept of pardon. These gentlemen resided
in different parts of the Union, and some of them had been on the side of the Cherokees
and missionaries, through the whole of their unhappy controversy with the state of
Georgia. But as the missionaries were at first, from their own view of their rights,
confident that they had been guilty of no crime, and would not, therefore, accept a
pardon; so now, having obtained the decision of the Supreme Court in their favor, they
were still less inclined to do anything which might imply that they had not a just claim
to an unconditional discharge, without the stigma of being pardoned criminals. From
time to time they submitted their case to the Prudential Committee, with the arguments
which were pressed upon them from different quarters. But the Committee saw no cause
for advising them to change their course.

More recently, however, and especially subsequent to giving the notice of the intended
motion in the Supreme Court, the subject was presented to the minds of the missionaries
in a somewhat different aspect; which, together with the posture of our national affairs,
induced them to examine the whole subject anew, and to lay the arguments in favor of
withdrawing their suit, which had been suggested to them by others, or had occurred to
their own minds, before the committee, which they did in a letter from which the sub-
joined paragraphs are extracted. Doct. Butler being at the time unwell, Mr. Worcester,
after mentioning that they had given notice of the intended motion, with some account
of the interviews which they had had with gentlemen on the subject, presents the following interrogations as containing the substance of the arguments presented by them.

What then are we to gain by the further prosecution of the case? *Our personal
liberty?* There is much more prospect of gaining it by yielding than by perseverance.
And if not, it is not worthy of account in comparison with the interests of our country.

Freedom from the stigma of being pardoned criminals? That also is a consideration
of personal feeling not to be balanced against the public good.

The maintenance of the authority of the Supreme Court? It is argued against us
that, if we yield, the authority of the court is not prostrated—only not tested; that, if
it be put to the test *now,* it is almost certain to fail; that the probability of prostrating
its authority is far greater than of maintaining it; that, if it were to be put to the test,
it ought to be done at a more favorable time.

The prevention of the violation of the public faith? That faith, it appears to us, is
already violated; and, as far as we can see, our perseverance has no tendency to
restore it.

The arresting of the hand of oppression? It is already decided that such a course
cannot arrest it.

The privilege of preaching the gospel to the Cherokees? That privilege is at least as
likely to be restored by our yielding as by our perseverance.

The reputation of being firm and consistent men? Firmness degenerates into obstinacy,
if it continues when the prospect of good ceases; and the reputation of doing right is
dearly purchased by doing wrong.

          *   *   *   *   *   *   *

In view of the foregoing considerations and some others which occurred to their
minds, all tending to convince them that little good was to be hoped from further
prosecution of the case; and that, as the law under which the missionaries had been
imprisoned had been repealed, they were much more likely to be speedily restored to
their labors among the Cherokees by withdrawing their suit, than by carrying it to
the extremity, the Committee expressed to Messrs Worcester and Butler the opinion,
that it was inexpedient for them to prosecute their case further before the Supreme
Court. It seemed to them also the part of Christian forbearance in the missionaries,
in the present agitated state of the country, to yield rights, which, in other circumstances, it might have been their duty to claim, rather than to prosecute them tena-

of nothing to effect the object desired. The story is too long and too disgraceful to be adequately treated here.[a] Dissensions within the tribe were encouraged, and by that means the Indians were finally worsted. It is generally conceded that there were two distinct factions, one headed by John Ross, the other by Major Ridge. Andrew Ross belonged to the latter and he, in conjunction with Eaton, negotiated the treaty of June 19, 1834,[b] which, against the official protest of his brother, was presented to the Senate for ratification. H. L. White, who had become politically estranged from Jackson, used his influence to defeat it and, to the disgust of the President, succeeded. The following spring, when rival delegations were in Washington, Ridge, as the representative of one, repeated the scheme, and, with the aid of Schermerhorn, drew up a preliminary treaty of cession and removal. Ross[c] was not consulted; but, as the treaty was not to take effect until agreed to in national council, there was yet time to strike one more blow for justice.

During the summer of 1835 all available forces were at work to close with the Cherokees.[d] Curry planned to reserve the annuities

---

ciously at the expense of hazarding the public interests." * * * ("Missionary Herald," XXIX : 109–111.)

Messrs. Worcester and Butler immediately acted upon the advice of the Prudential Committee of the American Board, and instructed their counsel, William Wirt, to stay legal proceedings. (Letter to William Wirt, January 8, 1833, "Missionary Herald," Vol. XXIX : 112.) At the same time they communicated their decision to the attorney-general and governor of Georgia, Charles H. Jenkins and Wilson Lumpkin, respectively. (Ibid.) Lumpkin chose to regard their reason for this decision, not change of principles but love of country, as an insult since it intimated that the State had been entirely in the wrong. The missionaries, therefore, sent the executive a second letter exonerating themselves from the charge of intending disrespect and saying that they left "the question of the continuance" of their "confinement to the magnanimity of the state" which was a respectful way of applying for a pardon. Governor Lumpkin did not deign to send a written discharge (Letter from Worcester, January 23, 1833, "Missionary Herald," XXIX : 113), but by proclamation, January 14, 1833, directed Colonel Mills, the keeper of the penitentiary, to release them.

[a] C. C. Royce has brought out many facts in his "History of the Cherokee Nation," but he does not seem to have used the Curry and Schermerhorn letters which reveal the extent of Federal cooperation. Moreover, these letters hint at much that was never intrusted to paper and the story is a very dark one.

[b] E. W. Chester had tried unsuccessfully to negotiate a treaty of exchange in 1832. In the course of the prosecution of his mission it had developed that some of the Cherokees wanted to emigrate to the Columbia River region. (Royce, pp. 263–264.)

[c] Unfortunately Ross had already made a false move. Thinking, as he said, to test the sincerity of the Government, he offered, February 25, 1835, to sell his country for $20,000,000. The Senate considered the proposition and came to the conclusion that the sum was too large. Ross then said he would take whatever the Government thought just and the Senate placed the figure at $5,000,000. That did not come within Ross's conception of justice, and he declined the offer. His enemies, however, profited by the transaction and it reacted against him later on; for Schermerhorn, whose profession did not save him from practicing gross deception, represented to the Cherokee adherents of Ross that he was a very Judas. In this way the reverend gentleman, as he boasted to the War Department, was able to gain many supporters of the treaty of New Echota.

[d] Curry to Herring, July 31, 1835, "Indian Office Letter Books," Letters Sent and Received, 1835–36, pp. 298, 308; Curry to Schermerhorn, July 30, 1835, ibid., pp. 304–305; Curry to Herring, August 20, 1835, ibid., pp. 309–311; Curry to Lieut. John L. Hooper, August 5, 1835, ibid., p. 312; Curry to Herring, August 20, 1835, ibid., pp. 322–324; Ross to Schermerhorn and Curry, August 22, 1835, "Curry Papers."

for the Ridge faction alone by summoning them to a separate council, but the Rossites came out in full force, and he was circumvented. The Ridge treaty came before the national council at Red Clay in October and was rejected, mainly because something happened that the white men had not counted upon—a temporary compromise between the opposing factions. Ross then prepared to set out for Washington, but was arrested by the Georgia guard on the plea that he was a white man residing, contrary to law, within the Indian country.[a] He certainly did have a large proportion of Scotch blood in his veins; but the charge, under the circumstances, was so absurd, being just as applicable to hundreds of others, that he was soon released.[b]

Schermerhorn had been sent by the Secretary of War to present the Ridge treaty to the Cherokee national council. That done he ought to have gone away. His mission was ended. Instead of doing so he lingered. He called another meeting for the third Monday in December, at New Echota, and, in excess of his instructions, submitted an entirely new treaty to the Indians. Accepted conditionally by them, it went to the Senate and there called out some bitter reflections upon the Administration and its Indian policy— all well deserved. John Ross protested, but in vain. The treaty was ratified and the Cherokees were doomed.[c] That as a nation they never consented to it needs no proof. Were one needed, we have but to note the correspondence of General Wool, who was sent into their country to put down any insurrection that might arise.[d] As victims of tyranny and injustice, many were eventually escorted West by General Scott and his army. More than one-fourth are said to have perished on the way.

The year 1835 was a turning point in the career of two other Indian nations—both southern. The inoffensive Caddoes, of Louisiana, negotiated, in July of that year, a rather peculiar treaty[e] with the Federal Government, whose representative was Jehiel Brooks.[f] They agreed to remove themselves forever from the territory of the United States, a course of action they seem to have been contemplating for a good many years. They were exiles, indeed, and yet who can say they did not choose the wiser course. Well might it have been for the Seminoles had they done the same, and, in some more hospitable clime, had found the refuge denied them in the everglades of Florida. The three years noted in the treaty of

---

[a] Curry to Cass, November 30, 1835, " Indian Office Letter Books," Letters Sent and Received, 1835–36, pp. 356–357.

[b] Curry to Cass, December 1, 1835, ibid., pp. 339–340.

[c] 7 United States Statutes at Large, 478–489.

[d] Indian Office MS. Records, " Cherokee Emigration Papers."

[e] 7 United States Statutes at Large, 470.

[f] Jehiel Brooks was, later on, accused of having resorted to fraud in the negotiation of this treaty. (Indian Congressional Documents, Vol. XXX; House Document No. 25, second session Twenty-seventh Congress, 1841–42.)

Payne's Landing expired in May, 1835, but the time of removal was extended for six months more. A fatal six months, weighty with all the disasters of a long and bloody war! The Black Hawk of the Seminoles appeared in the person of Osceola, more commonly known by his English name of Powell. It was he that found courage to voice the national protest against the fraudulent treaty of Fort Gibson, but J. Q. Adams was no longer President. Charley Emartla suffered the fate of McIntosh, and, when Wiley Thompson, of Georgia, refused to pose as a second Crowell, he also was pursued by a Nemesis. War broke out, and, prolonged by climate and mismanagement, lasted until 1842. The Indians were gradually subdued, piecemeal, and most of them forced westward. Some are still in Florida. General Gadsden, who had done so much to injure this unfortunate tribe, was one of the first to condemn the war. Professional jealousy was to a large degree his motive power but, none the less, he spoke the truth. There was no economic need for the removal of the Seminoles.

In his seventh annual message [a] Jackson commented in boastful terms upon all that he had accomplished for Indian consolidation. It certainly was a great deal. Pity it is that it is not a part of American history upon which one can look with any pride. Besides, Jackson retired from the Presidency leaving a very onerous burden for Martin Van Buren. The Cherokees were not yet removed or the Seminoles subdued. In those two affairs Van Buren followed the trail that Jackson had blazed; but in one other he acted as a New Yorker and independently.[b] The strenuous and continuous effort of the Ogden Land Company to remove the whole body of New York Indians had signally failed. Comparatively few had ever gone to Wisconsin. Among the many reasons that may be assigned for this, are an attachment to their native soil, a determination not to be overreached by speculators, an appreciation of the great value of their eastern lands, and, maybe more than anything else, a realization that the title to the Wisconsin tract was far from clear. The Menominee grantors had never ceased to dispute it; and, when in 1827 Cass and McKenney, under commission to execute certain provisions of the treaty of Prairie du Chien, negotiated that of Butte des Morts, the Menominees still refused to admit the validity of the contracts of 1821 and 1822, so the commissioners could do naught but leave the affair to the discretion of the President. They did, however, recommend, though to no purpose, that since the New York Indians had

---

[a] Richardson, III : 171–173.

[b] It is not intended to imply that other removals besides that of the New York Indians were not arranged for during Van Buren's Administration. On the contrary there were several, some of which have already been incidentally referred to. There remains to mention the Munsee, a consent to which, indefinite as to the time of fulfillment, was secured September 3, 1839. The main body of Wyandots did not treat for removal until March 17, 1842.

settled for the most part on the east side of Fox River they should be allowed to stay there and receive the land by a permanent title.[a] As time went on the uncertainty of tenure continued. In fact, the indecision of the treaty of Butte des Morts might almost be said to have increased it, and so the Ogden Land Company affected to believe. The Senecas positively would not emigrate, and J. Q. Adams, though ready to be acquiescent in a willing removal, should one be secured, would permit no compulsion.

When Jackson became President, the Ogden Land Company expected their interests, selfish as they were, to receive more attention than they deserved. They were soon relieved of such a misapprehension, for McKenney in June, 1829, instructed Jasper Parrish, who had reported the Munsees and Stockbridges willing to emigrate, that the General Government had no funds to assist the New York Indians in removing to Green Bay. The proper person to apply to was the governor. A subsequent letter to Justus Ingersoll, of Medina, indicated that, though unwilling to stand the expense, the United States was not loath to advise its agents, " under a guarded and discreet interview," to turn the attention of the Iroquois to Green Bay.[b] Even that did not satisfy Colonel Ogden, and he complained of Jackson's indifference or possible opposition, but only to receive the assurance that silence ought not to be so interpreted.[c] Meanwhile, the New York Indians at Green Bay petitioned the Senate for an adjustment of their differences with the Menominees. An investigation took place, but no conclusions were reached and the matter was referred back to the President. This resulted in the appointment of three commissioners, Gen. Erastus Root, James McCall, of New York, and John T. Mason, secretary of Michigan Territory, who were instructed to proceed to Green Bay and, waiving any decision as to the validity of the compacts of 1821 and 1822, simply choose a satisfactory location at that place for the New York Indians.[d] The commissioners repaired betimes to Wisconsin and proceeded to arbitrate between the Menominees and the Iroquois; but, knowing nothing beforehand of the facts in the case, were soon nonplussed by its perplexities.[e] They could not agree among themselves as to the extent of their own powers and failed to effect a compromise between the disputants.

About this time, when the United States Senate was not in session, a change took place in the Green Bay agency, Col. Samuel C. Stambaugh, of Pennsylvania, replacing Henry B. Brevoort. The change

---

[a] McKenney to Ogden, Troup, and Rogers, December 14, 1827, " Indian Office Letter Books," Series II, No. 4, pp. 178–180 ; McKenney to Col. T. L. Ogden, January 15, 1828, ibid., p. 253.

[b] September 21, 1829, " Indian Office Letter Books," Series II, No. 6, p. 90.

[c] McKenney to Ogden, December 28, 1829, ibid. pp. 209–210.

[d] Letter of Eaton, June 9, 1830, ibid., pp. 463–467.

[e] Colton, I : 147.

was momentous, for the new agent sympathized openly with the Menominees and chose to regard the New York Indians as land speculators,[a] which was not far from the truth. Stambaugh himself was much interested in the development of Wisconsin, and advised the Menominees to sell some of their land to the United States. Accordingly, in November, 1830, a delegation, though uninvited, started for Washington, the energetic Stambaugh in close attendance. On the 8th of February, following, Eaton and Stambaugh negotiated a treaty of cession [b] highly pleasing to the people of the Northwest.[c] It made a pretense of safeguarding the interests of the Iroquois, but really so hedged its begrudged concessions about with conditions that neither the Ogden Land Company nor the Indians could have consented to it. These conditions, which left the Menominee offer to the New York Indians open for three years only and provided that rejection of it should signify a final removal from the Green Bay lands unless the President willed otherwise, were stricken out by the supplementary article of February 17. One great objection still remained, the land offered was situated in a poor locality. Political influence, however, was strong enough to cause the insertion of the Senate proviso which, while not increasing the amount, improved the quality of the land that was to be conceded to the New York Indians. The treaty was finally ratified July 9, 1832. It was then the turn of the Menominees to be dissatisfied,[d] and George B. Porter, Territorial governor of Michigan, was asked to propitiate them.[e] He went to Green Bay for the purpose, and on the 27th of October gained their consent to a modification of the Senate proviso,[f] to which the New York Indians reluctantly agreed.[g]

The Senate proviso of 1832, besides altering the boundaries of the land intended for the New York tribes proper, arranged for a change in residence of the Munsee, Stockbridge, and Brothertown Indians who were to vacate the land on the east side of the Fox River and pass over to the east side of Winnebago Lake. This provision was left unchanged by Porter's treaty of October, and, during the year 1834, the Stockbridges took up their new quarters about 20 miles distant from their old location.[h] In 1836 Schermerhorn successfully negotiated for their removal, but the Senate refused [i] to

---

[a] Report to Secretary of War, 1831.

[b] 7 United States Statutes at Large, 342–348.

[c] Schoolcraft MSS., Library of Congress.

[d] George Boyd to Governor Porter, September 2, 1832, " Boyd Papers "—" Wis. Hist. Colls.," XII : 291–292.

[e] Cass to Porter, December 19, 1831, " Indian Office Letter Books," series II, No. 7, p. 497.

[f] 7 United States Statutes at Large, 405.

[g] Ibid., p. 409.

[h] " Missionary Herald," XXX : 417.

[i] Resolution, June 13, 1838.

ratify the instrument.[a] Finally, in 1843, the Stockbridges applied
for citizenship in imitation of the Brothertowns, who had made the

[a]Articles of a Treaty, made and concluded at Green Bay, Wisconsin Territory, September
19, 1836, by John F. Schermerhorn, Commissioner on the part of the United States,
and the Chiefs and head men of the Stockbridge and Munsee Tribes of Indians, interested in the Lands, on Winnebago Lake, provided for them in the Menomonee Treaty,
of February 1831, and assented to by them, October 27, 1832, and who now reside on
Winnebago Lake, and those that are still in the State of New York.

Article first. The chiefs and head men of the said Stockbridge & Munsee Tribes of
Indians, whose names are hereunto annexed, in behalf of their people, hereby cede, relinquish, & convey to the United States, all their right, title, and interest, of and to their
lands on the East side of Winnebago Lake, as provided for them in the Aforesaid Treaty,
for and in Consideration of the Covenants, Stipulations, and provisions contained in the
several articles of this Treaty, on the part of the United States.

Article Second. The United States, in consideration of the above cession, hereby covenant and agree to dispose of and sell the lands above ceded, for the benefit of the Stockbridge and Munsee Tribes of Indians; and after the deducting from the avails thereof,
the actual expenses incurred by the United States, in the survey and sales attending the
same, and such reasonable sum for the lands assigned to them by this Treaty for their
future homes, as the President may see fit, to fix upon it (should the Senate of the
United States require it) then the Nett Avails shall be disposed of as follows

First. The Lots and improvements of each individual of the Tribes shall be valued by
the Commission to be appointed by the President of the United States for that purpose,
and the fair and just value of the same shall be allowed and paid to the respective
owners thereof.   The Lot and improvements for the Mission to go to the A. B. C. F. M.
who are now in possession of the same.

Second. A sufficient sum is hereby set apart for the removal and subsistence of the
whole of said Tribes of Stockbridge and Munsee Indians and for their subsistence for
one year after their arrival at their new homes provided for them, by this Treaty.

Third The sum of Twenty Thousand ($20,000) dollars shall be and hereby is set
apart and allowed to remunerate the *Stockbridge Tribe* for the Monies laid out, and expended by said Tribe, and for the services rendered by their Chiefs and agents in securing the title to these lands, and removal to this Country; the same to be examined and
determined and paid out to the several Claimants, by the Commissioner and Chiefs as
may be deemed by them most equitable and just—The remainder of the Nett Avails shall
be invested by the United States in some safe and productive Stock or incorporated Company in the State of New York, and the interest thereof to be paid to the Chiefs of the
Tribe to be applied by them in such manner as may be for the best interest of the Tribes,
Whenever either of the Tribes or any portion of them are ready to remove after having
selected their new homes they shall be furnished with the means for removal by the
United States and for their one years subsistence to be reimbursed out of the Sales of
their lands and any Chief who removes his Tribe or any Party not less than 100 persons
shall be allowed & paid $500 for his services.

Article Third. This Treaty is on the Express Condition, that the Stockbridge and Munsee Tribes of Indians shall have the privilege first to go and examine the Indian country
Southwest of the Missouri River, at the expense of the United States, and if they find a
country to suit them which has not already been Ceded by the United States to any other
Tribe of Indians, and if the same equal to two Townships shall be conveyed to said Stockbridge and Munsee Tribes by Patent from the President of the United States according to
the provisions of the Act of Congress of June, 1830, then this Treaty shall be obliga-
tory upon the Stockbridge and Munsee Tribes of Indians in all respects and in every part
and article of the same. But if upon such examination they cannot find a Country to suit
themselves, that then it is expressly understood and agreed that only the East half of the
said tract on Winnebago Lake is hereby ceded to the United States; and the remaining
half shall be held by them in common, but the Munsees shall not be permitted to sell or
relinquish their right to the United States without the Consent of the Stockbridge Indians,
and in the event of the sale of the remaining half the Munsees shall be entitled to a
share of the same in proportion to their relative numbers in the amount to be invested or
divided for the benefit of the Whole ——— Eight Thousand dollars shall be set apart and
is hereby appropriated out of the monies arising from the sale of the same for the
removal of the Munsee Tribe of Indians from the State of New York, and their subsistence one year on their removal to the Indian Country South West of the river Missouri
and the balance shall be paid to the Stockbridge Indians according to the third item in
the second article of this Treaty.

Article Fourth. Since it is the desire of the Stockbridge Indians, that their lands shall
be sold to the best advantage for their tribe; it is therefore stipulated and agreed by the

experiment four years before;[a] but it involved them in a deal of trouble, since some of their number were very averse to a change in political status. This and the non-execution of the treaty of 1839,[b]

United States, that a Special Commission shall be appointed by the President by and with the advice and consent of the Senate of the United States, who is hereby authorized to sell and dispose of the said lands in any quantity or quantities at public or private sale as may be deemed best for the interest of said Tribes. Providing however that the same shall not be sold for less than the Minimum Congress price. It is understood that if the said Stockbridge Indians do accept of a country Southwest of the Missouri River, that then they will remove in two years from the ratification of this Treaty ; and if the whole of the lands at that time are not disposed of at public or private sale, by the Consent of the Chiefs and head men of the Stockbridge Tribe of Indians the whole shall be disposed of at public or private sale on such terms as may be deemed best for their interest and the said Commissioner shall also superintend their removal and make all the necessary disbursements and pay all the Claims under the provisions of this Treaty, and render an account of the same both to the Government of the United States, and to the Chiefs of the said Stockbridge and Munsee Tribes of Indians. And it is also understood & agreed that no preemption rights shall be granted by Congress on any of these lands.

Article Fifth. Perpetual peace and friendship shall exist between the United States and the said Stockbridge & Munsee Tribes of Indians and the United States hereby guarantee to protect and defend them in the peaceable enjoyment of their new homes and hereby secure to them the right in their new country to establish their own Government, appoint their own officers, make and administer their own laws and regulations, subject however to such Legislation of the Congress United States for regulating trade and intercourse among the Indians as they may deem necessary and proper. The lands secured to the Stockbridge and Munsee Tribes of Indians under this Treaty shall never be included within any State or Territory of this Union, without their consent, and they shall also be entitled to all the rights and privileges secured to any Tribe of emigrant Indians settled in said Territory.

Article Sixth. This Treaty when approved and certified by the President and Senate of the United States shall be binding on the respective parties.

In testimony whereof the said John F. Schermerhorn and the chiefs and headmen of the Stockbridge and Munsee Tribes of Indians have hereunto set their hands and seals, the day and year above written.

J. F. SCHERMERHORN
JOHN METOXEN.

In the presence of

GEORGE BOYD, *U. S. Ind. Agt.*
R. S. SATTERLEE L. M. *Surgeon U. S. Army.*

JOHN P. ARNDT	HENDRICK
CUTTING MARSH	his
M. L. MARTIN	JACOB x DAVID
W. L. V.—[*illegible*]	mark
W. B. SLAUGHTER	his
JNO. M. McCARTY	JONAS x THOMPSON
A. G. ELLIS	mark
D. GIDDINGS	JOSEPH M. QUINNEY
AUSTIN QUINNY	SIMON S. METOXEN
JACOB CHICKS	his
T. JOURDAN	Capt. x PORTER
JNO. W. QUINNEY	mark

The aforesaid treaty having been submitted & explained, by J. F. Schermerhorn Commissioner, it is hereby assented to and agreed unto, in all its provisions, and stipulations, in the presence of Chs. C. Brodhead, commissioner on the part of the State of N. York in behalf of the Munsees now residing in the State of New York. Oct. 15th, 1836.

his
JOHN x WILSON
mark

In the presence of

CHS. C. BRODHEAD
GEORGE TURKEY-*interpreter.*

("Treaty Files," 1802–1853, "Indian Office MS. Records.")
[a] Marsh's Scottish Report for 1842, "Wis. Hist. Colls.," XV: 175.
[b] 7 United States Statutes at Large, 580–582.

about which we shall have more to say later, finally induced the
so-called "Indian party," to apply for permission to emigrate
southward.[a]

After the Green Bay settlement of 1831–32, Jackson's indifference,
for surely we may call it that, toward the extinguishment of Indian
titles in New York returned and to so great a degree that it was variously commented upon; but if he could plead lack of funds and
excess of work as excuses in 1831,[b] he certainly could in the years
succeeding. It was the time of the Indian question and of the tariff,
and the contrast between the energy displayed in Georgia for removal
and that in New York probably contributed to the loss of many
Administration votes; for as Van Buren wrote to F. P. Blair,[c] September 12, 1842, the New York Democrats were then getting decidedly sore about the continued southern policy of their party. They
believed that all along the South had been benefited at the expense of
the North.

As a matter of fact, though, Jackson, while still remaining at bottom indifferent to the Iroquois in the Empire State, did make one last
effort to negotiate with them. This was in 1836. The motive power
was not the relief of New York itself, but of the Northwest,[d] and so
we find, as if preparatory to the statehood of Michigan, Governor
Henry Dodge starting out to extinguish the Indian title to Wisconsin
lands.[e] He succeeded with the Menominees,[f] but not with their neighbors; so his place, in so far as the New York bands were concerned,
was taken by the redoubtable Schermerhorn,[g] who, as it turned out,
was accompanied by very useful delegates from the St. Regis and Tuscarora Indians, men most "zealous," the commissioner reported,[h] "in
promoting the views of the government," and the treaty of Duck
Creek was successfully negotiated on the 16th of September. It had
been at first intended to hold a great general council of the New York
Indians at Buffalo, but Schermerhorn knew that if that were done
failure would be inevitable, since the Senecas were intrenched in their
old obstinacy and were managing to overawe the Cayugas who lived

[a] Marsh's Scottish Report for 1843, Ibid., pp. 178–179.

[b] S. S. Hamilton to James Stryker, May 20, 1831, "Indian Office Letter Books," Series
II, No. 7, p. 244.

[c] Van Buren Papers.

[d] All parties seem to have been anxious to have the Northwest relieved of its Indian
incumbrance at this juncture. In February, 1836, the Senate passed a resolution looking toward that end, and in the following March the Indian agent at Green Bay, Col.
George Boyd, transmitted to Elbert Herring the items of a proposed treaty with the
Menominees. ("Green Bay Files," 1835–1838, "Indian Office MS. Records.")

[e] Dodge's commission seems to have empowered him to treat generally with the frontier
tribes. ("Wisconsin Files," 1836–1842, "Indian Office MS. Records.")

[f] 7 United States Statutes at Large, 506.

[g] In connection with Gen. W. R. Smith, Governor Dodge continued the work of negotiating on the frontier, and in the spring of 1837 was treating with the Chippewas.
("Wisconsin Files," 1836–1842, "Indian Office MS. Records.")

[h] Schermerhorn to Jackson, October 29, 1836. Jackson Papers.

with them. Personally, the reverend commissioner was afraid of political criticism, for his methods " of removing prejudices and misrepresentations," as he called them, were none of the best. Clay's recent speech in Kentucky had been very abusive, and he was alarmed lest John Ross should contemplate some new move at Washington for frustrating his designs. " I expect," wrote he, " a violent and last opposition on the Indian question." His wish was to be present at the seat of Government when this attack should come, so as to correct misrepresentation; for, " after what has transpired," wrote he, " I need expect no very kind treatment from Judge White, Mr. Clay, or any of that class of politicians, and if they can make any difficulty in the ratification with the New York Indians, they will do it." His forebodings were correct, and Jackson's Administration closed without anything having been done to free it from the charge of indifference to the Empire State.

A different course of action was to be expected from one of her own sons, and Van Buren tried not to fall short of practical loyalty. A thing that would help him, and that really did, as will be shown in the sequel, although discreditable to the Indian, was the treachery of prominent chiefs. The Ogden Land Company had now abandoned all hope of converting Wisconsin into an Indian territory, and its only hope lay in a provision such as Schermerhorn had inserted in the treaty of Duck Creek—removal to the country west of Missouri. Toward this end all efforts from now on were directed.

It is scarcely necessary to go into the details of the treaty which, under the sanction of the United States commissioner, Ransom H. Gillet, was reported to have been negotiated at Buffalo Creek, January 15, 1838. Its repudiation is much more interesting, for it revealed the noble efforts of the Society of Friends in behalf of an oppressed and outraged people. Red Jacket had turned for help to the Quakers in 1827 and again in 1829, but their means were not equal to an interference just then. The old man's dejection moved them at last to active pity, and, from 1830 on, they labored for Seneca relief.[a]

The fraudulent character of the treaty of Buffalo Creek aroused their deepest indignation; and, in the winter of 1838–39, they appointed a committee to protest against its ratification. As a result, Van Buren authorized the Secretary of War to call an Indian council at Cattaraugus and receive testimony. The council met August 12, 1839. The Society of Friends was fully represented, and in the following November handed in to the President a formal exposure of the frauds. Van Buren demanded additional proof, which called forth the memorials of January 29, 1840, the one to him as President

---

[a] " Proceedings of the Joint Committee of the Society of Friends, 1847."

and the other to the Senate.[a] By the strangest reasoning, however,
the Senate resolved upon ratification March 25, 1840. It was said
to have been done by the casting vote of Richard M. Johnson at a
time when the senatorial friends of the Indian were for the most
part absent. The Society of Friends remonstrated to Van Buren,
who admitted that it was all a " most iniquitous proceeding." He
confirmed it, nevertheless. The treaty provided for removal to
Kansas, but the Indians never went there in any appreciable numbers, and their persistent refusal to do so proved the source of an
almost endless litigation in which their rights as against those of the
Ogden Land Company were always more or less of a secondary consideration.

The Indian State, which Calhoun had hinted at and Barbour had
planned, was never created, although Isaac McCoy did, under instructions from Eaton, lay out a seat for its government. During the
progress of removal in the South, the tribes frequently requested that
they might be assured of a regular government should they emigrate.
Doubtless, they would have gone readily if that had been done, but
it never was. The disencumbering of the Eastern States was the
main thing thought of, and all other interests, even though they
involved the fate of a race, were disregarded. The best criticism
that can be passed upon Indian removal is that it was a plan too
hastily and too partially carried into execution for its real and under-
lying merits ever to be realized. That it had merits none can gain-
say. But since it stopped short of self-government, for which some
of the tribes were even then well fitted, it was bound to be only a temporary expedient. The titles given in the West proved less sub-
stantial than those in the East, for they had no foundation in an-
tiquity. The Government gave them and, when it so pleased, defined
them. As a consequence, before the primary removals had all taken
place, the secondary had begun, and the land that was to belong to
the Indian in perpetuity was in the white man's market.

---

[a] " Proceedings of the Joint Committee of the Society of Friends, 1847."

A BIBLIOGRAPHICAL GUIDE TO PRIMARY AND SECONDARY AUTHORITIES.

ADAMS, HENRY. "History of the United States of America," 1801–1817, nine volumes, New York, 1889–1891.

> The best general history for the period covered, found particularly useful for a connected and scholarly account of the Ghent negotiations, but ought to be supplemented by the results of Captain Mahan's more recent investigations.

ADAMS, J. Q. Memoirs of, edited by Charles Francis Adams, twelve volumes, Philadelphia, 1874–1877.

> Strictly speaking, this is an edition of J. Q. Adams's Diary, and is very valuable for tracing the United States Indian policy from 1825 to 1829.

ADAMS, RICHARD C. "Memorial, with Brief History of the Delaware Indians."

> This is usually cited as Senate Document No. 16, Fifty-eighth Congress, first session. In many respects it is a mere sketch, but, as Mr. Adams is a Delaware Indian, it is especially interesting and is reliable as to its facts.

ADAMS, RICHARD C. "A Brief Sketch of the Sabine Land Cession," pamphlet, Washington, D. C., 1901.

> Indicates how intense was the desire of the Delawares and allied tribes to escape after 1830 from the jurisdiction of the United States.

ALDEN, TIMOTHY (Rev.). "An Account of Sundry Missions among the Senecas and Munsees," one volume, New York, 1827.

> A series of letters from 1816 on, giving a first-hand impression of Indian progress in civilization.

"AMERICAN ANNUAL REGISTER," 1825–1833. Eight volumes, published by G. & C. Carvill, New York.

> Contains material on the Georgia-Creek controversy, but only such as can be easily obtained elsewhere.

AMERICAN STATE PAPERS (Peter Force Collection), 1789–1837; first series, twenty-one volumes; second series, seventeen volumes.

> "Claims," one volume.
> "Commerce and Navigation," two volumes.
> "Finances," five volumes.
> "Foreign Relations," 1789–1828, six volumes.
> "Indian Affairs," 1789–1827, two volumes.
> "Military Affairs," 1789–1838, seven volumes.
> "Miscellaneous Affairs," two volumes.
> "Naval Affairs," four volumes.
> "Post-Office Affairs," one volume.
> "Public Lands," 1789–1837, eight volumes.

The two volumes on Indian Affairs, viz, Vol. I, March 4, 1789–November 18, 1814, and Vol. II, November 18, 1814–March 1, 1827, selected and edited by Walter Lowrie and Walter S. Franklin under authority of Congress and published by Gales & Seaton, are the most valuable printed source of infor-

AMERICAN STATE PAPERS—Continued.

mation about the Indians during the early years of the United States Government. The documents, taken directly from the Indian Office, are usually given entire, and arranged either consecutively by dates as they came into or were sent out by the Department or in groups as called for by Congressional resolutions. A close comparison with the originals bears witness to careful editing. The several volumes on " Military Affairs " and " Public Lands " occasionally contain Indian Office documents. For the student of Indian political relations with the United States Government the "American State Papers " are not only a primary, but also an original source, since many of the papers from which their contents were copied or extracted seem to have disappeared entirely.

ANDERSON, WILLIAM D. " Papers of."

The Rev. William D. Anderson was a missionary for a very short time to the Wyandots of Ohio. His papers, now in the possession of the Kansas Historical Society, deal with the period previous to 1815, but contain nothing that bears specifically upon removal.

ANDREWS, TIMOTHY (Major). " Papers of."

These deal with the Georgia-Creek controversy, and are to be found among the Indian Office MS. Records.

"ANNALS OF CONGRESS," forty-two volumes, Washington, D. C.

A record of the debates and proceedings of the Congress of the United States from 1789 to 1824. Practically, the set is divided into two series, the first covering the period from March 3, 1789, to March 3, 1791, and the second that from October, 1791, to May 27, 1824.

ARMSTRONG, PERRY A. " The Sauks and the Black Hawk War," one volume, Springfield, Ill., 1887.

Somewhat prejudiced politically. Brings out strongly Ninian Edwards's hostile attitude toward the Sac and Fox Indians and his untiring efforts to have them removed.

ATWATER, CALEB. " The Indians of the Northwest," one volume, Columbus, 1850.

In 1829 Atwater was added by Jackson to a commission already composed of General McNeil and Col. Pierre Menard for the purpose of conferring with the Indians respecting the mineral lands near the Mississippi River and south of the Wisconsin. His book is full of mawkish sentimentality and of pedantry concerning the origin of the American aborigines. Indeed, it has little historical value, except that it gives something of the contemporary view touching Indian removal, to which Atwater was steadily opposed. He was also opposed to the extravagant expenditure, under the plea of philanthrophy, of money for the Indians.

BARR, JAMES (Captain). "A Correct and Authentic Narrative of the Indian War in Florida," one volume, New York, 1836.

Of little value aside from the illustration it gives, in connection with Dade's massacre, of the lamentable condition of the United States Army at the time of the second Seminole war.

BARROWS, WILLIAM. " The Cherokee Experiment," in "Andover Review," February, 1887, VII : 169–182.

BECKWITH, HIRAM W. " The Illinois and Indiana Indians," in " Fergus Historical Series," No. 27, Chicago.

Of some slight value for the years from 1820 to 1825.

BELL, Mrs. HELEN D. " The History of a County," in " Mississippi Historical Society Publications," IV : 335–342.

Interesting for an account of the negotiation of the treaty of Doak's Stand, 1820.

BENTON, THOMAS H. "Thirty Years' View," two volumes, New York, 1854.

Although of the nature of recollections, is a fairly accurate and unprejudiced description of men, policies, and events from 1820 to 1850.

BENTON, THOMAS HART. "Abridgment of the Debates of Congress," 1789–1856, sixteen volumes, New York, 1857–1861.

BIDDLE, JAMES W. "Recollections of Green Bay in 1816–17," in "Wisconsin Historical Collections," 1 : 49–63.

A short reminiscent account of the pioneers and much that is interesting about the Menominee chief, Toma.

BIGGS, URIAH. "Sketches of Sac and Fox Indians," in "Annals of the State Historical Society of Iowa," July, 1865.

Useful for impressions of Black Hawk.

BLACK HAWK, "Life of Ma-ka-tai-me-she-kia-kiak or," one volume, Boston, 1834.

This is said to have been dictated by Black Hawk himself to the half-breed United States interpreter for the Sacs and Foxes, Antoine le Claire, in August, 1833, and afterwards edited and published by J. B. Patterson. Its authenticity was impeached by Governor Ford in his "History of Illinois;" but writers of well-known historical scholarship, like R. G. Thwaites have not hesitated to quote it as an authority.

BOYD, GEORGE, "Papers of, with Sketch of His Life," in "Wisconsin Historical Collections," XII : 266–298.

Boyd, in the capacity of Indian agent, first at Michillimackinac from 1818 to 1832 and next at Green Bay from 1832 to 1840, had an excellent opportunity of noting the relations between the white men and the Indians, and his papers are full of information on that score, particularly of the period of the Black Hawk war.

BRACKEN, CHARLES (General). "Further Strictures on Governor Ford's History of the Black Hawk War," in "Wisconsin Historical Collections," 1855, II : 402–414.

Makes out a short but rather strong case of prejudice and inaccuracy against Ford; but is itself prejudiced.

BRADY, CYRUS TOWNSEND. "The True Andrew Jackson" (True Biographies Series), one volume, New York, 1905.

Of general interest in the study of Jackson's personality, but has next to nothing to say about his Indian policy.

BRANNAN, JOHN. "Official Letters of the Military and Naval Officers of the United States during the war of 1812."

Inserted because it contains such documents of importance as Hull's "Proclamation to the People of Canada," July 12, 1812.

BRISH, HENRY C., "Papers of."

Brish, as United States agent, helped to move some of the Senecas and Delawares from Ohio, 1831–1834. These papers comprise his personal records of the very minutest transactions of that emigration and are now in the possession of the Kansas Historical Society.

"BRITISH AND FOREIGN STATE PAPERS," forty-six volumes, London, 1839–1865.

Correspond to though are less comprehensive than the "American State Papers," and include documents of various sorts, diplomatic dispatches, parliamentary papers, and the like, from 1814 to 1856. They were compiled by the librarian and keeper of the papers in the Foreign Office.

BROCK, SIR ISAAC, "The Life and Correspondence of," edited by Ferdinand Brock Tupper, London, 1845.

BROWN, HENRY. "The History of Illinois," one volume, New York, 1844.

Facts given largely from the pioneer point of view, very noticeable in the account of the Black Hawk war.

BRYMNER, DOUGLAS. "Reports on Canadian Archives," 1893–1894, one volume. Ottawa, 1894.

Is really a calendar of the State papers of Upper and Lower Canada separately for the years 1807 to 1813, an important semi-primary source for British relations with the northwestern Indians.

BUELL, AUGUSTUS C. "History of Andrew Jackson," two volumes, New York, 1904.

Is decidedly pro-Jackson and has nothing really new to offer on his Indian policy.

BULGER, ALFRED E. (Captain), "Papers of," edited by Reuben G. Thwaites for "Wisconsin Historical Collections," XIII: 10–153.

Has much on the condition of the Indians in the Northwest immediately after the war of 1812.

BURNET, JACOB. "Notes on the Early Settlement of the Northwestern Territory, one volume, Cincinnati and New York, 1847.

Presents a fairly good picture of pioneer life, but is inaccurate in details.

CALHOUN, JOHN C., "Works of," edited by Richard K. Crallé, six volumes, New York, 1888.

Although Calhoun corresponded so much about the Indians, there is comparatively little, one might say almost nothing, in his published works on the subject, and this is true, not only of Crallé's edition of his general works and of Professor Jameson's calendar of certain heretofore unpublished letters, but likewise of the Harper Brothers' collection of his speeches published in 1843.

CAMPBELL, JOHN ARCHIBALD. "The Creek Indian War of 1836," in "Transactions of Alabama Historical Society." III: 162–166.

Being two letters by a contemporary, both written long after the events.

CASTLEREAGH, VISCOUNT, "Correspondence, Dispatches, and Other Papers of," edited by Charles W. Vane, Marquess of Londonderry, London, 1852.

Volume X covers the period of the Ghent negotiations.

CATON, J. D. "The Last of the Illinois and a Sketch of the Pottowatomies," in "Fergus Historical Series," No. 3, Chicago, 1876.

Caton writes, as a contemporary, living in the neighborhood, of the removal of the Pottawatomies.

CHAMBERS, TALBOT W. "Memoir of the Life and Character of Hon. Theo. Frelinghuysen," one volume, New York, 1863.

CHAPPELL, J. HARRIS. "Georgia History Stories," in "Stories of the States" series, published by Silver, Burdett & Co., Boston, 1905.

Readable and accurate.

CHEROKEE NATION. "Address of Committee and Council to the People of the United States," 1830 (pamphlet).

An outline of Cherokee political relations with the United States.

CHEROKEE NATION, "Emigration Papers of," among Indian Office records.

CHEROKEE NATION, "Laws of," adopted by the council at various periods (pamphlet), Knoxville, 1826.

Useful as indicating progress in civilization.

CHOCTAW NATION, "Case of, against the United States" (pamphlet), Washington, 1872.

Contains a résumé of their political relations with the United States.

CHOCTAW NATION, "The Constitution and Laws of" (pamphlet), Park Hill, Cherokee Nation, 1840.

The constitution was made 1838; the laws bear date 1834–1839.

CHOCTAW NATION, "Papers Respecting the Rights and Interests of" (pamphet), Washington, 1855.

Contains several important documents bearing upon the violation of the treaty of 1820 and the non-execution of the treaty of 1830.

CHRISTIAN JOURNAL, THE, fourteen volumes, edited by Bishop Hobart, from 1817 to 1830.

Contains letters and papers bearing upon the Oneida Indians.

CLAIBORNE, J. F. H. "Mississippi as a Province, Territory, and State," Jackson, 1880.

Claiborne was one of the commissioners appointed by the United States, 1842–1843 to inquire into and adjudicate the claims of the Choctaws under the treaty of 1830. His account of the Choctaw removal and of the events occasioning it is short but fair.

CLARK, SATTERLEE. "Early Times at Fort Winnebago and Black Hawk War Reminiscences," in "Wisconsin Historical Collections." VIII: 309–321.

Has local interest, but little historical value.

CLARK, WILLIAM, "Papers of," in the possession of the Kansas Historical Society.

This collection of twenty-nine folio manuscript journals is somewhat inaccurately named, since it includes not only the records of Governor Clark, but likewise those of his successors in the office of superintendent of Indian affairs at St. Louis. They furnish numerous details, important and unimportant, in the history of Indian removal.

CLAY, HENRY, "The Life, Correspondence, and Speeches of," edited by Calvin Colton, six volumes, New York, 1857.

———. The same, with an introduction by Thomas B. Reed and a "History of Tariff Legislation from 1812 to 1896" by William McKinley, seven volumes, New York, 1897.

Clay was not interested in the Indians for their own sake, and his works furnish nothing for the investigator except in connection with the removal of the Cherokees, on which question he took, as was to have been expected, a decided stand against Jackson.

COHEN, M. M. "Notices of Florida and the Campaigns," one volume, Charleston, S. C., and New York, 1836.

Very serviceable for details of negotiations with the Seminoles, talks of chiefs, etc., relative to removal.

CQLTON, CALVIN. "A Tour of the American Lakes and among the Indians of the Northwest Territory in 1830," two volumes, London, 1833.

Excellent for an account of the New York emigration to Green Bay, probably obtained from conversations with Rev. Eleazer Williams, and for contemporary adverse opinions on the general subject of removal.

COPLEY, A. B. "Early Settlement of Southwestern Michigan," in "Michigan Pioneer Collections," V: 144–151.

Interesting for the subject in hand because of its biographical references to Isaac McCoy.

COPWAY, GEORGE (Kah-Ge-Ga-Gah-Bouh). "The Organization of an Indian Territory East of the Missouri River," one volume, New York, 1850.

Copway, a Chippewa chief, advocated before the Thirty-first Congress the erection of a new Indian Territory which should be an improvement upon the old, by offering an asylum to northern bands only, and by providing at the outset for Indian self-government.

CRAWFORD, W. H., "Papers of." Consult Phillips's "Georgia and State Rights," page 213.

CREEKS, "Emigration Papers of," MSS., among the Indian Office Records.
Relate to the final removal of the tribe from the country east of the Mississippi River.

CREEKS, "Examination of the Controversy between Georgia'and the." First published in the "New York Review," August, 1825. Based upon the documents.

CROWELL, JOHN (Colonel), "Defense of," MSS., among the Indian Office Records.
Submitted by the agent himself to the Government in vindication of his own conduct before, during, and subsequent to the negotiation of the treaty of Indian Springs. Consists of letters, affidavits, results of cross-examinations, etc.

CRUIKSHANK, E. (Major). "The Documentary History of the Campaigns upon the Niagara Frontier, 1812," collected and edited for the Lundy's Lane Historical Society.

CURRY, BENJ. F. ("Papers of "), MSS., among the Indian Office Records, addressed to various individuals, notably Schermerhorn, Wilson Lumpkin, and William Carroll, as well as to Government officials.
Such as were not originally intended for the Department seem to have been forwarded to Washington after Curry's death. All are of incalculable value when studied in connection with the Cherokee removal.

CUTLER, JULIA PERKINS. "Life and Times of Ephraim Cutler," one volume, Cincinnati, 1890.
Throws light upon the growth of Ohio and contains some documentary material.

DANFORTH, ELLIOT. "Indians of New York," in "Oneida Historical Society Transactions," VI : 152–203.
Instructive for conditions among these Indians during Jackson's régime.

DAVIDSON, ALEXANDER, and STUVÉ, BERNARD. "A complete History of Illinois," 1673–1873, one volume, Springfield, 1877.
Contains much eulogistic matter relative to pioneers, but is usually very fair in its account of the Indians.

DAVIDSON, JOHN NELSON. "The Coming of the New York Indians to Wisconsin," in "Wisconsin Historical Society Proceedings," 1899, pages 153–185.
A good general account derived from such secondary authorities as Colton, Ellis, etc.

DAWES, E. C. "The Scioto Purchase in 1787," in "Magazine of American History," XXII : 470–482.

DAWSON, W. C. "A Compilation of the Laws of Georgia," 1819–1829, one volume, Milledgeville, 1831.

DECIUS, "Letters of " (pamphlet), Louisville, 1805.
A series of charges, addressed to Secretary of State, James Madison, against W. H. Harrison. They contain some slight references to Harrison's work as superintendent of Indian affairs.

DILLARD, ANTHONY W. "The Treaty of Dancing Rabbit Creek," in "Alabama Historical Society Transactions," III: 99–106.
An account of Choctaw conditions in 1830.

DILLON, JOHN BROWN. "Decline of the Miami Nation," in "Indiana Historical Society Publications," I : 121–143.

Dix, Morgan (Rev. Dr.), (editor). "A History of the Parish of Trinity Church, New York," 1905.

Volumes III and IV contain many of the letters and other papers of Bishop Hobart, relative to the missionary work among the New York Indians.

Dodge, Richard I. "The Plains of the Great West," one volume, New York, 1877.

Contains a good criticism of the Indian treaty-making policy.

Doty, James Duane, "Papers of," edited by R. G. Thwaites, and published in "Wisconsin Historical Collections," XXIII: 163–246.

Doty was selected by Cass as official secretary of the United States exploring expedition of 1820, and this collection, pages 163–219, contains his journal, which supplements and, by Thwaites's comparison, accords with Schoolraft's narrative of the same expedition published in 1855. It furnishes material on the Indians only incidentally. The remainder of the papers here printed deal with the Territorial organization of Wisconsin.

Donaldson, Thomas. "The Public Domain; Its History, with Statistics," one volume, Washington, 1884.

Has a good exposition of the Indian status.

Drake, Benjamin. "The Life and Adventures of Black Hawk," seventh edition, Cincinnati, 1849.

Considering his nearness to the events, Drake, though somewhat of a hero worshipper, produced a fairly reliable and unprejudiced work.

Drake, Benjamin. "The Life of Tecumseh and of His Brother, the Prophet," one volume, Cincinnati, 1858.

Contains constant reference to the Harrison letters and other documentary material.

Dunn, Jacob Piat. "History of Indiana," in "American Commonwealth" series, one volume, Boston, 1888.

Has recently been issued in a revised and enlarged edition. Is perhaps the best secondary source for the early history of Indiana.

Edwards, Ninian, "Papers of," edited by E. B. Washburne, one volume, "Chicago Historical Society Collections," III.

Contains only a portion of the Edwards' collection. Those letters and papers that appeared in N. W. Edwards's life of his father are not here reproduced. The documents are useful for local and general politics, but do not contain much material on the Indians.

Edwards, Ninian Wirt. "History of Illinois, 1778–1833, and Life and Times of Ninian Edwards," one volume, Chicago Historical Society Publication, Springfield, 1870.

Contains some documentary material.

Ellis, Albert G. (General). "Life and Public Services of James Duane Doty," in "Wisconsin Historical Collections," V: 369–377.

Ellis, Albert G. (General). "Recollections of Rev. Eleazer Williams," in "Wisconsin Historical Collections," VIII: 322–352.

A touch of bitter personal feeling detracts from the dignity and true worth of this production. Nevertheless, it introduces us to the real Mr. Williams, and we understand, as never before, his relations to the Oneidas and allied bands.

Ellis, Albert G. (General). "Some Account of the Advent of the New York Indians into Wisconsin," in "Wisconsin Historical Collections," II: 415–449.

Events narrated some thirty years after they are supposed to have occurred yet, as Ellis was the assistant of Rev. Eleazer Williams and free

ELLIS, ALBERT G.—Continued.

from his vagaries, he was in a position to know the history of the New York Indian emigration intimately and well. His statements are very suggestive and in the highest degree helpful to further research.

EVARTS, JEREMIAH. "Essays on the Present Crisis in the Condition of the American Indians," one volume, Boston, 1829.

These essays, twenty-four in number, were first published in "The National Intelligencer" under the pseudonym of "Wm. Penn." They constitute a very fine exposition of the wrongs committed against the Indians and bear few traces of having been written from the absolutely missionary point of view.

EVARTS, JEREMIAH (editor). "Speeches on the Passage of the Bill for the Removal of the Indians," one volume, Boston and New York, 1830.

This is a collection of the principal Senate and House speeches against removal, April and May, 1830, and is very convenient for ready reference.

FAIRBANKS, GEORGE R. "History of Florida," one volume, Philadelphia, 1871.

Chapters XIX to XXIII inclusive deal with the Seminoles, and are fairly trustworthy.

FINLEY, JAMES B. (Rev.). "History of the Wyandott Mission at Upper Sandusky, Ohio," one volume, Cincinnati, 1840.

FINLEY, JAMES B. (Rev.). "Life Among the Indians, or Personal Reminiscences and Historical Incidents," edited by Rev. D. W. Clark, one volume, Cincinnati, 1868.

FONDA, JOHN H. "Early Reminiscences of Wisconsin," in "Wisconsin Historical Collections," V: 205–284.

Fonda, an early pioneer of Wisconsin, dictated the individual parts of this article to the editor of the "Prairie du Chien Courier," and it was in that paper that they first appeared. (L. C. Draper's edtorial note, "Wisconsin Historical Collections," V: 205.) Their shortcomings as reminiscences are more than compensated by their suggestiveness.

FORCE, M. F. (General). "Some Early Notices of the Indians of Ohio," one volume, Cincinnati, 1879.

A first-class report upon early conditions.

FORD, THOMAS. "A History of Illinois," 1818–1847, one volume, Chicago, 1854.

Exceedingly partisan and said to have been composed for personal vindication.

FOSTER, ARTHUR. "A Digest of the Laws of Georgia," 1820–1829, one volume, Philadelphia, 1831.

GAINES, EDMUND P., "Report of," MSS., among the Indian Office Records, being the results of his investigations relative to the Georgia–Creek controversy.

"GALES AND SEATON'S REGISTER OF DEBATES IN CONGRESS," thirteen volumes, Washington.

Cover the period from December, 1824, to March, 1837. Invaluable.

GALLATIN, ALBERT, "Writings of," edited by Henry Adams, three volumes, Philadelphia, 1879.

GARRETT, WILLIAM ROBERTSON, and GOODPASTURE, ALBERT VIRGIL. "History of Tennessee," one volume, Nashville, 1900.

On the text-book order, but contains interesting biographical sketches of such men as Crockett, Houston, Carroll, etc.

GARRISON, WILLIAM LLOYD, "Life of," as told by his children, four volumes, New York, 1885–1889.

Contains occasional references to Garrison's opposition to Jackson's Indian policy and to Georgia's treatment of the Cherokees.

GIDDINGS, JOSHUA R. "The Exiles of Florida," one volume, Columbus, 1858.

Has a place in an Indian bibliography only as throwing a little light upon the negotiation of early Creek treaties.

GILMER, GEORGE ROCKINGHAM. "Sketches of Some of the First Settlers of Upper Georgia, of the Cherokees, and the Author," one volume, New York, 1855.

A very egotistical book, but convenient for reference because of its documentary material, in particular the Gilmer-Wirt correspondence relative to the Cherokee case.

GREEN, CHARLES R. "The Indians of Huron County, Ohio," in "The Firelands Pioneer," XV : 1052–1073.

The subject-matter is entertaining and reliable though somewhat detached, as is often the case with the writings of local historians. For years Mr. Green has been collecting material on "The History and Traditions of the Marais des Cygnes Valley," which will greatly contribute to our knowledge of Indian removals.

GRIGNON, AUGUSTIN. "Seventy-Two Years' Recollections of Wisconsin," in "Wisconsin Historical Collections," III : 197–295.

The article concerns itself with recollections more of individual Indian chiefs than of historical conditions.

HALBERT H. S. and BALL, T. H. "The Creek War of 1813 and 1814," one volume, Chicago, 1895.

Professor Channing very accurately describes it as "often prejudiced" but "compiled from all available material, original, secondary, and traditional." (Larned, p. 169.)

HALKETT, J. "Historical Notes Respecting the Indians of North America, with Remarks on the Attempts Made to Convert and Civilize Them," one volume, London, 1825.

General, superficial, and frequently inaccurate.

HANSARD, T. C. "Parliamentary Debates," 1803 to date. Five series, London.

HANSON, JOHN H. "The Lost Prince," one volume, New York, 1854.

Contains a little material bearing upon Eleazer Williams's Indian interests, but not enough to make us think that in that respect also the pretender to French royalty had imposed upon the credulity of the author.

HARDEN, EDWARD JENKINS. "The Life of George McIntosh Troup," one volume, Savannah, 1859.

The chief value of this eulogistic biography lies in its collection of original material. Were the book itself more common, it might be regarded as the most accessible, because most convenient, repository of documents on the Georgia-Creek controversy. The author has introduced them chronologically and, in most cases, pointed out, in very fitting terms, their interrelation. As he says in his preface, "Troup's private correspondence must have been extensive; and, without doubt, much of it has been irrecoverably lost."

HARVEY, HENRY. "History of the Shawnee Indians, 1681–1854," one volume, Cincinnati, 1855.

A connected but very meager account, almost useless for purposes of reference.

HATCH, W. S. (Colonel). "A Chapter in the War of 1812," one volume, Cincinnati, 1872.

Hatch writes from memory. His chief fault is the use of too strong language. He pays high tribute to the character of Tecumseh and to that of the northwestern Indians generally.

HAWKINS, BENJAMIN, "Papers of." Consult Phillips's "Georgia and State Rights," p. 214.

HAYES, CHARLES W. (Rev.). "The Diocese of Western New York," one volume, second edition, New York, 1904.

Best and fullest general account of Bishop Hobart's relations with Eleazer Williams and the Oneidas.

HAZARD, SAMUEL (editor). "Register of Pennsylvania," 1828–1835, sixteen volumes.

Has little contemporary material on the Indians, but, beginning with Volume XII, offers an interesting series of articles on the history of land titles in Pennsylvania which involves a knowledge of the Indian's legal status.

HECKEWELDER, JOHN (Rev.). "A Narrative of the Mission of the Moravian Brethren's Church Among the Delaware and Mohegan Indians from 1740 to 1808," one volume, Philadelphia, 1820.

Very instructive for the early history of the Ohio Valley. William E. Connelley, the present owner of the original manuscript, is proposing to edit a new and more complete edition of it, the arrangement of which shall be as nearly as can be ascertained in line with the missionary's first intentions, the publishers having abbreviated and altered the original copy.

HERBERMANN, CHARLES GEORGE. "A French Émigré Colony in the United States," 1789–1793, in "History, Records, and Studies of the United States Catholic Historical Society," I, Part I, pages 77–96.

The material is based upon an article by M. Henri Carré in the "Revue de Paris," May 15, 1898, but is more interesting than that as a sidelight upon the events that necessitated St. Clair's expedition.

HILDRETH, RICHARD. "The History of the United States to 1821." Revised edition, six volumes, New York, 1882.

HOBART, JOHN HENRY (Bishop), "Papers of."

The manuscripts of the Right Rev. John Henry Hobart are among the archives of the Episcopal Church, preserved in a fireproof safe in room 46 of the Church Mission House, 281 Fourth avenue, New York City, under the guardianship of the acting registrar, the Rev. Dr. Samuel Hart. They consist of letters and other documents extending from Hobart's entrance to Princeton in 1791 to a short time before his death which occurred at Auburn, N. Y., September 10 (12?), 1830. The letters are from members of his family, especially his mother, from his classmates, and from other friends in the period to 1800. After that, they are from bishops, clergymen, and laymen of the Episcopal Church in America, also of the Church of England, and from distinguished persons on the continent of Europe. They are in number more than six thousand. About three thousand are indorsed and filed alphabetically in bundles. The others are inserted in the stubs of old voucher, or stock books, chronologically from 1802 to 1820. An index to the letters in bundles was published in the third volume of Doctor Dix's "History of Trinity Church" (Appendix pp. 487–497). In the bound volumes of the Hobart Papers are many letters from people connected with the Oneida Reservation in New York and a few that deal particularly with the proposed removal to Wisconsin. Many of the letters and other papers touching upon the Indians, in whose moral and spiritual welfare Bishop Hobart was vitally interested, were published at the time of their issue, the earlier ones in the "Christian Journal" and the later in the "Gospel Messenger." Some have more recently appeared in Doctor Dix's "History of Trinity Church."

HOBART, JOHN HENRY (Bishop), "Memorial of," a collection of sermons on the death of the Right Rev. J. H. Hobart, with a memoir of his life and writings, one volume, New York, 1831. Edited anonymously by John Frederick Schroeder, an assistant minister of Trinity Church in New York.

HODGSON, ADAM. "Letters from North America, Written During a Tour in the United States and Canada," two volumes, London, 1824.

The second volume has much concerning the civilization of the southern Indians and notes the Cherokee aversion to further cessions.

HOLST, HERMANN E. VON. "The Constitutional and Political History of the United States," 1750–1859. Translated by John J. Lalor et al., eight volumes, new edition, Chicago, 1899.

HULBERT, ARCHER BUTLER. "Historic Highways of America, sixteen volumes, Cleveland, 1902–1905.

Certain volumes and certain chapters in other volumes are of exceedingly great interest for the passing of the Indian.

HULBERT, ARCHER BUTLER. "Redmen's Roads; the Indian Thoroughfares of the Central West," one volume, Columbus, 1900.

HULBERT, ARCHER BUTLER. "The Old National Road; a Chapter of American Expansion," one volume, Columbus, 1901.

INDIANS. "Reports on," 1790–1834. Embodied in the reports of the Secretary of War.

INDIAN AFFAIRS, "Reports of the Commissioners," 1835 to date, Washington, D. C.

The Indian Office proper, as a regular and distinct subdivision of the War Department, was not created until 1835, and in that year the first Commissioner of Indian Affairs was appointed. The reports of this official dating from that time are full of matter relative to the past and present of the Indian.

"INDIAN AFFAIRS, LAWS, AND TREATIES," (Senate Document No. 452, Fifth Congress, first session.)

Compiled and edited by Charles J. Kappler, clerk to the Senate Committee on Indian Affairs, two volumes, Washington, D. C., 1903.

INDIAN COMMISSIONERS, "Annual Reports of the Board of," 1869–1905.

In 1860 a Board of Indian Commissioners was organized, responsible to the Secretary of the Interior, and assigned the duty of annually reporting upon Indian conditions and ways in which they might, if bad, be ameliorated. The reports contain many reflections upon past events that lighten the labor of the investigator.

INDIANS. "Documents and Proceedings Relating to the Formation and Progress of a Board in the city of New York for the Emigration, Preservation, and Improvement of the Aborigines of America, July 22, 1829." Compiled by Vanderpool & Cole, New York, 1829.

The contents of this publication include the constitution of the board, correspondence with Thomas L. McKenney relative to its organization, Jackson's talk to the Creeks, and his talk to the Cherokee delegation, etc.

INDIANS. "Laws of the Colonial and State Governments Relating to Indians and Indian Affairs from 1624 to 1831, inclusive," published by Thompson & Homans, Washington, D. C., 1832.

INDIAN OFFICE RECORDS.

The material in the second and in all succeeding chapters, except the third, is largely based upon the official records preserved in the Indian Office at Washington, D. C. These records have had a very precarious existence and are even now 'n a somewhat disorganized and perishable condition. They date from November, 1800, and at the time of my examination were

INDIAN OFFICE RECORDS—Continued.

to be found in files, bundles, letter books, report books, and index volumes. A description of the files and of their contents is given with reasonable exactness on pages 205–209 of the second edition of Van Tyne and Leland's "Guide to the Archives," issued by the Carnegie Institution.

The bundles are composed of certain records, classified according to subject-matter, such as "Indian Talks, the Mitchell Papers, the Curry Papers, the Indian Springs Treaty Papers, the Cherokee Bounty Land Papers, Reservation Papers of the Various Tribes, Spoliation Claims Papers, Cherokee Neutral Land Papers, and the Emigration Papers of the Creeks, Choctaws, Chickasaws, Cherokees, and Seminoles, respectively. I have not been able to find any special papers relating to the removal of any of the northern tribes.

The letter books, with one exception, contain copies of outgoing correspondence and may be classified as follows:

A. "Letters Sent."

1. Those dealing with miscellaneous affairs:

(*a*) "First series," six volumes, designated by letters, November, 1800, to April, 1824: Vol. A, November 17, 1800–April 20, 1804; Vol. B, April 23, 1804–July 5, 1809; Vol. C, July 8, 1809–December 31, 1816; Vol. D, January 8, 1817–July 31, 1820; Vol. E, August 20, 1820–October 27, 1823; Vol. F, October, 1823–April 26, 1824.

(*b*) "Second series," two hundred volumes, designated by numbers, March 18, 1824, to January 8, 1886.

(*c*) "Third series," ("Chickasaw Letter Books"), three volumes, designated by letters, January, 1832, to April, 1861: Vol. A, January, 1832–September, 1838; Vol. B, September, 1838–June, 1848; Vol. C, June, 1848–April, 1861.

2. Those dealing with Indian trade relations only:

(*d*) "Fourth series," four volumes, designated by letters, October 31, 1807, to April 11, 1818.

(*e*) "Fifth series," incomplete, only one volume, "D," extant, and that covers the period from July, 1820, to April, 1822.

B. "Letters Sent and Received."

(*f*) "Sixth series," one volume, 1835–1836. Relates chiefly to Cherokee removals.

The index volumes are valuable only as furnishing suggestions of papers to be examined and may be classified thus:

A. "Letters Received."

(*a*) "First series," thirty-three volumes, designated by numbers, January 1, 1824, to June 30, 1847.

(*b*) "Second series," three volumes, designated by letters, February, 1830, to November, 1836. Deals exclusively with emigration.

B. "Weekly Report of Letters Received."

(*c*) "Third series," one volume, January, 1832, to June, 1833.

C. "Letters Registered."

(*d*) "Fourth series." This system of recording the incoming letters was adopted about the time the Interior Department was created and continues to the present day.

From the foregoing analysis it is evident that, for the period covered by this thesis, there was no regular system of preserving the Indian records, which, at best, do not antedate the destructive fire which broke out in the War Office, November 8, 1800. Furthermore, the records have themselves been subjected to various removals, incident upon new building

INDIAN OFFICE RECORDS—Continued.

accommodations and upon the transfer of the Indian Bureau from the War to the Interior Department. It is matter of tradition that, when the last-named change was effected, the Secretary of War was so annoyed at the consequent loss of jurisdiction, that he took no pains to see that the papers were not tampered with in transit. Autograph fiends must have been in evidence, for the page bearing the signature of a prominent individual is sometimes mutilated or missing. The parts of a letter are often separated from each other and inclosures abstracted or misplaced. All this points to very rough handling which we may well suppose took place, inasmuch as the papers, after being carelessly sorted, were thrown into an ordinary transfer wagon. Removal has, moreover, not been their only misfortune. Such of them, as there was no immediate need of, were stored temporarily in the basement; and, on one occasion, it was discovered that a night watchman had disposed of some of them for waste paper. Fortunately the office managed to recover most if not all of them. A few years after the Civil War an alarm of fire in an opposite building caused the Indian Office to remove its records to an outside inclosure for safety. Some of them may have been lost. At all events, the occurrence aggravated the existing disorder. Pressure of current business and lack of facilities have prevented the arrangement of these manuscript materials in proper order for convenient examination. Nevertheless, so valuable are they that the research worker is well repaid for his trouble.

INDIANS, " Removal of." Article in " North American Review," January, 1830, XXX: 62–121.

Was pronounced by contemporaries to have had great influence in bringing about the passage of the removal act of 1830.

INDIAN RIGHTS ASSOCIATION, "Annual Reports of the Executive Committee of," 1883 to date, Philadelphia.

INDIAN SPRINGS TREATY PAPERS, MSS. among the Indian Office Records, bearing upon the negotiation and repudiation of the Creek treaty of 1825, and including the incoming correspondence of Campbell, Crowell, Andrews, Gaines, Troup, and others.

INDIANS. "A Statement of the Indian Relations with a Reply to the Article in the Sixty-sixth Number of the North American Review on the Removal of the Indians," published by Clayton & Van Norden, New York, 1830.

" INDIAN TREATIES AND LAWS AND REGULATIONS RELATING TO INDIAN AFFAIRS," compiled and published under orders of the Department of War, February 9 and October 6, 1825, Washington, D. C., 1826.

" INDIAN TREATIES BETWEEN THE UNITED STATES AND THE INDIAN TRIBES," 1778–1837. Compiled and annotated under the supervision of the Commissioner of Indian Affairs. Washington, D. C., 1837. (Printers, Langtree & O'Sullivan.)

More comprehensive than any other edition covering the same period. Includes not only extensive treaties, but also minor contracts of which there is often no trace in the seventh volume of the United States Statutes at Large. The compiler's notes are accurate and labor-saving.

INDIAN TREATIES BETWEEN THE UNITED STATES AND THE INDIAN TRIBES," 1778–1842, being the seventh volume of the United States Statutes at Large. Later treaties are included in the particular volume for the year in which they were individually ratified.

INGERSOLL, L. D. "A History of the War Department of the United States," one volume, Washington, D. C., 1879.

Its treatment of the Indian Bureau and its policy is superficial in the extreme.

JACKSON, ALFRED AUGUSTUS. "Abraham Lincoln in the Black Hawk War," in "Wisconsin Historical Collections," XIV : 118–136.

Superior to Nicolay and Hay's account, which R. G. Thwaites has declared to be based upon erroneous data.

JACKSON, ANDREW, "Papers of."

The collection of Jackson manuscripts belonging to the Congressional Library is minutely described by C. H. Lincoln in "The Literary Collector" for May, 1904. It is there estimated to consist of about 7,000 distinct papers—"letters, reports, and military returns—together with thirteen volumes of letter books and military records." More specifically one might say, that the collection comprises Jackson's own letter books, rough drafts of letters written by him, letters addressed to him, copies of letters passing between second and third parties, and, finally, attested copies of Indian treaty journals. Some of the last named are of incalculable value, because their originals have apparently disappeared from the Indian Office. Additional Jackson Papers are in the custody of the Tennessee Historical Society.

The examination of the Jackson collection in Washington is a most laborious process, for faded ink, poor writing, and still poorer spelling, increase the natural shortcomings of a very much mixed and discursive correspondence. Jackson was interested in many things, and he wrote energetically upon all. Fortunately for future investigators, the process of arranging, cataloguing, and calendaring is well under way. That done, surely we may hope that in a few years a well-edited publication of his more important works will appear, to say nothing of a really praiseworthy biography. At present the historical student is lamentably destitute of both.

JACKSON, HELEN HUNT. "A Century of Dishonor," one volume, New York, 1881.

Severe in its criticism of the United States Indian policy. None the less, its statements are in the main based upon facts. It is much to be regretted that the tone of the book is a trifle sentimental.

JEFFERSON, THOMAS, "Calendar of the Correspondence of," in Bulletins of the Bureau of Rolls and Library of the Department of State, Nos. 6, 8, and 10, Washington, 1894, 1895, 1903.

JEFFERSON, THOMAS, "Memoir, Correspondence, and Miscellanies from the Papers of," edited by Thos. Jefferson Randolph, four volumes, second edition, Charlottesville, 1830.

JEFFERSON, THOMAS, "The Writings of," edited by H. A. Washington, nine volumes, Washington, 1853–54.

JEFFERSON, THOMAS, "The Writings of" 1760–1826, edited by Paul Leicester Ford, ten volumes, New York, 1892.

JEFFERSON, THOMAS, "The Writings of" (library edition), A. A. Lipscomb, editor in chief; A. E. Bergh, managing editor. In process of publication, eighteen volumes to date, 1904, Washington, D. C.

More complete but less handy than Ford's edition, which, in its turn, is beyond all comparison with Randolph's and Washington's.

KENNEDY, JOHN PENDLETON. "Memoirs of the Life of Wm. Wirt," two volumes, Philadelphia, 1849, a new and revised edition, Philadelphia, 1850.

Volume II, Chapters XV, XVII, XIX, useful for a study of the Cherokee case.

KING, RUFUS, "The Life and Correspondence of," 1755–1827, edited by Charles R. King, six volumes, New York, 1900.

Volume VI, page 114 contains a letter to Edward King, February 12, 1818, relative to the treaty of Edwardsville and to Cherokee affairs.

LEA, JOHN M. "Indian Treaties of Tennessee," in "American Historical Magazine," VI: 367–380.

Advances the idea that Jackson, though determined to force the Indians westward, had no intention of acting at the behest of Georgia.

LEWIS AND CLARK EXPEDITION, "History of," edited by Elliott Coues from the original manuscript journals and field books of the explorers, four volumes, New York, 1893.

The Clark-Voorhis papers, described by R. G. Thwaites in Scribner's Magazine, XXXV: 685–700, being newly discovered personal records of Lewis and Clark, may possibly throw light upon the secondary objects of the expedition; for, although the explorers were to open up communication with western tribes, there is no indication in Coues's reprint of their papers that they were to prepare for the migration of the eastern.

LITTLE, HENRY. "A History of the Black Hawk War," third revised edition in "Pioneer Society of Michigan Collections," V: 152–178.

A good summary of the chief events, but the accuracy of the details may well be questioned. Little was 78 years old when he brought out this edition, and, while posing as the historian of the Indian's side, indulges in weak sentiment. His knowledge of the subject is not exhaustive.

LUMPKIN, WILSON, "Papers of."

Many of the Lumpkin letters are to be found in the bundle of Curry MSS. among the Indian Office Records, also in the Miscellaneous and Cherokee Files of the same office, and in Jameson's edition of the Calhoun correspondence. For information respecting the Lumpkin MS. autobiography, consult Phillips's "Georgia and State Rights," page 214; it has (1908) just been printed, we are informed.

McBRIDE, DAVID. "The Capture of Black Hawk," in "Wisconsin Historical Collections," V: 294–297.

A brief sketch of the betrayal of Black Hawk by Winnebagoes.

McCALEB, W. F. "The Aaron Burr Conspiracy," one volume, New York, 1903.

The latest work on the subject. Written from the standpoint of the Southwest. Based upon Jackson Papers, Mexican Archives, and contemporary newspapers. The strong feature of the book is the showing that Louisiana was not disgruntled at the time the conspiracy is said to have been plotted. Possibly the abandonment of the removal project may have contributed to her satisfaction.

McCALL, GEO. A. (Major). "Letters from the Frontiers," one volume, Philadelphia, 1868.

Not of much value except as throwing light upon the Indian character, and in that respect it is most useful for the Seminoles.

McCALL, JAMES. "Journal of a Visit to Wisconsin in 1830," published with a sketch of his life by his nephew, Ansel J. McCall, and a copy of the instructions from the Secretary of War of June 9, 1830, in "Wisconsin Historical Collections," XII: 170–205.

McCALL, JAMES. "Documents Illustrating the Journal of," obtained from the records of the Interior Department, and published in "Wisconsin Historical Collections," XII: 206–215.

Among these documents are the report of the commissioners, pages 207–214, and the affidavit of one of them, John T. Mason, September 20, 1830, to the effect that he does not concur in that part of the report bearing

McCALL, JAMES—Continued.

upon the validity of the New York-Menominee agreements of 1821 and 1822, because he regards it as gratuitous, the commission not having been authorized to investigate the claim of the New York Indians, but only to adjust their differences with the Menominees.

McCoy, ISAAC, (Rev.). "Papers of," MSS. in the possession of the Kansas Historical Society presented by John C. McCoy. Consist of missionary and family correspondence, from 1808 to 1847, besides journals, incomplete, from 1817 to 1841.

A very valuable source for research work on the actual removal of the Indians, especially of the northern tribes after 1830. McCoy surveyed, or superintended the survey, of several of the early reservations in Kansas and located most of the tribes that went there. The Government placed great reliance upon him, and his truly kindly disposition toward the emigrants softened the rigor of the Jacksonian measures.

McCoy, ISAAC (Rev.). "The Annual Register of Indian Affairs within the Indian Territory." A rare periodical.

Contains interesting particulars respecting the Indian emigrant's advent into the new country, his surroundings, and his prospects.

McCoy, ISAAC (Rev.). "History of Baptist Indian Missions," one volume, New York, 1840.

A record of the personal experiences of the missionary, his family, and his friends from 1818 on. Is more instructive as regards the Ottawas and the Pottawatomies than almost any other tribes.

McCoy, ISAAC (Rev.). "Remarks on the Practicability of Indian Reform, Embracing Their Colonization" (pamphlet), Boston, 1827. Reissued in a second edition with an appendix, New York, 1829.

McCoy, ISAAC (Rev.). "The Condition of the American Indians," an address issued from the surveyor's camp, Neosho River, Indian Territory, to philanthropists in the United States generally and to Christians in particular on the condition and prospects of the American Indians, December 1, 1831.

McKENNEY, THOMAS LORRAINE (Colonel). "Memoirs Official and Personal with Sketches of Travel among the Northern and Southern Indians, Embracing a War Excursion and Description of Scenes along the Western Borders," two volumes, New York, 1846.

Singularly destitute of anything very valuable. Like all McKenney's writings, it is, in the broadest sense, disappointing. A man connected with the Indian Office for so many years ought to have been able to furnish extraordinarily good material, and we are at a loss to know why McKenney did not. He became Superintendent of Indian Trade in 1816, and his memoirs contain a few reflections upon the manner of conducting that trade, but are otherwise quite uninteresting.

McKENNEY, THOMAS L. "Sketches of a Tour to the Lakes, of the Character and Customs of the Chippeway Indians, and the Incidents Connected with the Treaty of Fond du Lac; also a Vocabulary of the Algic, or Chippeway, Language, Formed in Part and as Far as it Goes upon the One Furnished by the Hon. Albert Gallatin," Baltimore, 1827.

McKenney was joint commissioner with Cass in negotiating the Treaty of Fond du Lac, but he is rather reticent on the subject.

McKENNEY, THOMAS L., and HALL, JAMES. "History of the Indian Tribes of North America with Biographical Sketches and Anecdotes of the Principal Chiefs, Embellished with 120 Portraits from the Indian Gallery in the Department of War at Washington," three volumes.

McKENNEY, THOMAS L., and HALL, JAMES—Continued.

Vol. I. "Biographical Sketches of Chiefs," published by E. C. Biddle, Philadelphia, 1837.

Vol. II. "Biographical Sketches of Chiefs," published by Frederick W. Greenough, Philadelphia, 1838.

Vol. III. "History of the Indian Tribes of North America," published by D. Rice & J. G. Clark, Philadelphia, 1844.

Some serious, sober facts, but much that is traditional, sentimental, and worthless.

McKENNEY, THOMAS L. "The Winnebago War of 1827," in Wisconsin Historical Collections," V : 178–204. Taken from the "History of Indian Tribes of North America."

McLAUGHLIN, ANDREW C, "The Influence of Governor Cass on the Development of the Northwest," in "Papers of the American Historical Association," III : 67–83.

McLAUGHLIN, ANDREW C. "The Western Posts and British Debts," in "Annual Report of the American Historical Association," 1894, pages 413–444.

Offers evidence from the Canadian archives of a more or less complete exoneration of the British in their attitude toward the northwestern Indians just prior to the war of 1812.

McMASTER, JOHN B. "A History of the People of the United States," 1783–1861, five volumes, New York, 1884–1900.

McMINN, JOSEPH, "Papers of." The archives of the Tennessee Historical Society contain forty-eight letters and papers signed by Governor McMinn. ("American Historical Magazine," V : 48.) They are published in "The American Historical Magazine," IV : 319–335; V : 48–66; VIII : 377–394.

Those in Vol. IV are of some value for Indian affairs 1818–1819 and those in Vol. VIII for Indian treaties 1815, 1816, and 1817. Other McMinn letters are to be found in the files of the Indian Office and are very important.

MADISON, JAMES, "Calendar of the Correspondence of," Bulletin No. 4 of the Bureau of Rolls and Library of the Department of State, Washington, 1894.

MADISON, JAMES, "Letters and Other Writings of," (Congressional edition), four volumes, Philadelphia, 1865.

Gaillard Hunt's edition of Madison's writings will probably throw additional light upon the Indian policy of the Government; but as yet it has come down only to 1790 [1807]. The life of Madison as written by both Rives and Hunt is quite barren of any information on the subject.

MAHAN, A. T. (Captain). "Sea Power in Its Relations to the War of 1812," two volumes, Little, Brown &'Co., Boston, 1905.

MAHAN, A. T. (Captain). "The Negotiations at Ghent in 1814," in "American Historical Review," October, 1905, XI : 68–87.

MANYPENNY, GEORGE W. "Our Indian Wards," one volume, Cincinnati, 1880.

Manypenny was a United States commissioner, 1853–1857, and chairman of the Sioux Commission of 1876, so that what he had to say was well worth while, but his tone is often petty and his statements show a defective memory or neglect to consult records easily accessible.

MARSH, CUTTING (Rev.), "Papers of."

The papers of the Rev. Cutting Marsh, missionary of the "American Board for Foreign Missions" and also of the "Society in Scotland for Propagating Christian Knowledge" to the Stockbridge Indians, 1830–1848, were deposited with the Wisconsin Historical Society. They include "fifty-five letters from and to Marsh bearing dates from 1830 to August 6, 1856,"

MARSH, CUTTING—Continued.

and of a journal, comprehended in "thirty-nine manuscript books, covering the period from May 2, 1830, to the close of the year 1855." (Wisconsin Historical Collections, XV: 39, note.) Some of these papers, namely, selections from or abridged reprints of Marsh's annual reports to the Scottish Society, May 2, 1830, to June 1, 1848, have been edited with notes by William Ward Wight and R. G. Thwaites for the Wisconsin Historical Society (Collections, XV: 48: 204). As it happens, the notes are really more interesting than the documents themselves; for they furnish numerous treaty and literature references, also a great deal of biographical data, while the Marsh reports, though comparable "in matter, form, and spirit to the 'Jesuit Relations,'" are chiefly concerned with educational and religious affairs.

MENARD, PIERRE, "Papers of," in "Chicago Historical Society Collections," IV: 162–180, from the originals in the possession of the society.

Such Menard papers as are here given are of little value, being Government commissions and the like. Secretary Armstrong appointed Menard sub-agent of Indian affairs in 1813, and ever after the man was intimately associated with the tribes of the Northwest.

MINER, JESSE, "Papers of," "Wisconsin Historical Collections," XV: 41–48.

Miner was the predecessor of Marsh at the Stockbridge mission in Wisconsin, and some of his papers, here edited by Wight and Thwaites and printed in full, passed with the Marsh papers into the custody of the Wisconsin Historical Society. They are of general interest only.

"THE MISSIONARY HERALD," containing proceedings at large of the American Board of Commissioners for Foreign Missions, Boston.

A mine of contemporary history, often overlooked but exceedingly valuable. The unavoidable complication of missionary affairs with the efforts to expel the Indians from Georgia render the numbers of the "Missionary Herald" from about 1826 to the end of the controversy a very fruitful source of information. They contain letters, official documents, statistics on Indian civilization, and missionary reports from all over the country.

MITCHELL, DAVID B., "Papers of." MSS. among the Indian Office Records, dealing with the causes of his dismissal from the position of government agent to the Creek Indians.

MONETTE, JOHN W. "History of the Discovery and Settlement of the Mississippi Valley," two volumes, New York, 1846.

The footnotes are usually very suggestive, and much of the text is still acceptable data.

MONROE, JAMES, "Calendar of the Correspondence of," in Bulletin No. 2 of the Bureau of Rolls and Library of the Department of State, Washington, 1893.

MONROE, JAMES, "Papers of." MSS. in the Library of Congress, "purchased under act of Congress of March 3, 1849, repaired, mounted, and bound under acts of March 2, 1889, and August 30, 1890.

Consulted more for the purpose of substantiating material found elsewhere than with the expectation of discovering anything additional to that accessible in print.

MONROE, JAMES, "Writings of," 1778–1831, edited by S. M. Hamilton, seven volumes, New York, 1903.

MOONEY, JAMES. "The Ghost Dance Religion," in Fourteenth Annual Report of the Bureau of American Ethnology.

Instructive for Tecumseh and Indian participation in the war of 1812.

MOOREHEAD, WARREN KING. "The Indian Tribes of Ohio—Historically Considered," in "Ohio Archæological Historical Society Quarterly," VII, part 1; pages 1–109.

Intended by the author to be preliminary to an extensive work on the Ohio Indians. As it stands, it is a mere sketch devoted mainly to events centering around Tecumseh. Moorehead has used Mooney, Drake, Atwater, Catlin, Schoolcraft, and Hatch extensively and has also gathered statistics for himself. He is very impartial.

MORSE, JEDIDIAH (Rev.), "Report of, to the Secretary of War of the United States on Indian Affairs, comprising a narrative of a tour performed in the summer of 1820 under a commission from the President of the United States for the purpose of ascertaining, for the use of the Government, the actual state of the Indian tribes in our country," one volume, New Haven, Conn., 1822.

Field in his "Essay toward an Indian Bibliography," pronounces this "the most complete and exhaustive report of the condition, numbers, names, territory, and general affairs of the Indians ever made," and surely he cannot be gainsaid. The volume in which the report is embodied consists altogether of four hundred pages, but only about one-fourth of them are taken up with the official communications to the Secretary of War. The remainder constitute an "Appendix" of statistics and documentary material or, as Morse himself says, "the body of his information." He visited many of the tribes reported upon personally, but not all. Instead of that he opened up a correspondence with individuals, often missionaries, in various localities, and from them gained what he could. In minor particulars these accounts did not always tally with each other, and Morse noticed discrepancies, but could not very well avoid them. His own idea in making the tour of 1820 was to look over the ground for the organization of "Mission Families." By that he meant colonization on a small scale for a specific purpose, or removal in a modified sense. Sincere in his endeavor, he spared no pains in unearthing information of all sorts, and the result was an honest, plain-spoken narrative that the student of Indian history dare not ignore.

NEILL, EDWARD D. "History of the Ojibways and Their Connection with the Fur Traders," in "Minnesota Historical Society Collections," V: 395–510.

Based upon official and other records.

NEW YORK STATE ASSEMBLY. "Report of Special Committee of," appointed in 1888, "to investigate the Indian problem of the State of New York," one volume, Albany, 1889.

F. J. Shepard very adequately and concisely sums up the content of this report in Larned's "Literature of American History:" "The report transmitted to the legislature, February 1, 1889, devotes 40 pages to a history of this people in New York, with special reference to the complicated Ogden land claim. The remaining 39 pages of the report proper describe the conditions prevailing on the several reservations, and are followed by appendices containing the full text of various National and State treaties with the New York Indians, land grants, legal decisions, and miscellaneous matter connected with the subject."

"NILES' WEEKLY REGISTER" of documents, essays, and facts, edited by H. Niles, 1811–1836, fifty volumes. Baltimore. Continued as "Niles' National Register" from September, 1836, to March, 1849, 25 volumes, Baltimore.

OSGOOD, HERBERT L. "The American Colonies in the Seventeenth Century," three volumes, New York, 1904–1907.

The last chapter in the first volume treats in a masterly way of Indian relations during the colonial period and of the beginnings of the reservation system.

OTIS, ELWELL S. "The Indian Question," one volume, New York, 1878.

A good general account of the United States Indian policy, but occasionally too sweeping in its conclusions.

PARKER, THOMAS VALENTINE. "The Cherokee Indians," one volume, The Grafton Press, New York, 1907.

PARKINGSON, PETER. "Notes on the Black Hawk War," in "Wisconsin Historical Collections," X: 184–212.

PARTON, JAMES. "Life of Andrew Jackson," three volumes, New York, 1860.

Parton more than any other of Jackson's biographers develops to a certain extent the Indian policy of his subject and submits or quotes from the documents.

PECK, CHARLES H. "The Jacksonian Epoch," one volume, New York, 1899.

PERKINS, JAMES H. "Annals of the West from the Discovery of the Mississippi Valley to 1845," published by J. R. Albach, 1846. A later edition brings the record down to 1856, published by J. R. Albach, 1857.

PERKINS, SAMUEL. "Historical Sketches of the United States, 1815–1820," one volume, New York, 1830.

Presents Creek affairs from a contemporary point of view, and is reliable.

PETERS, RICHARD. "Report of Cases Argued and Adjudged in the Supreme Court of the United States," 1828–1842, sixteen volumes, Philadelphia.

PHILLIPS, ULRICH BONNELL. "Georgia and State Rights," a monograph published in the Annual Report of the American Historical Association, 1901.

Contains an authoritative treatment of the relations of Georgia with the Creeks and Cherokees based upon a thorough research into the Georgia archives.

PICKETT, ALBERT JAMES. "History of Alabama and Incidentally of Georgia and Mississippi from the Earliest Period," two volumes, new edition, enlarged, Birmingham, Ala., 1900.

The work of Pickett ended with 1819, but Thomas M. Owen carried it on to the present century. The earlier narrative has not been superseded, and is invaluable as a secondary source, because its details were derived, "in part" from "original printed authorities," and "in part" from "interviews with Indian chiefs and white pioneers."

PIERCE, M. B. "Address (delivered at Buffalo) on the Present Condition and Prospects of the Aboriginal Inhabitants of North America with Particular Reference to the Seneca Indians," Philadelphia, 1839.

PIKE, ZEBULON MONTGOMERY. "The Expeditions of, to the Headwaters of the Mississippi River, through Louisiana Territory, and in New Spain during the years 1805, 1806, and 1807," new edition, now first reprinted in full from the original of 1810, edited by Elliott Coues, three volumes, New York, 1895. The Pike Papers recently discovered in the Mexican archives have some bearing upon Indian history.

POLK, JAMES K. "Papers."

MSS. in the Congressional Library, not yet arranged chronologically, and therefore for the most part a disorganized mass. They yield, on examination, very little that bears directly upon Indian affairs.

PORTER, JAMES D. "The Chickasaw Treaty of 1818," in "The American Historical Magazine," IX: 252–256.

Instructive for the circumstance of the leasing of the Chickasaw Salt Lick.

POTTER, WOODBURNE. "The War in Florida, being an Exposition of its Causes and an Accurate History of the Campaigns of Generals Clinch, Gaines, and Scott," one volume, Baltimore, 1836.

Contains the details of Florida Indian treaty negotiations, Gadsden letters, and one valuable letter from Eaton to Cass, March 8, 1835. Potter is inclined to take the Indian side unreservedly.

QUINCY, JOSIAH. "Memoir of the Life of John Quincy Adams," one volume, Boston, 1858.

Helpful for information respecting the political enemies of J. Q. Adams and their plans.

RAMAGE, B. J. "Georgia and the Cherokees," in "American Historical Magazine," VII: 199–208.

A mere sketch.

RANDALL, HENRY S. "Life of Thomas Jefferson," three volumes, New York, 1858.

REYNOLDS, JOHN (Governor). "The Pioneer History of Illinois," second edition, one volume, Chicago, 1887.

Concludes its account with 1818.

REYNOLDS, JOHN (Governor). "My Own Times," 1800–1855, one volume, published by the Chicago Historical Society, 1879.

Presents a contemporary view of the Black Hawk war in which the author participated.

RICHARDSON, JAMES D. "Compilation of the Messages and Papers of the Presidents," 1789–1897, ten volumes, published by authority of Congress, 1896–1899.

RIVES, WILLIAM C. "History of the Life and Times of James Madison," three volumes, Boston, 1859–1868.

ROOSEVELT, THEODORE. "Thomas H. Benton" (American Statesmen Series), one volume, Boston and New York.

Admirably delineates the character of Benton as a projector of western enterprise.

ROOSEVELT, THEODORE. "The Winning of the West," New York, 1889.

ROSS, JOHN, "Letter from, to a Gentleman in Philadelphia, May 6, 1837" (pamphlet), Philadelphia, 1838.

A clear exposition of Cherokee grievances against the State and National governments. An earlier letter to some one else but on the same subject and accompanied by a protest of the Cherokee delegates in Washington was published in pamphlet form in 1836.

ROYCE, CHARLES C. "The Cherokee Nation of Indians," in Fifth Annual Report of the Bureau of American Ethnology to the Secretary of the Smithsonian Institution, 1883–1884, pages 129–378, Washington, 1887.

Royce seems to have used for this very excellent account of Cherokee history material not generally accessible and the source of which he has failed to indicate. He also had free range of the Indian Office.

ROYCE, CHARLES C. (compiler). "Indian Land Cessions in the United States," in Eighteenth Annual Report of Bureau of American Ethnology, 1896–97, Washington, 1899.

A storehouse of valuable statistics. Nowhere can a better understanding of the Indian's retreat and the white man's advance be obtained. The maps are an important feature. The introduction by Cyrus Thomas

ROYCE, CHARLES C.—Continued.

is an historical survey, unintentionally comparative, but not exhaustive, of the different ways the Indian was regarded and treated by the individual English colonies, or the States growing out of them, and the individual European nations.

SAMPSON, W. H. "The Claim of the Ogden Land Company," being a letter dated May 12, 1902, and addressed to Howard L. Osgood, corresponding secretary of the Rochester Historical Society, reviewing the case of the New York Indians in controversy with the proprietors of the Massachusetts preemptive right.

SARGENT, EPES. "The Life and Public Services of Henry Clay," new edition, one volume, New York, 1848.

Introduced here because of its special reference to Clay's attitude toward the Cherokees, the victims of Jackson's Indian policy.

SCHOOLCRAFT, HENRY., "Papers of."

Two distinct collections, one in the Library of Congress and another in the Smithsonian Institution. The former is in a particularly bad shape, and its contents are of varying value. The Indian matter that they contain proved to be not so great as was expected. It is chiefly to be found in the correspondence with Governor Cass, and deals more with the natural resources of the Indian country than with social and political affairs. The Schoolcraft journals, so called, were a grievous disappointment. A good share of their bulk is taken up with newspaper clippings, suggestive, but often useless as speedy references, because date and source are unnoted. As a general thing the Smithsonian collection relates to a period subsequent to that covered by this thesis on Indian removal.

SCHOOLCRAFT, HENRY R. "Historical and Statistical Information Respecting the History, Condition, and Prospects of the Indian Tribes of the United States," six volumes, Philadelphia, 1851–1857.

A queer assortment of valuable and worthless matter. Schoolcraft spent most of his life among the Indians, but his interest centered more in the natural resources of the country than in its native inhabitants, and more in their sociological than in their political conditions.

SCHOULER, JAMES. "History of the United States of America," five volumes, New York.

SCOTT, NANCY N. (editor). "A Memoir of Hugh Lawson White," one volume, Philadelphia, 1856.

Includes selections from his speeches and correspondence, and among these are some bearing upon his criticism of Benjamin Curry and the Cherokee removal.

SCOTT, WINFIELD (Lieutenant-General), "Memoirs of," two volumes, New York, 1864.

Adversely as the reviewers have rated this personal account, it is none the less interesting for events in which Scott was a prime mover, viz, the Black Hawk war and the Cherokee removal.

SENECA. "The Case of the Seneca Indians," printed for the Society of Friends, Philadelphia, 1840.

SENECA. "Report on the Memorials of the Seneca Indians and Others, Accepted in the Council of Massachusetts," Boston, 1840.

SHEA, J. G. "Indian Tribes of Wisconsin," in "Wisconsin Historical Collections," III : 125–138.

A sort of summary of ethnological and etymological facts based largely upon the "Jesuit Relations" and other narratives of early French writers.

SMET (Father), JEAN DE, " Life, Letters, and Travels of," 1801–1873. Edited from the original unpublished MS. journals and letter books, and from his printed works, with historical, geographical, ethnological, and other notes; also a life of Father De Smet, by Hiram Martin Chittenden and Alfred Talbot Richardson. Four volumes, New York, 1905.

De Smet's labors were chiefly among the Indians of the far Northwest, from St. Louis to the Straits of Juan de Fuca. In 1838 he was sent with Father Verreydt and two lay brothers to found a Catholic mission among the Pottowatomies at Council Bluffs, Iowa, and other remnants of eastern tribes transferred to new lands west of the Mississippi. From that time dates his famous series of letters.

SMITH, GEORGE GILLMAN. " The Story of Georgia and the Georgia People," 1732–1860, one volume, Atlanta, 1900.

Suggestive for economic conditions.

SMITH, HENRY. " Indian Campaign of 1832," in " Wisconsin Historical Collections," Vol. X : pp. 150–166.

L. C. Draper, on page 150, gives an account of this production as follows: It " was written in 1833 at the request of the conductors of the *Military and Naval Magazine*, published at Washington, and appeared in August of that year as written ' by an officer of General Atkinson's brigade.' It was thus prepared while the recollections of that frontier service were yet fresh in his memory. He left a copy in manuscript, which was furnished by his daughter, Mrs. A. W. Snyder, of Rockford, Ill., to the *Journal*, of that city, in which it appeared August 12, 1882, and copied into the Milwaukee *Republican-Sentinel* of the following 17th and 24th of September. These two copies have been carefully collated, and errors corrected."

SOCIETY OF FRIENDS, " Proceedings of an Indian Council, Held at Buffalo Creek Reservation April, 1842, and Printed for the " (pamphlet), Baltimore, 1842.

In reality a formal protest against the recent ratification of the Buffalo Creek treaty, the Society of Friends being extremely indignant at that occurrence, inasmuch as they had made " a full exposure of the objectionable means used to procure it."

SOCIETY OF FRIENDS, " Proceedings of an Indian Council, Held at Cattaraugus, June, 1843, and Printed for the " (pamphlet), Baltimore, 1843.

SOCIETY OF FRIENDS. " Proceedings of the Joint Committee Appointed by the Society of Friends for Promoting the Civilization and Improving the Condition of the Seneca Nation of Indians," Baltimore, 1847.

SPRAGUE, JOHN T. (Colonel). " The Origin, Progress, and Conclusion of the Florida War," one volume, New York, 1848.

Relation of incidents very similar to Fairbanks's.

STAMBAUGH, SAMUEL. " Report on the Quality and Condition of Wisconsin Territory," 1831, in " Wisconsin Historical Collections," XV ; 399–438.

" Copied from the original MS. on file in the War Department at Washington."

STONE, WILLIAM L. " Life and Times of Red Jacket, or Sagoyewatha," one volume, New York, 1841; new edition, Albany, 1866.

The standard authority on the history of the great Seneca opponent of Tecumseh.

STRONG, MOSES M. " The Indian Wars of Wisconsin," in " Wisconsin Historical Collection," VIII : 241–286.

Covers in detail the Winnebago war of 1827 and the Black Hawk war of 1832. Places much reliance upon Black Hawk's autobiography.

STRONG, NATHANIEL T. (Seneca chief). "Appeal to the Christian Community on the Condition and Prospects of the New York Indians," one volume, New York, 1841.

An amplification of and, in a sense, an answer to some of the facts presented in "The Case of the Seneca Indians."

STRONG, NATHANIEL T. "A Further Illustration of the Case of the Seneca Indians," one volume, Philadelphia, 1841.

SUMNER, WILLIAM G. "Andrew Jackson" (American Statesmen Series), one volume, New York, 1883.

SWAIN, JAMES B. "The Life and speeches of Henry Clay," two volumes, New York, 1843.

TAYLOR, E. L. "The Ohio Indians," in "Ohio Archaeological and Historical Society Quarterly," vol. VI, part 1, pages 72–94.

Not of much account except in the particulars furnished on the relative territorial position of the tribes in Ohio.

TEXTOR, LUCY ELIZABETH. "Official Relations between the United States and the Sioux Indians." (Leland Stanford Junior University Publication), Palo Alto, 1896.

A masterly treatment of the Sioux troubles, prefaced by a full résumé of the United States Indian policy.

THATCHER, B. B. "Indian Biography," two volumes, New York, 1832.

THWAITES, REUBEN GOLD. "The Story of the Black Hawk War," in "Wisconsin Historical Collections," XII: 217–265.

By all odds the best secondary authority on the Indian hostilities of 1832, the correct and important facts of all earlier accounts being here brought together in one continuous narrative.

THWAITES, REUBEN GOLD. "Notes on Early Lead Mining in the Fever (or Galena) River Region," in "Wisconsin Historical Collections," XIII: 271–292.

An abstract of these notes appeared in the "Report of the American Historical Association," for 1893.

TOCQUEVILLE, ALEXIS DE. "Democracy in America," translated by Reeve, two volumes, Boston, 1873.

Contains some slight but interesting reflections upon the Indian policy of the United States. De Tocqueville felt that the removal project was too thoroughly executed.

TURNER, FREDERICK JACKSON. "The Significance of the Frontier in American History," in "Report of American Historical Association" for 1893, pages 199.

Footnote references especially helpful.

TURNER, ORSAMUS. "Pioneer History of the Holland Purchase of Western New York," one volume, Buffalo, 1850.

TURNER, ORSAMUS. "History of the Pioneer Settlement of Phelps and Gorham's Purchase and Morris' Reserve," one volume, Rochester, 1851.

This and the preceeding work, though concerned primarily with the settlements of western New York, deal with different phases of New York Indian history as modified by the Massachusetts preemptive right in that region. Both are overflowing with information, much of it extraneous or of local and temporary interest only.

TYSON, JOB R. "Discourse on the Surviving Remnant of the Indian Race in the United States," delivered October 24, 1836, before the Society for Commemorating the Landing of William Penn. Philadelphia, 1836.

Note the unfavorable comments upon the effect of the removal act of 1830.

UNITED STATES, " Public Documents of."

(1) " State Papers, Reports of House Committees," first session, Seventeenth Congress, Report of Select Committee, January 7, 1822, on the execution of the compact of 1802.

(2) " State Papers, Reports of Committees," second session Seventeenth Congress, Vol. I.

(3) " State Papers, United States Executive Documents," No. 57, second session Seventeenth Congress, Vol. IV: Resolutions of the Georgia legislature, December 5, 1822, and accompanying documents; also a memorial from the general assembly of Missouri.

(4) " State Papers, House Executive Documents," No. 59, second session Nineteenth Congress, Vol. IV: Message of Governor Troup, November 7, 1826; report and resolutions of Georgia legislature, December 1826, together with various documents, treaties, etc., relative to the execution of the compact of 1802.

(5) " House Journal," first session Twentieth Congress. (1827–8.)

(6) " State Papers," first session Twentieth Congress, Vol. VI, No. 233: Information as to Indians that have emigrated west, called for by House resolution March 22, 1828. No. 238: Correspondence respecting Creek treaty of November 15, 1827, called for by House resolution March 22, 1828. No. 248: Correspondence relative to charges against Crowell since January 1, 1826, called for by House resolution April 9, 1828. No. 263: Correspondence relative to Lovely's purchase, Arkansas, called for by House resolution April 10, 1828.

(7) " State Papers," House Executive Documents No. 91, second session Twenty-third Congress, Vol. III: Memorial drawn up by Cherokees in council at Running Waters, November 28, 1834.

Senate Document No. 512, parts 1 to 5, Twenty-third Congress, first session, December 2, 1833–July 30, 1834. Contains a large collection of correspondence concerning the emigration of the Indians.

UNITED STATES STATUTES AT LARGE, 1789–1893, twenty-seven volumes, Boston and Washington, 1850–1893.

UNITED STATES. " Treaties and Conventions Concluded between the United States of America and Other Powers since July 4, 1776," Washington, 1889.

UPHAM, CHARLES W. " The Life of Timothy Pickering," 4 volumes, Boston, 1873.

Contains constant reference to his services as Secretary of War and ex-officio in control of Indian Affairs.

VAN BUREN, MARTIN, " Papers of," MSS. in Library of Congress.

Contain scarcely anything on Indian Affairs.

WAIT, THOMAS B. " Wait's State Papers and Public Documents of the United States," third edition, twelve volumes, Boston, 1819.

Contain Presidential messages, memorials to Congress, etc., but nothing that cannot be obtained just as conveniently elsewhere.

WALKER, FRANCIS A. " The Indian Question," one volume, Boston, 1874.

A superficial account of the United States Indian policy by a former Commissioner of Indian Affairs.

WASHINGTON, GEORGE, " Papers of."

Among the Congressional Library collection of Washington's papers are six volumes, bound separately from the others, entitled " Letters to and from the War Department, 1789–1800." In addition there are scattered letters from Knox of a private character.

WELLINGTON, DUKE OF. " Supplementary Despatches, Correspondence, and Memoranda of Field Marshal Arthur Duke of Wellington," edited by his son, London, 1862.

Important for an insight into the Ghent negotiations.

WHEELER, HENRY G. " History of Congress, Biographical and Political," two volumes, New York, 1848.

Describes the rise of a small party in the Senate opposed to Jackson, chiefly on the score of the Cherokee removal.

WHITE, GEORGE (Rev.) " Historical Collections of Georgia," third edition, one volume, New York, 1855.

" Compiled from original records and official documents," some of which it quotes in whole or in part. It is rich in statistics, and in biographical accounts of the governors and other prominent men of Georgia.

WHITTLESEY, CHARLES (Colonel). " Recollections of a Tour Through Wisconsin in 1832," in " Wisconsin Historical Collections," I : 64–85.

A running narrative of the Black Hawk war, plain-spoken, impartial.

WIGHT, WILLIAM WARD. " Eleazer Williams, His Forerunners, Himself," in " Parkman Club Papers," No. 7, vol. I, pp. 133–203, Milwaukee, 1896.

J. N. Davidson, " Wisconsin Historical Society Proceedings," 1899, page 167, says :

" This monograph is a model of its kind—thorough, accurate, painstaking, and just."

WILLIAMS, EDWIN. " Statesman's Manual of Presidents' Messages, Inaugural, Annual, and Special from 1789 to 1846."

WILLIAMS, JOHN LEE. " The Territory of Florida," one volume, New York, 1837.

Very inaccurate as regards the account of the Indians.

WILSON, HENRY. " History of the Rise and Fall of the Slave Power," three volumes, Boston, 1872–1877.

The scattered references to the interplay of policies, affecting alike the negro and the Indian, are not well supported by historical evidence.

WINSLOW, EDWARD (Judge). " Papers of," selected and edited by Rev. W. O. Raymond under the auspices of the New Brunswick Historical Society, St. John, New Brunswick, 1901.

" Shed much light upon the attitude of the Loyalists in the American Revolution and the circumstances that attended their settlement in the maritime provinces at the close of the war." They also furnish some information about the period just before the war of 1812 and the war itself. Such as are here printed are excellent for an idea of the feeling entertained by the Canadians against the Americans, but are comparatively destitute of anything about the Indians, who partly occasioned that feeling.

WOOLLEN, WILLIAM WESLEY. " Biographical and Historical Sketches of Early Indiana," one volume, Indianapolis, 1883.

YONGE, CHARLES DUKE. " The Life and Administration of Robert Banks, Second Earl of Liverpool," three volumes, London, 1868.

Important for the Ghent negotiations.

INDEX TO INDIAN CONSOLIDATION.

065924